HONORING the CODE

Conversations with Great Game Designers

Matt Barton

CRC Press
Taylor & Francis Group
Boca Raton   London   New York

CRC Press is an imprint of the
Taylor & Francis Group, an **informa** business

AN A K PETERS BOOK

CRC Press
Taylor & Francis Group
6000 Broken Sound Parkway NW, Suite 300
Boca Raton, FL 33487-2742

Printed on acid-free paper
Version Date: 20130226

International Standard Book Number-13: 978-1-4665-6753-5 (Paperback)

Library of Congress Cataloging-in-Publication Data

Honoring the code : conversations with great game designers / Matt Barton.
  pages cm
  Includes bibliographical references and index.
  ISBN 978-1-4665-6753-5 (pbk.)
  1. Computer games--Authorship. 2. Computer programmers--Interviews. 3. Computer games--Design. I. Barton, Matt, interviewer.

  QA76.76.C672H675 2013
  794.8'1526--dc23

2012050924

Visit the Taylor & Francis Web site at
http://www.taylorandfrancis.com

and the CRC Press Web site at
http://www.crcpress.com

I dedicate this book to my wife, Elizabeth Barton. I can still hear the bells ringing on the hill.

———————————————————————

Contents

Acknowledgments, vii

Web Materials, ix

CHAPTER 1 ▪ Honoring the Code 1

CHAPTER 2 ▪ John Romero, Architect of *Doom* 5

CHAPTER 3 ▪ Rebecca Heineman, Archmage 27

CHAPTER 4 ▪ Tim Cain, Game Designer X 45

CHAPTER 5 ▪ Brian Fargo, Patron of Wizards 61

CHAPTER 6 ▪ Chris Avellone, the Iconoclast 75

CHAPTER 7 ▪ Chris Taylor, the Problem Solver 83

CHAPTER 8 ▪ Howard Scott Warshaw, the Sad Clown 97

CHAPTER 9 ▪ Jon Hare, the Rock 'n' Roller 105

CHAPTER 10 ▪ Ralph Baer, the Father of Videogames 129

CHAPTER 11 ▪ David Fox, the Mindbender 137

CHAPTER 12 ▪ George Sanger, "The Fat Man" 155

CHAPTER 13 ▪ Mark Soderwall, Mentor to Graphic Artists 173

CHAPTER 14 ▪ Megan Gaiser and Rob Riedl, Gamemakers for Girls 191

CHAPTER 15 ▪ Paul Reiche and Fred Ford, the Toymakers of Gaming 203

INDEX, 219

Acknowledgments

I'm indebted to the many wonderful designers, artists, musicians, producers, publishers, and coders who donated their time to share their stories with me. I'm grateful to have met so many of my childhood heroes and learned so much about their work and lives. It's comforting to know that these men and women are just as intelligent and charming as their games.

I'd also like to thank the many fans and supporters of my "Matt Chat" YouTube program, the original platform for these interviews. Without their comments, suggestions, research, help, and fine ale for my Rather Excellent drinking horn, none of this would've been possible.

Web Materials

A chat forum and venue to watch video of original interviews is available at the author's website, Armchair Arcade

http://armchairarcade.com.

CHAPTER 1

Honoring the Code

If you're reading this book, then I'm guessing you feel like I do about videogames. They're fantastic, awesome, great, amazing, spectacular, the best damn thing in the universe. They have just as much (if not more) cultural importance to me than any book, movie, or album. Videogames aren't a waste of time. Time is a waste of videogames.

I encourage you to adopt a similar attitude. Next time someone scolds you for all the time you spend gaming, please thank them sincerely for wasting theirs.

Are videogames art? Considering some people still ask the same of a Picasso or a Pollock, I really don't think I'm going to be changing anybody's mind about *Pac-Man*. Fortunately, I don't need to do that here. I can already tell you're on my side about all this. We can appreciate videogames because we've been playing them since were old enough to roll a quarter into a slot or press play on a tape. But I want you to take one further step, and go from being a simple consumer of videogames to a connoisseur.

As with any field of creative endeavor, there are those who wish to do more than simply experience the art. We want to know something about how it was made, and by whom, and for what reason. We wish to get into the head of the artist to understand the confluence of energy, passion, and craziness that somehow results in a masterpiece. The creators of great videogames are not normal people. Just talk to them. Yet they think we're nuts for actually paying them to make these things. Now, that's not to say they wouldn't like more money. With more money they could make more games! Oh, and eat! (See Figure 1.1).

According to celebrated game designer Danielle Bunten Berry, "No one ever said on their deathbed, 'Gee, I wish I had spent more time alone with my computer.'" Perhaps. But I bet there are plenty of game developers who've said, "Gee, I need more time! I promise I'll die as soon as I've finished this one last level!" (See Figure 1.2).

I wrote this book primarily to fill what I see as a social and cultural void in our beloved games industry. Although we have plenty of great resources out there to help aspiring game developers learn the *technical* skills they'll need to make great games, there is not nearly enough historical material on the *culture* that made all this possible—the wild and crazy pioneers who blazed the trails and established the industry as we know it today. I'm not just talking about being able to line up names with game titles. If you want to be successful in

FIGURE 1.1   Some gamers have spouses who discourage their gaming. Mine makes me delicious gaming-themed brownies.

any field of game development, whether it's game design, programming, graphics, sound, or publishing, you need to know some things about the people who stand out in those disciplines; the ones the current professionals admire and wish they could be like.

Nothing is going to make a better impression during a job interview than showing you fit in. That means talking and thinking like a member of the group, not like a résumé with a voice chip. It means being aware of the industry's history, its defining moments, and key people. If you read these interviews carefully, not just for content but also for style and emotion, you will be much closer to achieving that goal.

It's also vital to get a sense of how past developers have dealt with huge, sweeping changes in the technology that drives this industry. Inevitably, you too will find yourself confronted with a paradigm shifter like the CD-ROM, 3D graphics cards, the Internet, or the mobile revolution. Who can say what new technology is just around the corner, ready to make the bleeding edge games of today look like *Pong*? You may not be able to predict the future, but you can prepare for it by learning equally from the triumphs and failures of great game developers. And knowing what *Pong* is definitely wouldn't hurt either.

I wish that everyone had the opportunity I had to meet and chat for hours with the people in this book. Each has a unique story and approach to what they do, as well as considered and well-thought-out advice for anyone aspiring to a career in the games industry.

FIGURE 1.2 As a game historian, I've worn lots of hats over the years. This stylish number is a 3D imager for the Vectrex gaming console.

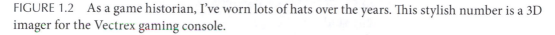

There are things you can learn in five minutes across a table from John Romero, George Sanger, or Becky Heineman that you're just not going to get in any other way. But I've done the best I could to bring out their personalities and share them with you.

Some might wonder how I selected which interviews to include in this volume. It was tough. I tried to go for a diverse mix, and also for people who had contributed to multiple eras or genres, or had experience hiring, teaching, or mentoring newcomers. Obviously, there are some names I would like to see here that, for whatever reason, aren't. But one thing's for sure—everyone here has something valuable to offer. I also favored people who are now developing games for mobile devices or have experience with independent game development.

We're now living in the midst of a new "Golden Age" of gaming, but only a few developers are poised to take full advantage of it. The big game changer is the ability to make a "commercial quality" game with a small team—mostly using free tools—and getting the whole thing funded with a crowdsourcing application like Kickstarter. The mobile revolution has opened up whole new demographics for game developers to tap—as well as cool new gameplay mechanics. Almost everyone interviewed here has something to say about these critical, paradigm-shifting developments in the industry.

I also tend to favor people who make the style of games I play the most: adventures, role-playing games, and real-time strategies. Since my foreign language skills are limited to a few words of Klingon, I naturally gravitate toward English speakers. Finally, I wanted people who wouldn't just be repeating that story about the pizza with the missing wedge or that Jay Wright Forrester book for the 69,105th time. Believe me, there is no shortage of wonderful game developers out there who, for whatever reason, have just not been given the chance to tell their story.

Many of the people in this book are quite active online, whether on Twitter, Google+, or Facebook. I haven't bothered to include their addresses, since there's a decent possibility they'd be invalid by the time you're reading this. In any case, it's easy enough to search for their accounts or profiles on these services (or whatever new services spring up), and worthwhile to keep tabs on their current projects. I'm also pretty sure that they'd be willing to answer your questions about anything they've said in these interviews, provided you do so politely. I'd also recommend being succinct and grammatically correct. Nothing seems to irritate a developer more than a long, poorly worded, and poorly punctuated e-mail. If it's not worth writing it out clearly, it's not worth your time or theirs.

I also wrote this book for an entirely different reason, one that gives the book its title. I am concerned that we are squandering an invaluable opportunity by ignoring our gaming legacy. Perhaps it's the nature of the industry, but there's an insatiable and self-destructive view out there that the only games that matter are the ones that are coming out next week. There's a tendency to dismiss older games—and the people who worked on them—as obsolete. This is an attitude I find not only arrogant but irresponsible. Our pioneers aren't going to be with us forever. Several of gaming's early greats, such as Danielle Bunten Berry (*M.U.L.E.*), Daniel Lawrence (*Telengard*), Paul Steed (*Wing Commander* and *Quake* artist), and Gary Gygax (*Dungeons & Dragons*), have already passed on to the great beyond, and with them, the opportunity to ever interview them again.

It's also sad, I think, that the pioneers who are still with us are seldom treated with the same respect and veneration we'd give to a musician, novelist, or moviemaker of their stature. It's not just that their greatest achievements are often no longer available for sale but routinely and wantonly downloaded illegally as "abandonware." Indeed, many of them say that they're fine with the practice simply because it's the only means open to them to enable gamers to still enjoy their games. While I'd still love to see them being properly compensated for their past work, what bothers me much more is that a lot of modern gamers simply don't appreciate or aren't even aware of their masterpieces. When Jon Hare or Brian Fargo can go to game development conference and not be instantly surrounded by adoring fans and admiring colleagues there's something terribly wrong. Do you want to be part of an industry that treats its greatest artists and their games like disposable tissue? I didn't think so!

In short, we all have a duty, as game developers and gamers, to honor the code. These are our industry's Bob Dylan's, John Lennon's, and Madonna's. Let's treat them and their work, no matter how dated it might seem at the moment, with the respect they deserve.

Now then, let's get started. There are some people I think you should meet.

CHAPTER 2

John Romero, Architect of *Doom*

Interviewing John Romero is like asking forty questions of a hurricane. At forty-five, Romero still has the energy, enthusiasm, speed, and desire to blow things up as of a sixteen year old. Even at crowded Game Developer Conferences, he's easy to spot, zooming from booth to booth and surrounded by a crush of adoring fans eager for autographs, insights, or perhaps a lock of his famous mane of hair. Anyone who doesn't know his work can be brought around quickly enough: "What? You don't know? That's the guy who did *Doom, Quake,* and *Wolfenstein 3D*! Duh!" That's right. John Romero is one of the core members of id Software, the tiny company that single-handedly introduced the world to the first-person shooter. But more than anything else, he's the rock star of the gaming industry. Unlike the vast majority of developers—including his fellow id founder John Carmack, who seem to shun attention and personal publicity—Romero revels in the spotlight, thoroughly at home in a big crowd of fans. He stands out in this often quiet and reserved profession, always dressed in stylish clothes that probably cost more than my car—and a hairstyle that wouldn't look out of place on a the cover of a romance novel (see Figure 2.1).

I first met John at a hotel in San Francisco, at the Game Developer Conference of 2009. My friend Bill Loguidice and I were there to interview developers for a documentary film, and Romero was an hour late. Everyone else was ready to call it quits and go home, but I insisted that we wait. Eventually, John texted to say he was on his way. Another hour later, he rushed into the room and began talking like a machine gun. Even though none of us had ever seen him before, he conversed with us like old friends, and when Bill mentioned some obscure game for the Apple II, John's eyes lit up like a demon. As much as John loves the high-tech, cutting-edge stuff that defines his own contributions to the industry, his first and greatest love will always be the old Apple computers and games played by a few hundred people—many of whom have long forgotten about them and the teenage hackers that created them.

FIGURE 2.1   John Romero, rockstar of the gaming world.

But John Romero hasn't forgotten anything or anyone. Pioneering Apple II programmers such as Bill Budge (*Pinball Construction Set*), Jordan Mechner (*Prince of Persia*), and Nasir Gebelli (*Gorgon*) mean as much to Romero as Chuck Berry, Buddy Holly, and Elvis Presley meant to The Beatles. After two intense but enjoyable hours of interviewing, John treated us to dinner, quizzing us about every game ever created for the Apple II. At one point, he handed me the earbud of his iPhone and challenged me to identify the tune playing on it. I instantly recognized it as the theme from *Spelunker,* an obscure 1983 platform game by Tim Martin. It was a bonding moment.

The following interview took place in February 2010. Unlike the previous interview, during which we focused on general questions about the games industry, this time I wanted to zero in on his own life and career, to learn how someone like us becomes someone like John Romero.

How did you learn to program, John?

Let's see. When I started programming in 1979, the first computer I saw was a mainframe [at Sierra College in Rocklin, California; John was eleven years old]. There was a terminal connected to a mainframe that was in the next room—it was an HP 9000, a massive room-filling computer. The room next to it was full of terminals, all connected to it on a time-share system. The next room was full of Burroughs computers, which, I don't know what they ran—maybe CP/M. I never even used it and nobody else did, either. There was another room, but they didn't put anything in it until 1981, two years later. Finally, they filled it with Apple IIs. That was when I first saw the Apple II.

Looking over the students' shoulders, I saw that it had color and it made noise—the terminals didn't do that; they were black and white, and text only. It sounded like it could do something, and I had never seen an Atari or a Commodore 64 at this point, so it was still pretty early. Anyway, I started asking the students what commands they knew for turning on the screen, colors, and dots, and lines and all that stuff. Most of them didn't know, but some of them did, and I wrote down HGR, plot, color, all that kind of stuff. Then I started to just play around with it. I was in ninth grade.

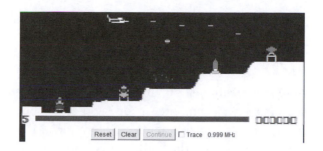

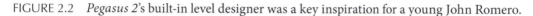

FIGURE 2.2   *Pegasus 2*'s built-in level designer was a key inspiration for a young John Romero.

I was up there at the local college because they had a computer, and playing games for free was great. I didn't have a lot of money. I was just delivering papers, and that didn't make that much. I spent all the money I made on *Pac-Man*.

These computers didn't have many games on them. But there was a place called Capital Computers in the next town over. That was pretty much an Apple store, and they had the games in Ziploc™ baggies hanging off the wall. It was funny because it was a big empty store with stuff hanging off the walls and nothing in the center eating up space. I remember seeing *Pegasus 2** for the first time (see Figure 2.2). I thought it was pretty cool even though it was mostly a black-and-white game. It was neat because it let you create your own levels with the paddle. You could create your own heights for terrain and then play through your own level. I thought this was really, really smart. Did you ever see *Pegasus 2*? It was the first game that I'd seen [with a level editor] until *Lode Runner* [by Douglas Smith].

No. Was the editor like the one in Lode Runner?

An interesting story about *Lode Runner*—do you know what the original name of the game was?

No idea.

The original game was *Miner,* before Doug sent it to Broderbund. Doug lived in Seattle and was older than the other kids in the neighborhood. A couple of the kids used to come over and test his games for him—like a free QA [quality assurance] team. They thought his game was just awesome. They wanted to make the levels, too. So Doug thought that maybe he should put a mode in that let you make levels. So he did, and those kids made a ton of the levels that were in the game—it wasn't all Doug. It ended up that one of these kids was Daron Stinnett, the executive producer of *Dark Forces, Jedi Knight*, and *Outlaws*, so he's been involved in games for a long time, and it all started on *Lode Runner*.

So Pegasus 2 and Lode Runner set you on the path of becoming a level designer?

Yeah, after I got *Lode Runner* I started playing around making levels. I didn't spend too much time doing it, because I was more interested in trying out a lot of different games,

---

* Olaf Lubeck's Apple II clone of the popular arcade game *Scramble*.

and I was doing a lot of programming. *Lode Runner* came out in 1983, and that was when I first learned assembly language, and after I learned that it was all I could do—I spent all my time trying to write code.

What made you want to move from just playing games to actually making them?

Well, I loved games, and seeing a computer made me think—whoa, free games! I don't pay money to do this? Then, on the actual mainframe terminal, I wanted to see if I could make some, too, because the games [on the mainframe] were really lame, and I thought I could do something better. So [the students] said, yeah, you can program it in HP BASIC. So I said, wow, how do I do that?

I got a bunch of basic information on line numbers and such, and the first program I started writing was a text adventure modeled after *Adventure*[*] because that was on the mainframe there. But I'm playing arcade games, right, and you'd go to the mainframes and the games on them were crap, and I wanted to make the games from the arcades on the computer so I wouldn't have to pay money to play them!

What's funny is that's exactly what happened in the marketplace anyway; everybody was copying from the arcade games and selling them on the computer. The arcade machines were the design templates for all the actual home computer games.

I didn't have a [floppy] disk back then, so the stuff I typed in [was being deleted] every time I went away. Disks were like ten bucks back then.

When I started high school, I figured out that the Capital Computer store was only a mile from my school, so after class I'd walk over and ask the guys that worked there if I could play the games hanging off the walls. I got to see a bunch of games that had just come out. That was the first place I saw *Gorgon*.[†] Anytime I had lunch or whatever, I'd go to the computer room at school, wait until after school, then walk down to the computer store, and then try to come back to the activities bus to get a ride back home.

I spent as much time as I could [in a computer lab]. At home, I'd tell my stepdad all the stuff that I was learning, and he started thinking that it'd be a really good idea to get a computer for home. So he did; he spent $3,000 and got a huge Apple II setup with a printer and even got the Microsoft Softcard for it that had a Z80 and CP/M. So it's like I had two computers, a CP/M and the Apple II. I spent all my time on the Apple II; as soon as I got home, I was on the machine until [my parents] made me go to sleep. It was all about BASIC and trying to make games.

I loved playing games, and programming was really fun—it was a different kind of fun that I'd never experienced. Learning how to code is not any normal part of a kid's existence. You learn how to go outside and screw around, but you don't know anything about programming. But it was really fun to do. So my goal became to actually make *good* games. I started making game after game, and in each one, I'd try to do one new thing. So in one

---

[*] *Adventure* is also known as *Colossal Cave Adventure* and was written by Will Crowther and Don Woods. It's a foundational adventure game composed entirely of text; players input commands such as "GET TORCH" and "GO WEST" to interact with its game world. Crowther's version was released in 1976, and Woods released his expanded version a year later.

[†] Nasir Gebelli's 1981 clone of the arcade hit *Defender* for the Apple II. Gebelli wrote it using E-Z Draw Assembly language.

game, I'm going to draw graphics; in the next, I'm going to use the paddle; in the third, I'll have the player shoot something; then a game with sound effects.

By 1982, I'd reached the end of what you could do in BASIC on an Apple II. I was drawing shape tables, using my main loops to do the minimum amount of stuff. I was even using Microsoft Task compiler, which could compile BASIC into binary, and was faster, but unreliable. I needed to learn assembly language.

In the December of 1982, several things happened. We were going to move to England in January. I asked my mom for a book—*Assembly Lines: The Book* by Roger Wagner. Jeffrey Stanton wrote a book called *Apple II Arcade Game Design* [that I also wanted]. I also got the December '82 issue of *Creative Computing,* which had an Apple Cart section written by David Lubar, a games programmer. He showed a bunch of assembly language and was talking about what it did, which showed how to *and* out and *or* in shapes on the screen—and I was like, oh, my God! So, I had my mom get me a subscription to *Creative Computing* as well.

Then we moved to England, and while I was able to bring my books with me, the computer had to go by boat—and that took six months [*laughs*]! I had to learn assembly just with the books and hand assemble my code and use an op code look-up table to write it all out, drawing out my bitmaps, turn that into hex … The school had Apple IIs, so at lunch I could go in and type in all my hand assembled code and watch it work on the computer. I had to do that for a couple of games—writing everything down on paper, hand assembling it, and then going to school to type it all in. I learned assembly without an Apple II. When it finally came, then I could spend a crazy amount of time programming. '83 and '84 were big programming years for me.

Was there anyone else working with you, or were you doing it all by yourself? What did the other kids at school think about your games?

Mostly it was all just me. It's funny, but I didn't make [my games] for anyone else. I started to figure out that it'd be cool to publish these games in a magazine. I used to get *Nibble* magazine and *A+* and *Insider,* the three Apple magazines. I saw that they published programs in there, so I sent them some of my early stuff, but they rejected a shit load of that stuff. Just a bunch of rejections [*chuckle*]. There was either too much assembly language— no one would type it in because it was just a wall of text, and that's not useful for anyone typing it in because they won't learn anything. If I didn't write it in assembly, though, it'd be too long [to print in the magazine]. And sometimes the games were just … bad.

I had to figure out the game that would be fun and with code [that I could] comment on to help people learn stuff. So I hit on the magic formula with a game called *Scout Search.* I figured I could write all the stuff like high scores in BASIC, which would be very short, and then write the real core stuff in assembly, and then I [would still have room] for my comments. So I did that. Actually, *Scout Search* was so short they just put a hex dump in there for the assembly language—they didn't even bother to annotate it. That made it fit to two pages [*laughs*]! Every time I made a game after that, it got published, because I knew what they needed. So [my games] got the cover of *Nibble* for three years in a row—'87, '88, and '89. *Scout Search* was published in the June issue of 1984 [at this point, John was sixteen years old].

FIGURE 2.3 Growing up in the '70s, John Romero was more interested in computer clubs than discothèques.

Did you have any buddies at school, John? Girlfriends? (See Figure 2.3).

I … was like the super computer geek guy. All I cared about was programming, I didn't care about girls or anything. I basically made up a bunch of utilities and games, and I'd write little flyers for them and hand them out at computer clubs. I was trying to market myself by myself. But that's all I cared about.

In Roseville, California there was a computer club and a class. The kids in there knew I was dedicated, and some of them were decent programmers. The feel in that class was like—I was too far ahead of those guys. In California, I had to take P.E. Go to England, and they said, yeah, you don't need two years of P.E., just one. So I said I'd already done my one, can I do computer class? [*Laughs.*] They said, "Well, it's a BASIC programming class, and you're coming in at the second half of it." I said, "Look, that is not even an issue." [*Laughs.*] So I talked to the teacher, telling her about my assembly language, BASIC programming, my games … I showed her the stuff that I had, the games that I'd written with shape tables and graphics.

She was impressed. She said that I could get into class—that was the first day. The second day of school, I come in, and she tells everybody else to work on something and tells me to go with her. We got in her car and drove across base—this was a U.S. Air Force base—we went to the area called the Aggressors Squadron, where the pilots are. Apparently, she'd been out the night before, and started talking to a captain and telling him all about this brand new kid from California. So, he's like bring him in, because we can put him to work. He was a really cool guy.

[The captain] wanted to show me the vault. It was like a bank vault, where you had to say some code words to open it. Everyone inside would hide their stuff when someone came through. He takes me to the very back where there's a Cromenco mini-computer and a terminal. He said, "Do you think you can program that?" And I just looked, saw they had some books and stuff, and said, "Yeah, it'd be easy." So he asked how often I could work. I worked there for a couple months in the summer.

All the other kids knew about this, so I was the programming god over there. In high school, there was no programming competition, at all. I got A's in computer class ... I did an independent study class that was just playing Atari 2600 games all day long—I got an A in there [*laughs*].

When other kids were modeling themselves after star athletes, actors, or musicians, John was worshipping the best programmers of his day. I ask him who inspires him the most.

Nasir Gebelli is my favorite. He's my number one programming god, my idol. He's awesome.

What makes Nasir so good?

Early on, seeing Nasir's games, I really liked the speed of the games—great speed. He was reaching further than other people, with *Horizon 5* and *Zenith*, this 3D work that he was doing. Sirius Software [where Nasir worked] came out with a bunch of action games, and Nasir made nine in just the first year. He was chain smoking, drinking coffee, and turning out these games. He never had a program that would save his code; he typed them directly into memory on the Apple II. There was no source code or comments. He'd type in one line, it'd be converted to machine code, then he'd type in the next line. There were no symbols; nothing. No source code for anything. He had to keep the whole game in his head. He kept doing that all the way up to *Secret of Mana* [a 1993 game for the SNES]. He used the same mini-assembler built into the Apple II. I liked the focus on speed. Games that were really fast and fun. [Sirius Software's other programmers] Mark Turmell, Larry Miller—they were all awesome.

When I look back at it, id Software really mirrors what Sirius Software was—super fast games, trying to do something new. Nasir's stuff was the first fast game on the Apple II.

[Romero then talks about another of his idols, Bill Budge.] I tracked [Bill] down for my Apple II party, and he never wants to talk about what he did on the Apple II. Not interested in talking about it ... He didn't want to talk about his game programming past, which for me is insane. I can't even understand why somebody wouldn't want to talk about the cool games they made; that's just bizarre. I just don't understand programmers like that. That kinda sucked ...

In fact, when I'm around other people, and they don't ask me questions about *Doom* or *Keen, Wolfenstein, Quake,* or whatever, I think that's weird. I mean, I'm right here, you can ask me anything—I got all the answers for all those games if you just want to ask ... I will fucking talk about *Doom* and *Quake* all day long.

What about *Commander Keen*, though?

Keen was the first real breakthrough (see Figure 2.4). I had been at Softdisk [a software company in Shreveport, Louisiana] for about two years. The whole time I was there, I didn't get to actually make games—I was porting some of my games to the IBM or PC disks ...

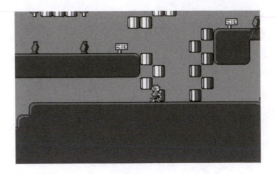

FIGURE 2.4 Who would have thought that the same team who produced the cutesy *Commander Keen* series would go on to create some of the most violent games in computer game history?

But I wasn't able to make games, and I *had* to make games. So I talked to the president and told him that I was going to leave if I couldn't make games—I'd go over to LucasArts. He was like, "Whoa, let's try to keep you here. We'll start a games disk." I told him I needed two months to do the games, and he was okay with that. The whole company ran on monthly cycles—two months was a stretch, but they could do it. Back then, I was like, two months—awesome! [*Laughs.*] But I needed a team of people; I needed another coder, an artist, and an editor guy—somebody to take care of all the business so I could just code. Four people, in the room.

I'd been programming my whole life, from '79 until '90—eleven years of me by myself coding. This was the first time I was going to code with someone else; the first time I would be part of a team. I could not wait.

While I was working for Softdisk, I also sent them games on the side. I sold them a game called *Substalker* that I'd written in double hi-res on the Apple II, and on that same disk they published a game called *Tennis* by John Carmack. It was a hi-res game, too. I saw the game and liked the smooth animation; I could tell the guy was a good programmer. I can look at a screen and tell you who wrote the program—that is Tony Suzuki [*Star Blazer*], Nasir, or Bill [Budge] … Just by the graphics techniques and movements and stuff. I knew the stuff cold. Looking at John's *Tennis* game, I could tell. So I asked if I could get him. They said, "Yeah, we've tried hiring him twice already and he's turned us down." So I said "let's do it again," because I knew he wouldn't say no to me. And I'd bring Lane with me, the editor. He was also hardcore Apple II, Apple IIGS, and Mac programming—he knew 68K assembly … I knew the Commodore 64, the PC assembly, Apple II … Each of us knew three computers with only one of them overlapping. When Carmack came down, we totally blew him away. He was like, "Man, I'm gonna learn so much stuff if I go there!" Before the place [had nothing to offer him], but now he was going to have a badass time.

He accepted the job. He was totally excited, and moved his stuff down from Kansas City.

What kind of guy was Carmack? I've always pictured a Spock-like character.

Well, back then he was pretty normal. As time went on, he became more … logical, more closed off and not very social. His social aspect went away as he had to focus more on complex thoughts, like 3D and VSPs, and shaders … Everything that he learned was becoming more complex, and it closed him off. But at the beginning, he was just a normal guy like everybody else. He vandalized stuff back in high school, went to juvenile hall, he was just a normal dude.

When I met him, we'd just talk and hang out and stuff. When we finally got to working on stuff, and got into the same room and started working on the first issue [of the games disk] … They'd waited so long that the first disk had to be done by the end of August. And we were starting at the beginning of August. They were really sorry about it, but to market it and blow the doors off and stuff we needed two games in one month instead of one game in two months. We could do that, but it was going to be ports of stuff we'd already done.

While John [Carmack] was waiting for us to start, he'd written a game called *Catacombs* on the Apple II and sold it to Softdisk. I had written a game on the Apple II two years later called *Dangerous Dave*. We decided to port those games to the PC; nothing creative, just get it done. We worked insane hours every day, the entire month, and got those games done. John did *Catacombs* in CGA, but I decided to do mine in CGA, EGA, or VGA—and you could switch video modes at any time. You could be jumping in the air and switch video modes! It was the first game ever on the PC that could do that.

While I was writing these, I had a book called *Power Graphics Programming* by Michael Abrams. It taught me the hard part, which was the EGA drawing and latch code and stuff. I gave it to Carmack and told him it had everything he needed to know about programming graphics, especially the part about the panning registers for EGA and smooth movement; you're going to have to use that. So on our next game, John started using the CRT address register, which could tell the computer where to start looking in memory to draw the screen. If he kept on changing the CRT register to go down a line, he could have a smooth *Xevious*-scrolling background [a vertically scrolling arcade game].

We were making these games together. I was making tools and doing the levels, and he was doing the actual scrolling and the game engine, movement of the ship and stuff. That first game was so awesome—it was great being on a team and doing this stuff so fast.

Then John started playing around with the horizontal scrolling. That's when he did the *Dangerous Dave and Copyright Infringement* demo that he'd set on my desk.* As soon as I saw the panning on the screen I was totally blown away. Because I knew every game on the PC—there was no game I hadn't seen on the PC, and they were all very similar to each other. There was nothing breakthrough on the PC at that time, and this was 1990, and the PC had been around since '81, and EGA was very popular. But for Softdisk, EGA was too ahead of their subscribers. They were still CGA people—that's why *Dangerous Dave* and *Catacombs* had to have CGA. John's vertical scrolling trick was fine for CGA, but the horizontal panning was EGA-only. We couldn't use it at Softdisk.

But I knew when I saw the horizontal scrolling that we had a Nintendo on the PC. Boom! Here it is. I just said, "We're out of here." I just knew that Softdisk couldn't do jack with this tech; it'd just be buried, just like everything else that they published. I knew that this was groundbreaking, and no one had ever seen it before.

---

* This demo was an unauthorized clone of *Super Mario Bros.* for the Nintendo Entertainment System.

Before we'd been in a team environment, John hadn't done any crazy, brilliant stuff, and I hadn't either. But when we got together, it was crazy coolness. So that was the start of id Software, when I saw that demo.

We got a deal with Scott Miller who'd been trying to contact me for months, ever since he saw *Pyramids of Egypt*—this game I had written for Softdisk's *Big Blue Disk*. He wanted me to make a clone of that game for him. He thought it'd sell like crazy. I said, "Scott, you don't want a copy of that. There's something way cooler. Let me show you this!" So I showed him the *Copyright Infringement* game and he was blown away—he knew the market. He was like, "Okay, I need a trilogy of games like that—with that scrolling trick." We wrote up a proposal and asked for $2,000 to show that he was really serious. So he sent us the check and for three and a half months we spent all of our time making the original *Commander Keen* trilogy. We put it out, it sold like crazy, and we decided to leave Softdisk and start id immediately.

But [*Keen*] was a breakthrough technology—it was Mario on the PC. I have reviews from 1991, from when the game came out, and it was just like when *Doom* or *Quake* came out years later: "Oh, my God, groundbreaking insanity! The smoothest thing I've ever seen on a PC …" Everybody forgets how revolutionary it was with the scrolling tech for gaming on the PC, because after that a lot of games started appearing with that trick.

Coming back to this idea of moving from doing solo work—controlling every aspect of a game's design and development—to being part of a team. I know there were big advantages, but do you think something was lost, too?

Team efforts really started in 1985. Before that, they were all single programmers; the guy's name is on the front of the box, just like any book you see in the bookstore. Those programmers had their own techniques, their own character, their own humor … But the other thing they had was [platforms]. The kind of games you wrote on the Apple was different than what you wrote on the Atari [800] and different than what you saw on the Commodore [64]. Each of those systems, and I'm not counting software that got ported across the board, like the Adventure International stuff and Infocom. But the games that were originally written on those systems were part of their own culture on that machine. Games on the Atari 800 all feel different than the games that were written on an Apple. And it's not just the API that you had to go through to put stuff on the screen. On the Atari 800, everyone used the player/missile graphics to put sound and graphics on the screen. Everyone went through the same API that way, nowadays, everyone goes through DirectX [or OpenGL] for Windows games. Games looked similar on the Atari 800 because they used the same hardware techniques. On the Apple II, though, there was no API to write to, so you had to figure out how to put [your pixels] on the screen. It was like here's a bunch of memory, put values in [it], and stuff shows up on the screen. Whereas on the Atari, it was set up a bunch of stuff in memory, then tell the registers where it's at, and then [it] draws it on the screen—it's very smooth, arcade-quality stuff. But all the built-in hardware limited people's expression of their creative thoughts. To be smooth, they had to put [their graphics] through Atari-dictated hardware and API stuff. On the Apple II, Woz [Steve Wozniak] dictated color and memory layouts but no hardware support at all. So you had to be more creative, and that's why I can look at a game on the Apple II and tell you who made it.

The games that were written on the Atari were very different than those written on the Apple. *Droll, Lode Runner,* and *Choplifter* are very different than *Maxwell Manor, Preppy, Canyon Climber* and those kinds of games that were written on the Atari. And those are very different than *Wizball* and *Impossible Mission* on the Commodore 64. People back then [chose a machine] and they stayed there—it was their world. They based their games on whatever had come out before [on that system]. Their ideas, and inspirations, and gaming culture were all within that same set of games that they'd been exposed to. It was very interesting when Windows came out, and—BOOM! Now there's just one culture. [Even if you] write on the Mac, you're using OpenGL, you're supporting both systems. So you don't see any Mac-centric game designs like you did [back in the '80s], like *Continuum* and *Dark Castle. Dark Castle* is a classic Macintosh game. It was its own thing on that machine back then. Black and white. Now that whole thing is gone … It's been leveled by the OpenGL and DirectX 10 APIs. Now it's really up to the artwork and the animation to try to express something. It's really hard to express the quirkiness of a design in a large team. With a small team, you can get at it. But it gets ironed out with a bigger team—the QA team says, "Hey, what's that?" And it gets removed.

Speaking of creative and original games, do you get upset that so many games that came out after *Wolfenstein 3D* are basically just clones of it? Do you feel guilty that so many games coming out now are first-person shooters?

No, I love them. I don't feel guilty at all. [After] we did *Wolfenstein,* during that year it was all copies of *Wolfenstein. Ken's Labyrinth, The Fortress of Dr. Radiaki, Isle of the Dead,* just really bad knockoffs. They didn't have that quality level we achieved. After *Doom,* we saw a bunch of *Doom* clones, and those were much better. *Dark Forces* is a great *Doom* clone. That was the first one out—if you don't count *Heretic*—and they used our engine, which is why they had a head start. But the reason why *Hexen* and *Heretic* were out there is that I wanted to see more games. I wanted more shooters, and there was nothing out there that was of the quality that I wanted to play. They'd been done by these really bad shareware guys or these really crappy engineers. I really wanted to see really pro developers making really cool 3D stuff, so that's why I got Raven to make these games. I've always been excited to play shooters. I never thought, "Oh, man, I wish I hadn't done that!" I think it's awesome.

You've definitely succeeded in inspiring other developers to make them, John! Let's talk about *Wolfenstein 3D*. Obviously you had some great inspiration, too (see Figure 2.5).

The inspiration was *Castle Wolfenstein,* from Silas Warner in 1981. MUSE was his company; him and Ed Zaron had started that company. [*Castle Wolfenstein*] was a really groundbreaking game, and everybody recognized that. It is the original stealth game—the pre-*Splinter Cell* game; the original one. It was a huge impact on me. I played that game so much I figured out how to get through every single castle. Every time you ran *Wolfenstein,* it [gave you] a new castle. The exits in every single room are the same; [only] the contents

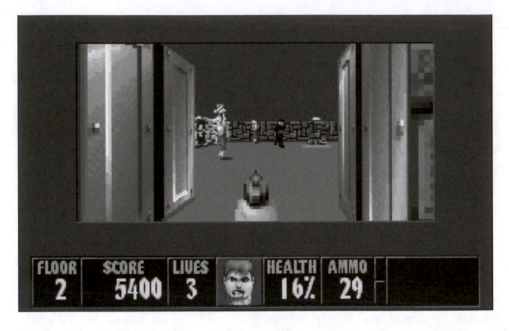

FIGURE 2.5 Whereas its namesake is a complex game of stealth and strategy, *Wolfenstein 3D* followed a simple design principle: Keep 'em shooting, stupid.

of the rooms change. So if you know the layouts of each castle, you can run through and get to the exits very quickly. That's how much I played that game … [I wish I had asked Silas] why he put that annoying screen craziness [when you hit the walls]. Maybe he thought he needed that in there to scare you. But I think when you have nine keys to shoot and nine keys to move out—it's already nerve-wracking enough. But it was such an amazing game.

In 1991, when we were thinking about what our next game was going to be after *Keen* … We'd just done this 3D game texture-mapped game called *Catacombs 3D* in EGA. It's probably the only 3D EGA texture-mapped game ever made. But it came out way earlier than *Ultima Underworld*, which came out a week after *Wolfenstein* did. We wanted to make another 3D game like *Catacombs* for Scott, and we wanted it to be a trilogy. One of the ideas that Tom [Hall] had was to call it *It's Green and Pissed*. It was set in a research lab, and scientists have created mutants that are killing everybody, so you go in and blast your way out.

Hmmm, sounds familiar.*

[*Laughs.*] I was like, no way, that's the oldest story in the book. I totally don't want to play that game. So I asked, why not just make *Wolfenstein* in 3D? Carmack and Tom and I all had this simultaneous, "Ahh, yes!" Why wouldn't we want to do that? It'd be amazing! All three of us immediately knew we had to make that game as soon as I mentioned it. We didn't even need design docs. That game had hit each one of us hard ten years earlier.

---

* This is essentially the plot of *Half-Life*, a famous first-person shooter released in 1998 by Valve Corporation. I suspect Romero is taking a dig at them.

What did the release of *Wolfenstein 3D* mean for id?

It was a turning point. Because it was fast, and it was violent, and the sound was awesome; it was our first digitized sound, coming out of a Soundblaster instead of AdLib. We had a bunch of new stuff coming out with *Wolfenstein* … 3D texture mapping in VGA. It was the first time we made a gun game, where it wasn't a wizard's hand or a tank turret. This was a first-person shooter. The key controls were the first FPS-key controls. The sound, and the violence, and the speed—all of those things were huge. This was a huge increase in PC entertainment. That game was seventy frames per second. I was really proud of it, because this is the kind of game that I've always wanted to play.

We knew what *Wolfenstein* was because it was a really simple design. It was more complex when we started, but we scaled it back. We knew the core of the game had to be speed. Anything that slowed us down had to be removed. We [originally] had code for dragging and searching dead bodies, and stuff like that, but that stopped you from killing, from mowing shit down. So we got rid of that stuff. We knew that it would be difficult enough for people use a mouse in 3D and a keyboard at the same time. We knew we needed to keep it simple, so people wouldn't have to think about it—just worry about what's around the next corner, and know they need to just mow down everything that they see.

In *Hovertank,* there were scary monsters but also people you needed to rescue. You *could* mow them down, but that was useless—you needed to save them to get more money to get to the next level. It wasn't pure simplicity like *Wolfenstein,* where it was just kill everything in sight. I think boiling it down, getting rid of all the pauses—just a blast-a-thon through this fast castle … That ended up being the best way to keep the core pure. We were technically the best thing out. It was a very clean, simple design that didn't complicate what the player would want to do.

After *Wolfenstein*, did you ever want to go back and create more *Keen*-type games?

No. *Wolfenstein* and *Keen* are like night and day. *Keen* is a fun, happy, safe game—the only time I feel any fear is when I'm in a really difficult spot and I might fall off. That's very different than a chain gun mowing down a screaming Nazi. That feeling in *Wolfenstein* was what I wanted to get out of a game. And we needed to do it better. We needed to perfect it in *Doom.*

It took a year to make *Doom,* even with six people working on it. In January of '93, when we started working on it, we put out a press release that had everything we wanted to put in the game. We told everybody: this is *Doom,* and it'll be out at the end of the year. Everything was groundbreaking, and we hadn't done any of it yet [*laughs*].

But we *knew* we could do it. It was like predetermined.

We did have challenges during the [development], first of all with the engine being fast enough. When Carmack started writing it, it was fast enough, because our level design wasn't inspired. I was working on a tool to make the levels, and Tom was making them. But he was really unhappy. Tom is not a killer kind of guy. He's a *Keen* kind of guy. Tom's levels were like *Wolfenstein* but with diminished lighting—it had the same floor and ceiling height, and four walls … It was like that because our story was set in a military base, and that's what rooms and hallways [in a real military base] look like. They're right angles.

It felt like we were still in *Wolfenstein*. It had cooler textures. Adrian [Carmack] had gone from the primary colors of *Wolfenstein* and completely redid the way he did them. He got away from the clean look to a dirty look. We told Adrian *Star Wars* was a really successful movie, and one of the really key things was that it all looked *used*. It wasn't clean and shiny. So we wanted our base to reflect that used feel. We felt it was important for the believability of this space. So that's what Adrian did—slime and dirt and all that kind of stuff.

But anyway, Tom was having trouble. [John] Carmack had told him to get some books on military buildings—architecture books. And they were boring [*laughs*]! So I decided to try making levels. I wanted to solve this problem. I didn't want it to look like *Wolfenstein*. So I played around, looking at all the variables I had: floor, ceiling, height, and lights. We had to grok this stuff because nobody had done this before. Carmack had written his code in a very optimized way to allow a top, middle, and bottom texture. You could turn off the middle texture, and then you'd have a window. A sector is an enclosed area that has a floor, ceiling, and light value—that's it. It was very basic data structures, and that's all that the level editor used to create the levels. I started playing around with height, making ceilings really, really high up, and putting balconies in the walls. I made a room that ended up being in E1-M2. That was the first room that had the *Doom* look. When I made it, I got Kevin and Adrian (the art guys) to check it out. I'd played around with stairs leading up to it, changing light values, making recessed stuff. I wanted to demonstrate the feeling of going from a closed-in area, down a hallway, and now you're upstairs—now that was different. Whoa, stairs! Then you go up, and the room opens up into this huge thing. They were like, "Whoa!" Yeah, *that's* what I'm talking about!

I hadn't used any straight walls. Nothing was straight. I showed them a curving hallway with stairs going up it into a huge room with angles. This was something that couldn't be made in *Wolfenstein,* and it was really, really cool. Even [John] Carmack saw it and said, "Oh, yeah!" So that was it. Forget everything you knew about making buildings in *Wolfenstein*. Don't be afraid of how many line segments you need to make an area. Hide stuff in secret areas …

It took about four months to get that *Doom* look. We had the basic monsters in there. We got Bobby to send us some sounds, and that really changed things. But the really interesting thing was that *Doom* was shaping up so well, so quickly. Tom left in August of '93, and we brought Sandy Petersen on to make the levels for episodes two and three.

Doom was the only game I'd played where the emergent behavior of the monsters felt unpredictable. The way they wandered and the way they found you—the things that they would do, like the way different monsters would attack each other. That's what demons would do, right? Even if you made the level, the game would always have some mystery to it. The game comes alive when it runs. When the AI is working, you're taking in the environment, the music, the sound effects—it was the first game that really came alive. It felt mysterious. You could never trap people in *Wolfenstein;* the door opens, and here comes the guy. But in *Doom,* we had sound flooding. So if you had a window or any opening between areas and shot your gun, the sound will trigger the monsters in the other area. It was the coolest thing ever. It was the Holy Grail (see Figure 2.6).

FIGURE 2.6 *Doom* is the definitive first-person shooter. 'Nuff said.

Did you realize then that you'd made one of the best games of the decade?

Oh, yeah, we knew. We knew we had made the best game *ever*, and we knew that because we were gamers. We had new technology—and the multiplayer was insane. It's still my favorite multiplayer game of all time, because there's nothing else that feels that way. The [development of *Doom*] was so smooth it really felt like it was just our destiny.

So you didn't have any roadblocks along the way? No bugs?

There was *one*. At id, we looked at Nintendo for everything. We judged our own quality based on their games. The thing about a Nintendo game is that you will run forever. They have their QA process down to a science. They would never let a game come out that had a glitch on the screen.

That's what we wanted, too, but we didn't have a QA team. The developers *were* the QA team. As precise as we were with our programming, and as advanced as we were with our design, we used all of that [intensity] on testing our game as well.

We left the game running on everybody's computers to see if anything would happen. We didn't want to see one single thing wrong. But randomly, computers would just lock up forever—it'd be running in demo mode, and then it'd freeze. It was random. Carmack was trying to nail it down and finally found out what it was: we were using the timing chip in the PC to time the refresh. We weren't clearing the timing chip, and when it flipped over, it got locked into this check that's never going to happen again, ever. So Carmack zeroed in on that and fixed it in the level loader. And that fixed it! It was only a two-day bug, but it was a very insidious one.

Considering how ambitious *Wolfenstein 3D* had been, and then *Doom* pretty much surpassed it in every way, trying to up the ante again for *Quake* must have been pretty daunting.

Quake was a very difficult game to make. The first *Keen* series took three months. *Wolfenstein* took six months. *Doom* doubled that to a year. After a year of working on *Quake*—that was the hardest year on the team. With *Wolfenstein* and *Doom*, after only two months [we had enough of the engine assembled] to start making levels. With *Quake*, the engine wasn't ready for a year.

I designed all the level editors for the other games, so I was working on *Quake*'s as well. I was experimenting with the design, wondering what it was going to look like. But it wasn't just me and John; we had nine people working on it. But except for the people who'd been on *Doom*, these people had never been through a development cycle. They didn't know what it was like, and it was really hard on them to keep working on stuff that they had to throw away. American [McGee] kept making level after level for Carmack's engine, and then having to throw it away. Write something up in the scripting language, then have to throw it out when Carmack changed the scripting. There was a point where American wanted to get rid of a whole area of textures—an Aztec one—and I had to go in and tell Adrian that he needed to create a whole new theme. Carmack didn't want to grow the team, so we didn't. And I was too busy, so I couldn't do it. It was really hard making a game for a technology that didn't exist yet.

After that year, everyone was mentally busted. We had a big meeting, and I told them— "Okay, *now* the game is ready to be made. *Now* we can put in all of that world class effort to make an awesome game design on an awesome engine!" And everyone else was like, "We're done." [*Laughs.*] Mentally, they were finished. They just wanted to crawl under a rock.

I was disappointed. I really wanted to do an awesome new game design … Everybody could see how big of a toll it took on people who hadn't done it before. They couldn't even think anymore. So that's how that decision came to just slap *Doom* weapons in there and call it a game. It wasn't the same place anymore. We used to all know what we were going to do, but these new people—these new elements at id—it wasn't the same place. So I said, okay, but it wasn't the next level I was hoping for. In January, I called Tom and told him when *Quake*'s over, we're leaving (see Figure 2.7).

I worked on *Quake* for seven months. Even though it was a clone, it took amazing hard work. On June 22nd, on a Saturday of '96—everyone was so broken … American had left, and we didn't even know where he was. He'd just snapped. That day, when I put the game together and put it out on the 'Net, I was there by myself. Nobody else was there. Everyone was broken.

Well, despite all the turmoil at id, what did the critics think of the finished product?

They loved it. In February, we'd put out *Q-Test*, which was a test of *Quake*'s multiplayer ability. We wanted to see if people liked it. It was the first huge thing.

When we were making *Doom*, people knew it was coming. *Wolfenstein* had ignited everybody, and the user groups were full of people talking about *Doom*. They were inventing stories about what *Doom* would be like. But it was even bigger with *Quake*, because we'd already proven what we could do. They had faith that *Quake* was going to be [great].

I knew IRC (Internet Relay Chat) was going to be crazy about it, so I went on there and told everyone it was being uploaded. It was a huge nuke.

FIGURE 2.7 *Quake* was a huge financial success, but Romero was disappointed. Essentially *Doom* with improved graphics, it wasn't the breakthrough product he wanted to make.

After all your disappointment with the creative issues on *Quake*, you cofounded Ion Storm and started work on *John Romero's Daikatana*. Obviously you had a lot more creative control over that. Did you finally get to do all the revolutionary stuff you'd wanted to do with *Quake* in that game?

Daikatana took three years; it doubled *Quake*'s schedule. I'd say that it was a lot more fun to make than *Quake* because there were no creative issues. It was my game, clear and simple. So there was nothing like with *Quake* where I lost faith in everything because we had to slap *Doom* weapons in there.

I really wanted to push the boundaries with *Quake,* and I knew that it was something we could've done—we were used to pushing all the boundaries. With *Daikatana,* though, I made a shooter-formula-type game, because the risk of making [an overly ambitious game] was too much for a new company [Ion Storm]. I didn't want to take a big risk on our first game, so I made something more traditional. I didn't do the crazy, revolutionary thing that *Quake* would have been. That's why *Daikatana* is still a traditional looking game. We did have a bunch of incremental improvements, [but some of those] weren't done well—like the sidekicks, and we got knocked for it.

First of all, I made a mistake in making *Daikatana* an expert level FPS. I did that because I wanted a game that'd be fun for me, and I wasn't really concerned about people who weren't really good. It was designed to be hard, and that's not a good mass-market design at all. But for people who want an expert FPS, this is a really fun game to play. If you can work with the sidekicks and understand how they work and how to control them—you have no issues. But if you're [too lazy] to figure them out, then it's frustrating to play.

[By contrast,] the sidekicks in *Ghost Recon* were a very safe design. They didn't jump; they were locked to the ground like you were—they moved really slowly. It came off really well, but with *Daikatana,* I wanted sidekicks that could do what I could do in the game. But that kind of programming was hard to do, and they didn't pull it off right. The sidekicks can get killed by doors and dumb stuff like that. But it was more fun to make than *Quake.* Sure it took two times as long, but we created a 120-person company and were making four games at once. I hired a bunch of people that'd never made games before. And then with my team leaving halfway through, that didn't help either [laughs]!

There were all these internal politics … I didn't want to have any part of them. I just wanted to make a game. Tom and I weren't part of it, but they affected the teams, and half of mine decided to walk out.

What was causing all the conflict?

Just people who should've never been in any position of power being super subversive. I don't want to go into detail, because the last thing I want to do is kick up the dirt on people and have to defend against a lawsuit. But it should've never happened, and if people were focused on making games, it never would have happened.

I had to deal with being the CEO of this big company, making four games, an office in Austin … *Daikatana* was the first game that I hadn't made with my own hands. I designed it, but I didn't execute it. It was a team that'd never made a game before who were executing it. If you haven't ever made a game before and don't know how to polish a game, it's just bad shareware. I did a lot of work polishing and straightening it out, but the PR stuff was *definitely* not fun.

Are you referring to the ad that said, "John Romero will make you his bitch?" (See Figure 2.8).

"John Romero's about to make you his bitch," is what it said. [*Long silence.*]

What were you thinking?

The person who was my marketing person—when I hired him, I'd already made the deal with Eidos. Here's the number of games we were going to make; here's the money, it was done. But, being a marketing guy, all he wanted to do was market. I told him not to worry about marketing anything yet because we didn't have any games ready. But being a marketing guy, all he wanted to do was market, so if he couldn't market our games he'd market our people. He was making ads with just us—the founders of the company—in the magazines. "Here's Ion Storm—suck it down!" He was putting out these image ads, just trying to get a rise out of people.

With *Daikatana,* he had our ad agency do something really aggressive, and when he showed it [the bitch ad] to me I told him, "I'd *never* say that to anybody." "John Romero's about to make you his bitch"? [*Laughs.*] Okay, first of all, I've never called anyone "my bitch" in my life and never will, because that's gay [*laughs*]. I'd say, "I'm going to kick your ass" or "I'm going to blow your head apart." I'm going to do something to you, but I'm not going to have sex with you, so I'd never say that.

FIGURE 2.8 The "bitch ad" was unquestionably the worst advertisement in the history of PC gaming. It destroyed Romero's reputation, reducing him to the butt of jokes and outright derision.

But he's like, "Come on, it's funny! Don't be a pussy!" It was his job, so I just said whatever. But I really should have said, "No way in hell are you putting that out." That ad ruined my connection to the fans in the community. It was calling them bitches. That's not anything I ever wanted to do, but that's what it looks like, and I have to take responsibility for that.

Did you get angry e-mails from fans about it?

No, I didn't get e-mails, but I did get angry forum posts that ripped on me and Ion Storm. Up until that ad, we hadn't seen anything bad. As soon as I fired [the marketing guy], though, all the bad stuff started happening; all these sites ripping on Ion Storm [started popping up]. *Bitch-X, Evil Avatar,* and *Fat Babies*—all those sites came into existence ripping on us. People inside the company that hated the founders hosted all the internal stuff. The people we got rid of were trying to destroy us. It was all sabotage. That's what happened.

But it was *still* more fun than *Quake* to make [*laughs*].

This whole "bitch ad" thing … all the machismo, the aggression, trash talk. The first-person shooter is still a male-dominated genre. Do you think that stuff like this is why so few women are into first-person shooters and prefer other types of games?

I think women are just as diverse as men when it comes to games. Some women get FPSs and they totally understand it. But a lot of women don't. A lot of women don't want that intense focus and dedication that it takes to be good at FPSs. But some do. If you go to any

CPL event or professional gaming type events, you'll see women all over the place. One of the best death matchers in the world is Cornelia. She lives in L.A., and she's been a top death matcher for years. She will destroy any guy. NVIDIA and ATI hire her to sit in their booth playing the latest FPS and just taking on any guy who'll go against her.

Any guy but you, right?

No, she will destroy me. She's at that level. Games are so well programmed nowadays, that there exists a wide range of skill inside an FPS. There's a separation now between people who are really good and professionals. It's like basketball—people all over the world love basketball and lots of people are good at it. But you also have those people who are just supernatural. Those guys are going to move up. That totally exists in FPS gaming. It requires skill, psychology, and strategy.

When you're playing against somebody and you have to map their patterns—this stuff happening in their brains—that's when it gets really exciting. There are Queen of the Hill tournaments now—just women playing death match. There are tons of them. It's a subculture, and there's a lot of very good women.

Do these women talk as much trash as the guys do?

I haven't really heard any. My girlfriend would do that. She'd beat me all the time, but we knew each other well. In a public setting, though, not many women would do that—not many guys, either. I would, though. I'd startle people in death matches by calling them names. It was a psychological advantage.

You're a guy that a lot aspiring game developers—especially young people—look up to. They want to be the next John Romero. What kind of advice would you give a teenager who was trying to make the next *Doom*?

Well, if you want to make a really great game, you have to be with a really great team. Identifying a great team, though, is really, really hard. You're not going to know that at the beginning, because you have no experience.

There's [a lot of different jobs in the industry]. The writing, the sound, the music, QA. Those are all on the outside. Art, programming, and design are the core. They get the most intensity.

The number one thing you need is a good attitude. You're going to see your stuff get canceled constantly. So you need to know that the journey of making a game is the reward. When the game is out, it's done, so make the making of the game as fun as you possibly can. To make a really fun game, you have to have fun making it. If you're not having fun at work, your game is going to suck.

It takes a lot of hard work, especially for the core disciplines, to get to the level where you could make something like a *Doom* or a *Quake*. It takes a lot of years. When we made *Doom*, I'd been programming for fourteen years. We'd all been programming for the same amount of time—we were experts, a small team of four people who were really good at what they did. We were like the Beatles or Led Zeppelin. To make crazy, world-class stuff, you have to be really good, and you really need to be positive, because good people want to be around positive people. If the economy sucks, or it's hard to get a job; if you're a positive person, you won't have a problem, because you'll have a great network.

Network as much as you can; it's really important. If you want to get good at something, find somebody who is really great at it, seek them out at GDC [Game Developers Conference], and make them a friend as fast as you can. Ask them what it takes, what they do to get good. Be serious, be positive—those are the two things that will help you push forward.

Do you think it's harder today to get a good job in the industry than it was when you started?

Well, since 1995, when Windows 95 came out, everybody has been on one machine—Windows. It's not very hard; it's just one system, and a lot has not changed over time. But to live through all the generations of hardware that I've lived through, and gone through, and discarding knowledge every time you go through another big change … Oh, I know BASIC, throw that away. Now I know 6502, throw that away. Now I know 8086, garbage. PASCAL, garbage. Throwing all that stuff away—even though the Windows platform has been around for fifteen years, there are still changes happening, and you have to stay up on them. If things change overnight, get ready to change overnight.

The biggest questions I get asked: "Hey, I want to make a game, I have a little team, but how do we get money from publishers? How do we get money to start a company?" The cleanest, global advice I can give people about starting a company and making a game: Don't *ever* ask anyone else to give you money to make a game. You need to do it yourself, at home, on your own time, because that's the least risky thing you can do. Don't quit your day job. You're doing this in your free time, which shows really good dedication, and you're going to test a team out if you're asking for their time like that. If you can meet up after work and actually finish making something, you've got a team. And you'll win more than most people can understand.

The more that you rely on people outside of your core people, the more let down you'll be. Other people just don't have the passion that you will. And you need people together in the same room to get the synergy, the culture. Internet groups fall apart. So, kick ass, and be positive.

CHAPTER 3

Rebecca Heineman, Archmage

It was early evening as I sat down to chat with Rebecca Heineman, known to most of her friends, colleagues, and fans simply as "Burger." The nickname seems a bad fit for this energetic and charismatic woman, whose passion for coding and game design are as infectious as her impish grin.

Becky's roots in the videogames industry go back, well, to its roots. She first gained notoriety by winning the National Space Invaders Championship in 1980, a feat she credits more to patience than prowess. She also spent time at Avalon Hill, the famous wargame and board game company, which began adapting some of its lineup to the computers of the early 1980s, when machines like the Apple II and Commodore 64 were the playground bullies. Becky's job was to port games like *London Blitz* to the even humbler Atari 2600. During this time she was a fourteen year old, but it was easier to lie about her age than to tell the truth. Who would believe someone so young could know so much? (See Figure 3.1).

Most of her fans probably know her best for her tenure at Interplay Productions, which she cofounded with Brian Fargo in 1983. While at Interplay, Becky designed *Tass Times in Tonetown,* a quirky, irreverent, and highly innovative point-and-click adventure published in 1986. She also did the heavy lifting on Interplay's famous computer role-playing game *Tales of the Unknown: Volume I*, better known as *The Bard's Tale*. A longtime fan of the genre, Becky would go on to write *The Bard's Tale III* in 1988, widely considered the best game in the series. She also designed the critically acclaimed *Dragon Wars* in 1989, which met with lackluster sales despite its bold innovations and meticulous design. She also earned a reputation for her many excellent conversions of popular games to the Apple IIGS, Macintosh, and many other platforms.

However, unlike most of those early coders, who hit or missed in the '80s before eventually moving on to other careers, Burger has remained a key player. She is now the senior engine programmer at Ubisoft Toronto and was recently an essential member of Microsoft's Kinect team.

During my chat with Becky, I couldn't help but wonder if this were really the person so often described as a hermit and a loner; a brilliant hacker who kept herself barricaded in a cubicle. Of course, at that time she was named William Salvador Heineman, a classic case of a woman

FIGURE 3.1 Rebecca "Burger" Heineman, a woman of many talents.

trapped in a man's body. In 2003, she began the transition to womanhood and now identifies as a lesbian. While it is tempting to separate Becky's personal life from her many achievements as a programmer and designer, I can't help but wonder if she owes some measure of her success to her willingness to veer away from convention and take the roads less traveled.

I found this on your website: "Who am I? I'm a forty-six-year-old woman, computer programmer, game designer, writer, engineer, pastry chef, markswoman, loving mother of five even though my kids have grown up and moved on." Do you feel that pretty much covers everything? Markswoman, really?

Yes. I used to have a Ferret 50 caliber, long time ago … Not anymore, I don't have any firearms. They've long since disappeared in the divorce, etc. But I used to go out with some friends shooting, and here's a little piece of trivia: In the game *Wasteland*, in the packaging there's a picture of Alan Pavlish, Michael A. Stackpole, and so forth all dressed as *Mad Max* road warriors—the guns they're holding are mine.

I understand that you also like to bake cakes.

Yes, I do, cakes, pies, cookies … I have kids, and they always loved it when mom cooked them stuff. I had this cake recipe I did called "Death by Chocolate," and right now it's a favorite for my son Jacob and my son William. Every birthday, I have to bake them that cake. It's called "Death by Chocolate" because you start with chocolate fudge cake mix, and I pour it in a Bundt cake pan, and then I put M&Ms or little chocolate baking bits, then another layer of cake mix, until the pan is full. Then I bake it, take it out, and ice it with chocolate icing, and then put Hershey's Kisses all over the cake or sprinkle it with M&Ms.

So, essentially just one bite would make you gain five pounds. My sons can't get enough of it, and I'm like, crap. There goes my diet.

Have you ever played *Portal?*

Yes, and it's not a lie. In fact, that's a fun story. Microsoft has a tradition in my department in the advanced technology group that every time it's your anniversary of being hired, you're supposed to bring a pound of M&Ms for every year you've been there. So my first anniversary, I made a Death by Chocolate cake with one pound of M&Ms baked into it, and then I went around the office area and made "Cake This Way" signs. Over the cake were big signs saying "Not a Lie" with big arrows pointing down to it.

How did you get started in the games industry? Apparently, it was a National Space Invaders Championship in 1980?

I had a friend named Tom Whicker. He and I would play videogames all the time. I didn't have much money, so I had a 2600 and an Apple II, and I was copying the cartridges—I designed my own "dev kit," shall we say—because I was just too flat broke. But he had every single cartridge made. So I would grab it and copy it from him. We played *Slot Racers* and *Space Invaders* all the time (see Figure 3.2).

Atari announced that there was going to be a *Space Invaders* tournament at the Topanga Canyon Plaza sometime in July in 1983. Tom was convinced that I was good enough to win it. I was like, "Yeah, right." So he drives me up, and as it's my turn, I start playing and I'm so bored playing this game. I was talking with the judge because I had nothing better to do. I was like, "Oh, I just lost a base," and play, play, play, play, and another hour would go by. Base, play, play, play. "What's my score?" And he said, "You've got like 83,600 points."

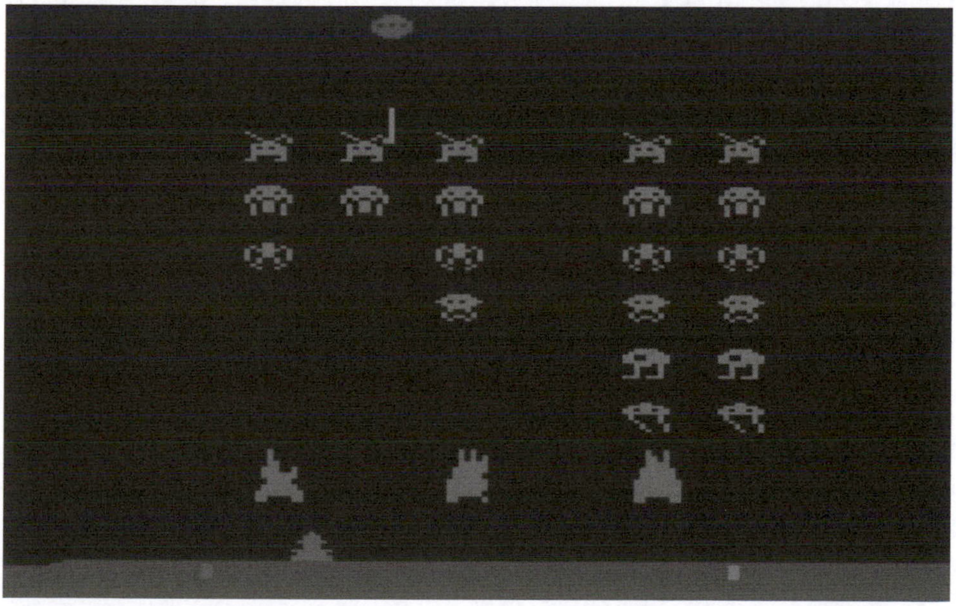

FIGURE 3.2 The Atari 2600 version of *Space Invaders* helped Becky blast her way into game development.

And of course, my reply was "Is that good?" As it turns out, it was more than double the second place player. They announced that I was the winner. I was like, "You're kidding me? I'm going to New York for the finals?"

So, in November I flew by myself to New York City to play in the championships. Just so you know, back then I was a loner. I lived by myself. I flew to NYC, met the other contestants. The kid from Dallas, we kept calling him Tex, and the kid from Chicago was being sponsored by some appliance store. He had this big t-shirt on him and was like the total sponsor hog. Of course, when the game was played, the aliens landed on him in ten minutes. So he got kicked out.

So they finally started the game. They had five TVs, five Ataris, and they gave each one of us a shirt with our cities on it. Mine said Los Angeles. It was sudden death. We'd just play the game, and we'd get three bases, maximum difficulty level, and the idea was to see who'd be the last man standing. After an hour and forty-five minutes, only the guy from Chicago was out. Everyone else was still just killing the aliens. They had a whole bunch of press behind us, and they were getting antsy, because an hour and forty-five minutes of *Space Invaders* does get kind of boring. So then they just said, "Okay, so that concludes the *Space Invaders* tournament!" I was like, "Does that mean we can stop playing?" I just reached over and yanked out the cartridge, and said "That's it! I'm done with this game!"

I wanted the Atari 800 computer that was the second place prize. The fifth place was a $50 gift certificate, the next one was $100 worth of stuff and a videogame collection, but the Atari 800 computer—oh, gosh—I really wanted one. Because the grand prize was a standup arcade game, and I didn't want that. So they then said fifth place goes to Chicago, fourth place goes to Texas, third place went to Hing Ning of San Francisco. I was sitting there going, "I got the computer! I got the computer!" And then when they said the computer goes to Frank Tetro of New York, I went "Crap!" Then they said, "The winner of the *Space Invaders Tournament* is the kid from Los Angeles!"

So they asked me how I felt. "Uhh, uhh." But because I won that tournament, I got to meet up with Arnie Katz and Bill Kunkel of *Electronic Games Magazine* and started writing some articles for them on how to beat videogames. I was a consultant for a book called *How to Master the Videogames* and *How to Master the Home Videogames.*

After about six months, I let Arnie Katz know that I knew how to program the Atari 2600. And he was like, "That's impossible, you're just a kid." Well, I'd made my own dev kit. And then he said that a company in Maryland named Avalon Hill was really looking for anybody who could program the Atari. I said, "Sure!"

So they called me up and within ten minutes said, "You're hired. Here's a plane ticket, come work for us. And you are eighteen, right?" And I said, "Yep!" In reality, nope. I lied my ass off for a couple years because I started in the videogame business when I was fourteen.

I worked for Avalon Hill and taught them how to program the 2600. I worked on *London Blitz* and *Out of Control.* Then I started going from company to company, doing some work for Time Warner on a Play Cable system, then did some consulting, but I wanted to leave New York. My friend Alan Pavlish kept saying there was a company named Boone Corporation who could really use some VIC-20 programmers. So I said, "If it gets me back to California, please!"

So I got a job there and was doing *Chuck Norris Super Kicks* and *Robin Hood* contracted by Xonox. We had a running joke in the office that if you were being bad, you'd get stuck with a Xonox game. So I must have been bad because I worked on three of them.

After that, I started working on some original titles: *Final Eclipse* that never got shipped and an original version of *The Demon's Forge* done by Brian Fargo. I was redoing some of the graphics routines for him, but then Boone Corporation folded. We were all fired. That's when employees of Boone, Brian Fargo, Troy Worrell, Jay Patel, and myself with an investor named Chris Wells, got together and thought we could do better. Brian got us a contract with *World Book Encyclopedia* doing some cheesy chain titles, and we created a company named Interplay.

I still remember when we were signing the lease. The guy asked about the name of the company. I didn't know. "It was 83 production place. Interplay Production!" Okay ... Of course, the first two years of Interplay, we had all these companies calling us about "Intercourse" and "Foreplay" productions and requesting our catalog of X-rated stuff. But that started my videogame career. I was at Interplay for eleven and a half years.

How did you learn to program?

I learned to program because in 1977 I got an AMES 65 kit computer. In high school I got interested in the TRS-80 and the teacher didn't know what to do with it, so I started playing with it. Then, later on, I met a friend with an Apple II. They were hot off the press. I had to have one. I kept going to his house, all the time, so I could play with his Apple II. And he got annoyed with me showing up at his place because he wanted to use it.

I had a paper route and saved up my money. I bought a used Apple II from some guy around the L.A. airport. I started getting cassette tapes for games, but then later on I started getting curious about the mini-assembler. The manuals for the Apple II were all written for programmers, so you'd look at all this code and be like, "What the heck is this stuff?" So I started reading it, studying it. Looked at the disassembler; 800L was my friend for many years. But then I learned how to make hardware. It shouldn't be hard to make a memory card, wire it up, get parts from Radio Shack—back when you could get parts like that from Radio Shack. When I started playing with the Atari 2600, I went to a BBS and saw how to make a copy cart. Ah! I made a RAM cart because I was too cheap, but what if I used that same technique and wired it to a cartridge—I molded it together into a dev kit. I could take a cartridge, plug it in, download it, save it to disk, upload it to ram, turn on my Atari, I could play the game!

But then I noticed that when you took the ROM cartridge and typed 800L, it made sense. It was 6502 assembly, just like the Apple II. From that, I started disassembling the code. I did a disassembly of *Freeway* by Activision, reverse engineering it from binary code all the way to what looks like the real source code. Every line is explained. That was me learning how to program the Atari 2600.

After that, Avalon Hill hired me, and was actually paying me to do this stuff that I'd been tinkering with all these years. I was like, "They're paying me to do this? Cool!" I kept striving to get better and better and better, and now here it is almost an eternity later, and I'm an expert in Power PC, ARM, Intel, AMD 64 ... The stuff I'm doing right now you'd require multiple college degrees to do—proud or not, I never went to college. I learned all this just by cracking books and doing it.

How long was it before you met people with the same or superior level of skill?

It took years before I found anybody. I remember meeting a friend who worked at Softdisk—a guy named John Carmack. He and I started talking about code and so forth, and he was one of the few people talking at my level. Other than that, for many years—even now—I have to dumb down my conversations with people. It's frustrating, but now I know at least a dozen people who I can talk to without having to dumb down anything.

Is John Romero in that category?

No. John Romero is a good programmer, but he's not an expert. He's not a great programmer. He doesn't do engines. Carmack did all the heavy lifting.

I know you're a big fan of *Wizardry*. It seems to come up again and again in my interviews with classic game designers. What is it about that game that makes it so special?

Simplicity. Absolute simplicity. The ability to tell a story with such minimal graphics. If you remember, back then, the only kind of games were text adventures—so your mind did everything. But it was really reading a book. But they took it a step further, and put the maze with the little Turtle graphics and static picture. It was the first game that introduced grinding. In fact, if you play *World of Warcraft*, it's still *Wizardry* grinding! We had a joke during *Bard's Tale*: What's the story of any RPG [role-playing game]? Start weak, get strong, kill the evil fill-in-the-blank. That's every RPG ever (see Figure 3.3).

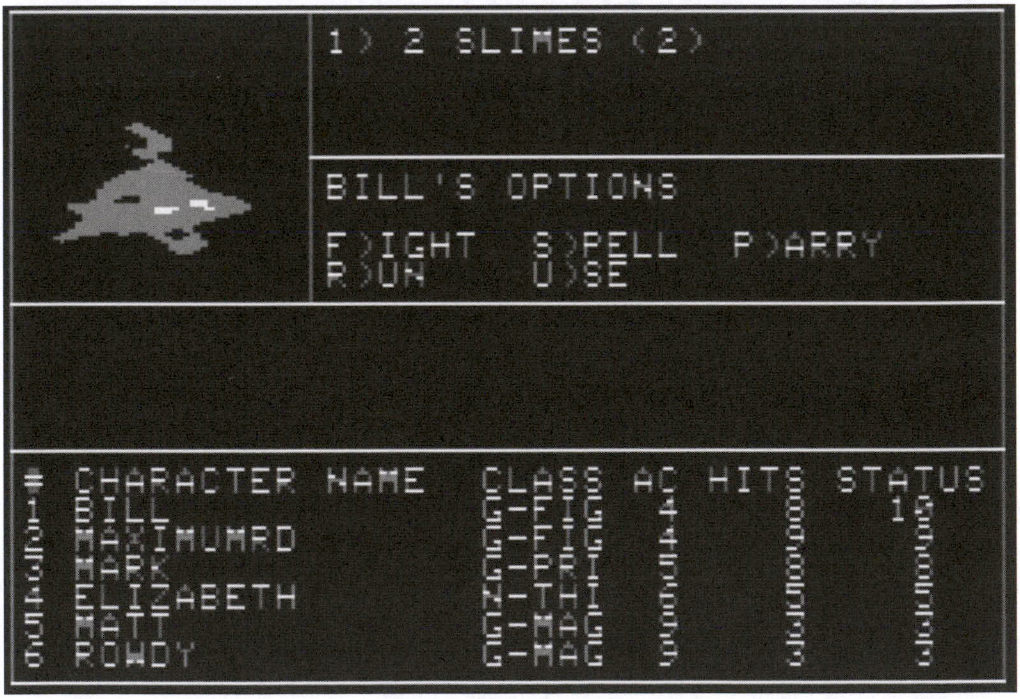

FIGURE 3.3 Sir-Tech's *Wizardry* (1981) had a tremendous influence on an entire generation of computer game developers. Becky attributes its success to its minimalist approach to role-playing.

Wizardry introduced the concept of a party. The idea of start weak, get strong, kill the fill-in-the-blank. As you were doing the grinding and leveling up the characters, you actually felt really bad when one of your characters died.

It was like, "Crap!" I remember when one of my characters died, I was like, "Shit, damn it! I gotta go all the way back to the Temple of Cant." But once you get one character killed, if it's a critical character, the rest of your party may not make it back. The stress and suspense—very few games today capture that kind of terror. And they did it with just line drawings and little postage stamp sized pieces of art.

You worked on some adventure games. *Mindshadow, Borrowed Time, Tass Times in Tonetown.* **Is that your favorite,** *Tass?*

Yes, because basically it's as close as you can get to an acid trip without taking acid.

So, you've done a lot of acid in your day?

Nope, I'm totally drug free from birth. But that doesn't mean I can't have psychedelic nightmares and try to make good games out of them.

It's a cult classic (see Figure 3.4).

Yeah, because it really innovated a lot of things. It really started the point-and-click adventure. Now the graphics look dated, but a lot of the concepts feel brand new. You were able to click on things. I had hot zones on every piece of art, so if you clicked on the give button and went to a character and clicked on him, it'd automatically type in "give to that person's name." You could click on two things to interact with both of them. I had all kinds

FIGURE 3.4 *Tass Times in Tonetown* is a cult-classic graphical adventure game. It debuted in 1986 for a variety of platforms.

of jokes and puns in there. Everything about it was so off the wall and twisted. The unit of money was guitar picks. The whole point of the game was that a crocodile was buying up the land and evicting everyone—a slumlord. You had a crack newspaper reporter who was a fluffy little Terrier named Ennio. Everyone dresses up like punk rockers as envisioned in the '80s, and when you first show up, dressed in normal clothes, they all look at you as though you were dressed like they are as if you were here. So they say, "Man, you're weird looking! Get some real clothes!" It was just so different. The soundtrack was good, too. *Tass Times* was the first game to ship on the Apple IIGS, and it used all thirty-one voices on the Ensoniq chip. Very few people did that since.

I've been holding off on this question for a while, but I have to know. How'd you get to be called "Burger"?

Remember when I told you I was flat broke? When we founded Interplay, we didn't pay ourselves much. We were starving. When I was at Boone Corporation, I was being paid $12,000 a year. Slave wages. I was a kid; I didn't know any better. My entire life was get up, go to work, work until I'm too tired, sleep, repeat. Didn't have time for cooking, and I didn't have any money.

There was a place called Hamburger Stand. They sold 29-cent hamburgers. Since I spent most of my time at the office, I didn't want to walk over, buy a burger, and walk back. So I'd buy a bag of twenty of them. Blow six bucks, get twenty burgers, go to my office, and put them in a drawer. I was too cheap to buy a refrigerator—well, really too broke. Every so often I'd open the drawer and eat a burger.

I had an office mate who was a health food nut, constantly complaining about how I should eat right, exercise like he did. One day I was working all through the night. I didn't leave. It's the morning, and he comes in, sits across from me. I'm still working. Around 3 p.m., I'm done. Burger time! I pull open the drawer, reach in, put the bag down, grab a burger, and start munching. Wasn't thinking anything about it. That's when my co-worker looks at me, looks back, looks at me—and it dawns on him that the bag has been there for who knows how long. Those burgers are pretty firm.

He just loses it. He jumps up, his chair goes flying, he goes, "That burger is insane! That burger is insane!" He runs out. I'm sitting there like, "What's with him? Whatever." Then later Brian Fargo comes in and asks what I did to him. I didn't do anything. What's going on? My co-worker had gone to the restroom and tossed his cookies. That's how disgusted he was.

So then, the rumor started. "Did you eat any burgers lately?" So they started calling me Burger. I played along. "Okay, I'll get a burger. I'll eat a burger." Later on, unbeknownst to anybody, I had an issue with the name I was given at birth. So I would rather be called Burger than by that birth name. "Just call me Burger." For the next twenty years, that was my name. Everybody called me Burger. Now my name is Becky. I finally shed the name Burger.

After *Tass Times in Tonetown* I was finally earning a real salary. Then I started eating real food. It was also when Brian Fargo started developing a taste for sushi. I didn't want to eat anything else but burgers by then—I was in a rut, McDonald's, Wendy's, Arby's. Brian took us to a sushi place. I was like, "Ew!" But the rumor was that I would eat anything.

Brian said, "I don't know what's in that tray, but if you eat a big helping of it, I'll pay for your meal." Free food? I was so there. It wasn't bad! Today it's my favorite food.

What was your involvement with *Bard's Tale*?

Brian Fargo had a high school buddy named Michael Cranford, and we were playing *Wizardry* all the time. Cranford was doing a *D&D* [*Dungeons & Dragons*] session where he was the game master. All throughout Interplay we thought we had to do a *Wizardry* killer. So, the project was given to Cranford to go ahead and write *Tales of the Unknown,* and that is the name of the game. They thought we were going to call it *The Bard's Tale,* and the sequel would be *The Arch-Mage's Tale,* and later on *The Thief's Tale.* But the title was going to be *Tales of the Unknown.*

The problem was Cranford; while he was okay coming together with the scripting and so forth, he couldn't do high-performance graphics. That's what I did. So, at this time in Interplay, I was becoming the tools programmer, or the technology programmer. I wrote all the graphics routines, I did all the sound routines, the animation. I also did the graphics editor, called Quick Draw. Apple later used that name—damnit, I should have copyrighted it. But I wrote the art program that all the artists were using. The tools, the extractors, every single piece of software, so all the heavy lifting work, I wrote that. Whereas Cranford wrote the actual game logic and the text instruction and some disk routines. I remember we had wars because I would write in an assembler called Merlin and he was using Orca/M. So I would have to write it in Merlin, then translate to Orca/M or give it to him for translation, and we were constantly back and forth. It made a rift between us.

Once *Bard's Tale* was almost done—we had a couple bugs left, Cranford had fixed them—Cranford then had the final floppy disk, and he came in and held the disk hostage. He told Brian to sign a contract, which changed the terms of the deal with him and Interplay, or he was not going to give the disk to Brian. He was going to sell it himself or something of that nature. We needed the money, so Brian signed the contract, and Cranford gave the disk, and the game shipped. Thankfully for Interplay, it made us a boatload of money.

However, that contract had a clause in it that basically said that the sequel, *The Destiny Knight,* was Cranford's and Cranford's alone. I did do some more functions, more assembly, more routines for Cranford, but basically the engine is *Bard's Tale I.* He just changed the scenario code. He recycled all the code I wrote, used all my tools.

Unfortunately, when Cranford plays *D&D* as the dungeon master, he plays it so that if everyone in the party dies, the DM wins. This is totally against how *D&D* works—the DM is not supposed to be a participant, he's supposed to make it fun for everybody. That showed up in the way *Destiny Knight* played. *Destiny Knight* was a very difficult game. In a way it was because Cranford actually said if people get killed, he wins. I was like … Okay.

Once *Destiny Knight* was done, the contract between Cranford and Interplay ended, and that's when I said I wanted to do *Bard's Tale III.* I have ideas, let's get Michael Stackpole involved so we can have a professional writer, and I'm just going to take all of Cranford's code—because I considered it a P.O.S. [piece of shit]—flush it down the toilet, and start from scratch. All the graphics routines I kept. But I improved upon them, and I added multisized dungeons, increased animation frames with better compression. I even came

FIGURE 3.5 *Bard's Tale III*, released in 1988, is widely regarded as the best game in the series.

up with two-voice audio on the Apple II, which was not really done except for music programs. This was in a game where music was an integral part of it (see Figure 3.5).

I was even able to shove in some Monty Python references, Sir Robin's tune "Bravely ran way," which lets you run from combat. When you go to the temples, they say "*dona eis requiem*" and you're healed.

I also introduced female characters—for obvious reasons! I was so pissed with Cranford, I kept saying, "Where are the girls?" He said, "Girls don't play this." If he only knew … I also added new character classes, geomancers, necromancers, and so forth. All of this stuff, and I only added one more disk because I used some really sophisticated compression algorithms. At the same time I was doing this game, I was doing the graphics routines and all the tools for *Wasteland*. That's why *Wasteland* has similarities in the graphics and monsters—it's the same code. It was my code I wrote.

Coming back to Cranford. I received an e-mail from him in which he wanted to "correct" me on a few things. He goes into a spiel and claims you had nothing to do with *Bard's Tale I* and *II*, that you were a hermit, out of touch with the larger process. What's the guy's deal?

Two things. Why don't you ask him to explain to you how the graphics routines work? How did he do the animation? He probably won't be able to tell you, because I'm the one who did it. That should right there tell you the truth.

As far as me being a hermit, there's a semblance of truth to it. Due to the fact of certain aspects of my upbringing, and the fact I was running away from my transgenderism, I did intentionally lock myself in a room because I did not want to face the world because I was embarrassed about how I looked, about how I was. I harbored this big secret, and I didn't want anyone to know. I wanted everyone to call me Burger because I didn't want them to call me that other name.

So, unfortunately, he is right. I mentioned earlier that my workday was get up, go into work, work until I'm too tired to work, leave. As far as out of touch, well that's his word against mine. I produced all these games, I wrote all these games, I made a lot of money for Interplay, my track record speaks for itself. I'm the one who wrote all the ports, I did the IIGS versions, the C-64, the fast-load drivers. There was so much stuff in there—right now I'm taking my old *Bard's Tale* code and porting it to iPhone. And that's because I wrote the frickin' thing. So …

I've tried to contact him about this, but he didn't respond.

Well, the trouble is that after *Bard's Tale II,* Michael did *Centauri Alliance.* He took the code drop he had of *Bard's Tale II* and used that as a base for a sci-fi game. I understand it wasn't a commercial success. It wasn't going to make him millions.

Then he went to college for, of all things, a philosophy degree, and then he went into theology. In fact, if you look in *Bard's Tale II,* many of the cities in the game are lifted directly out of the Bible. He got religion into him. I haven't spoken to Cranford since my transition, so I don't even know what he thinks about it. But I'm certain that since that letter came after my transition, he may also think ill of me because of it, which would go against his religious beliefs.

I wanted to talk a little about *Dragon Wars* (see Figure 3.6).

The Bard's Tale IV until three months before we shipped it!

So many innovations on the engine. What are your thoughts on *Dragon Wars*?

I think it was my best work. As you saw from *Bard's Tale II* to *III;* it was a huge leap in technology. As I was making *Bard's Tale III,* I was already making notes about where to take the engine next. So once we finished *Bard's Tale III* and got it out the door, I took a

FIGURE 3.6 *Dragon Wars* was released in 1989. It features a skill system and auto-mapper.

clean sheet of paper and wrote the *Bard's Tale IV* engine. This engine was totally using *Windows* and stuff like that, I had a huge screen for the graphics so it was a majority of the screen, but I still had little bars. I thought, what if we just had the name of the character and graphic bars for your health and magic—so we could put more information in a smaller space. But it was the same design, with the pillar with the magic spells, the box on the bottom for the text. I had pop-up windows. I had daylight, sunsets, I even had versions that actually had the sun moving behind the graphics. We ran out of space for that one. The auto-mapping was in a pseudo-2D, and I even had the ability to print, because I wrote printer drivers for all the popular printers then. If you hit control-P, it would detect what printer you had and actually print out. All of these little innovations were done.

I wanted a story. Mike Stackpole was busy doing novels and wasn't available, but we got Paul O'Connor. He started working on the scenarios. I actually found the book of all his notes and all my programming notes and everything. I just told him, design me a game and let me figure out how to make it real. So he just went nuts; there was this gigantic map and all this text, all this stuff. I said, "Hell or high water, I will figure this out!" And I will shove all this game into a couple of floppy disks. And I did.

One of the problems was that Paul O'Connor, just like me with *Bard's Tale III,* made the scenarios very linear. I wanted this game to be truly open-world. You start off in the Purgatory, but I intentionally put six different ways to get out of that city. And each one takes you on a completely different side quest. You can then go back to the other cities, but you could take them in any order. I wanted it so that no matter how it was, only when you were powerful enough to defeat Namtar, the bad guy—until then you could play it any time, in any way. That was a huge challenge, and one of the problems was that the stories I was given were like—if you defeat this castle, which talks about this war you won—but you didn't necessarily win it. I must have written a novel's worth of text in addition to what Paul did to fill in all the blanks. I even wrote extra side stories about princesses, and this brother and sister, and even had a place where you ended the game because you ended up ruling a kingdom. Even though it was technically a good ending, you didn't actually win the game because Namtar is still running around. But now you have to protect your kingdom.

It was everything I could think of on what would be the next-generation game, and, honestly, if the series had kept going, I would have done another engine with more innovations, and who knows what *Bard's Tale* or *Dragon Wars* would look like today had I continued to improve the series. It may have been *World of Dragon Wars* for all I know. *Dragon Wars* is one of the titles I'm most proud of for my entire career.

You wanted to continue making *Bard's Tale* games. Why did you make *Dragon Wars* instead of *Bard's Tale IV*?

EA wouldn't let us. What happened was that *Bard's Tale III* and *Wasteland* were shipping, and Interplay was a developer; EA was our publisher. So EA was getting a pretty big chunk of our revenue because that's the usual way it works with a developer and publisher relationship. We were coming out with another series of games; we wanted to do our own publishing. We wanted to use a company for our own distribution. This is where the rift began.

There was a bidding war going on, and Electronic Arts and Mediagenic went to war over who would publish Interplay's products. We were coming out with *Dragon Wars,* *Battlechess,* and *Neuromancer.* On all these titles, we were really set to take off. The trouble was that we went with Mediagenic. EA was pissed off, to say the least.

The publishing deal we had with *Bard's Tale* was that even though we owned the code and the scenario and so forth, the name *Bard's Tale* was trademarked by Electronic Arts. So if we wanted to release a game called *Bard's Tale,* we had to pay a licensing fee to Electronic Arts. They wouldn't even let us do it. They said, "Oh, you want to use the name? Publish through us." Push came to shove, and that's when Brian came to me and said, "Okay, we're calling it *Dragon Wars.*" I looked him dead in the eye and said, "You do know there's no dragons in the story?" "Well, it's *Dragon Wars* now."

So I had to come up with, at the last minute, a story that had a dragon in it, and put little quips every now and then that said there were dragon wars in the past. But since the game was only a month or two away from shipping, I couldn't redo the actual ending of the game to make a battle of the dragons. So, it's a running joke that we shipped a game called *Dragon Wars* with hardly any dragons in it.

That sounds like a *Monty Python* skit.

Very much so. But in spite of the critical acclaim *Dragon Wars* got—I mean it got five out of five stars, it got everybody raving about it—nobody knew what it was, and Interplay didn't have the budget to actually advertise the game properly. So, it did make money, but it wasn't a *Bard's Tale* runaway success.

What hurt me was that Electronic Arts was actually doing a *Bard's Tale IV* on their own. They had a team in Redwood Shores doing a *Bard's Tale* game because they owned the name. Of course they couldn't use any of my code, they couldn't use any of our art, but they could use the name. There was karma on that one, because after four years of development, they ended up killing the title.

There was a time when I had some of my team come up with a scenario for a *Bard's Tale IV* that I pitched to Electronic Arts, but they said the franchise was too old. Crap!

Do you think the setup with publishers and developers stifles the creativity of the designers?

In many ways, yes. What most people tend to forget, and because I've worn the CEO hat with Contraband and Logicware—this is a business. We need to make money because the paychecks I had to write to people were coming from a bank account that only had so much money. Once that money reached zero, everybody gets laid off. Whereas many people would like the id software model—it'll be done when it's done—most companies don't have that luxury, especially big companies with shareholders. They need to have profits every quarter. The only way to do that is to minimize their risk and go formula. Formulas are sequels or licensed titles like *Harry Potter* (the game). Those are the safest bets. Licensed properties—EA sports—they license NFL, NBA, NHL, NASCAR … There's your thing. Of course, lately they've been trying to branch out with new franchises like *Mirror's Edge,* but they still want to create a franchise they can milk over time.

One thing we actually found at Interplay, which I was raising the red flag all the time over, was that Interplay's greatest contribution to the gaming world was that we took risks. We came up with a lot of games that no one would touch because they were so off the wall—like *Tass Times in Tonetown,* I mean, who in the hell would come up with that and actually ship it? We did! *Neuromancer* was based on a book, but we did *Battlechess.* It's just chess with the pieces beating the crap out of each other. *Earthworm Jim, Boogerman, Clay Fighter,* all these games that Interplay did—we had a gimmick, but a lot of the publishers said, a game with clay warriors? Why don't you just make *Mortal Kombat V?* We made a lot of games that would have never seen the light of day. The trouble is that we did too many of them, and the company eventually ran out of money, which is why Interplay had to die and eventually be rebirthed as a company that was Interplay in name only—what exists today.

Companies like Electronic Arts, if they were to do a title that was risky and didn't have some real meat to back it up—to make people not afraid—it's a hard sell. It would kill the person's job. How would you like to be an executive producer who green lights a game that's never been done before, and the game tanks? You're fired. Nobody wants to get fired. So, they need to come out with *NASCAR 7,* then you can blame it on the NASCAR license. Oh, *Need for Speed,* maybe they don't like that type of game anymore, but we can still milk the franchise. It's not something innovative that's at fault, it's just the franchise is tired. Blame something else, so the executive producer can keep their job.

That's where, right now, in my opinion, indie games is where it's at for innovation. Who would do *The World of Goo, Minecraft* … Indie games are done by a couple of people locked up in a closet. They don't have anybody to answer to, so they can write something that's brand new and, in fact, doing something new and innovative is what gets them attention. Look at Introversion. They did *Uplink, Darwinia.* Those games, when you see them, are pretty out there. They made some money. Bingo! That is where the new ideas come from.

At a big company, if you were an executive producer and somebody gave you the idea for *Darwinia,* could you tell your CEO that *Darwinia* would absolutely, positively make you a million dollars? It's a hard sell. If it makes a million, you'll be a star. You'll be executive VP. If it bombs, well, the door is right there. With that kind of a choice, it really stifles the executive producer's ability to green light titles as innovative as *Darwinia.* Hence, the reason the vast majority of games these days are sequels, movie tie-ins, or some sort of celebrity hook.

One of my pet peeves right now is that a lot of videogames these days, for example, *Command & Conquer III,* have all these big-name actors in the cut scenes they film at a sound stage. Does that really add to the game? Did that really make the game a better game? I thought I was buying a videogame. I didn't think I was buying an interactive movie. I want to play a game. So many games these days are supposedly a first-person shooter, but you walk around a couple corridors, kill a couple formula monsters, and the game freezes as it plays a cut scene with voice actors. Then you continue on. Why don't I just buy the DVD and watch the movie? It's less work on my part. In fact, many games like *Bioshock* or *Dead Space*—I didn't play the game. But I pretty much did; I went to YouTube and watched people do a run through. As far as I was concerned I just watched the movie.

A game that did first-person shooter right: *Portal.*

One of my favorites.

Where are the cut scenes? Is there a cut scene in there? The only one there is that you actually get to see the cake. Other than that, it's just listening to GLADOS taunt you and go completely mad. Otherwise, it's the game. All about the game.

So you don't think that game would've been better if every few minutes it would have taken you out of the game and shown you fifteen minutes of cut scenes with some big-name actors?

I would have thought that they wasted a couple million dollars. Think about it, they saved a couple million dollars they could use to do *Half-Life III*, to be released in 2017. We hope.

I saw where someone had asked you if you could design any game, what would it be, and you said *Wasteland II*. I know a lot of gamers who would love to see that. Is there any possibility at all that you might do it?

Ask Brian.

He's the one with the keys to the franchise?

Talk to Brian Fargo. Leave it at that.

Speaking of him, what did you think of his *Bard's Tale* game?

[*Sticks finger down throat, makes gagging noises.*] When he first described it to me—he wanted to do a parody role-playing game. In my opinion, the *Bard's Tale* that Brian released was *The Princess Bride*. Even though it had Cary Elwes as the bard, the humor and everything was *The Princess Bride* and was not *Bard's Tale*. *Bard's Tale* is a game, a gritty role-playing game, with a party of fighting monsters in a fantasy role-playing setting. It wasn't *The Princess Bride* or *Shrek*. Now, the game that was shipped was one Brian wanted to make, so that's fine. But I disavow any connection to that *Bard's Tale* game.

If I were allowed to do *Bard's Tale IV*, I would do what I did in *Dragon Wars* but with the next technology. It would have 2011 technology. I would make something that would be pretty damn awesome. I just need someone to give me ten million dollars to do it. Unfortunately, my pockets—let me look in my purse. There's fifty bucks in there.

Maybe we can do a petition?*

Woohoo!

One last thing I wanted to ask you about was your port of *Half-Life* for the Mac. What happened with that?

Let's just say that someone at Apple—who will forever remain nameless, get someone drunk long enough and you might get the name, but that doesn't matter—overestimated the number of sales that would be potentially sold on the Mac. Let's understand this. This

---

* This interview was conducted before *Kickstarter* appeared on the scene.

was 1998, 1999. The Macintosh was dying. Sales of Mac games—I was doing them, selling them through Logicware—we would sell between eight thousand to forty thousand units. Anything that sold forty thousand units was stylin'. That's an awesome sale.

They fund the development of our project, fund our company, and we bust our asses. I worked on it—Andrew Meggs, I gotta give a shout out to him. I specifically hired him—Andrew, want to work for me, you'll work on *Half Life*. He said, I'll be there tomorrow morning. Everybody at Logicware had some hand in that game. It was a labor of love, and we made that game rockin'. We were playing against PC versions—in fact, we had a special server that was totally interactive and everything.

We were about three weeks from master. We just had some minor bugs here and there, just a little polish needed to be done. We were all set to do the maintenance to do the game forever. We were really into *Half Life*. We wanted this franchise to live forever, and we were gonna do it.

Then the orders started coming in. Okay, *Half Life* is now available for preorder, not to the general public, but to stores. The stores said, we love this game, we'll take fifty thousand copies! Of course, someone at Sierra was saying, where's the extra digit? Shouldn't there be an extra digit there? Of course, they asked the people at Apple—but they never quote sales figures.

Things happened. Things where people were upset. We were oblivious to all this; we were just working. Then one day I get a phone call and my friend at Sierra told me "Are you sitting down?" "No, but I can be." "Please sit down." So, I sat down. "We're cancelling *Half Life*." So at that point, I just dropped the phone. I picked it up and asked them to repeat it. "We're cancelling *Half Life*. Thank you very much for the work, you did a great job." "But what if we publish it? We'll pay you money." "Nope." It was set in stone. It was done.

It was pretty dismal when I went over to the team and called them together. We were paid in full, we got our early completion bonus. Take three weeks off. You can work on *Half Life* if you want, but we are going to avoid answering the phone right now and lay low. There's going to be a shit storm, and, yeah, we all ducked.

The press started going wild, saying Logicware screwed up the port. We didn't do anything! We were sitting there playing the game amongst ourselves, and saying, it's really great. There were all these companies, Mac Play, etc., and they all contacted Valve and threw money at them. Please let us publish it instead! Nope. Nope. That was the answer. Nope.

As a result, we were told to take the code and bury it. And it's been buried away since.

We don't want to end on that tragic tale.

It was pretty depressing. Oh, my God.

Think about all the Mac users.

Oh, we took flak for a year for that. They were convinced it was canceled because we screwed up. If they only knew!

As someone who has so much experience, going all the way back to the 8-bit platforms, all the ports and everything, I want to know what is your favorite 8-bit and 16-bit computer.

The 8-bit has to be the Apple II. That was by far the most versatile computer I've ever used. Even to this day, it's still more versatile. If I wanted to do a peripheral, it was trivial.

I must have wire wrapped twenty to thirty different peripherals, some that even became commercial projects, like my Harmony hand scanner. There was a Focus hard drive. Of course my Apple II development kit—I even did a card that let you control a 1541 disk drive so I could do my development on an Apple II, write it to a C-64 disk, and put it on the C-64 and run the game. That's how I was doing my ports. I had my source code on an Apple II.

Later on, they evolved it to the IIGS. I remember for many years the only way you could pry a IIGS away from me was from my cold dead fingers. It wasn't until '96 or '97 that I finally moved up to a PC. And that was a sad day for me. I really couldn't use the Apple II anymore. That was it.

As far as 16 bit is concerned, it would have to be the Amiga. The OS was way ahead of its time, the guru meditation errors were my friend, many, many times, usually because I had a bug that caused it. It was just so well done. And of course it got revived with the 3DO, because that console used a derivative of the Amiga OS.

That's all my questions. Anything else you want to add?

Don't do it—it's a trap!

I'm one of the old-timers who is still in the business. Most old-timers have retired or gone on to greener pastures. What drives me is that I constantly want to learn, better myself as an engineer, better myself as a person. I'm constantly looking for the next best thing.

If someone were to wave a big check in front of me and say, "Becky, could you do *Wasteland II* or *Bard's Tale IV*…" I may be turning in my resignation wherever I'm working.

Right now I'm working at Ubisoft at Toronto, working on the next *Splinter Cell* game, doing their engine work, and enjoying every minute of it. Previously I worked on Kinect, the camera and the motion capture stuff. All I can say is that I ain't done yet. Let's see what I come up with in the next ten years.

Do you think Kinect is going to take off?

It's awesome. The moment I saw the proof of concept demo, I knew Microsoft had something. I was privileged and honored to be part of that. I got to work on the camera, the micro controller on it, the coding in the camera itself. I did the code optimizations that run in the 360. I put a lot of blood, sweat, and tears into that—and along with over 100 engineers who worked many hours. There were lots of pizzas and late nights because we believed in this thing. Microsoft of all people! They allowed this thing to be done.

It's one of the few times I saw a major company take a huge risk. This camera could have easily never gotten past the design stage. We kept working at it, trying to make it so that all you had to do was a put a camera in a room, stand in front of it, it recognizes you, and you can play the game. Nothing else. That was our thing—we didn't want to make it so that you had to program it, do these poses—no, it had to be done automatically. When I got off that project, it was doing that. Now that I got to play the retail version, I'm so proud to have been part of that project.

What's even better is that people have reverse engineered the driver to the camera. Just seeing what people are doing on YouTube with the depth camera—to me, that camera just opened up the door to a whole slew of new innovations. I predict that in the next three years, we'll see some games that nobody ever thought of because that camera let them do it.

It's been an honor chatting with you.

It's wonderful to talk to you.

The pleasure was all mine!

If you got more questions, you know where to find me. Also, a little plug—I also do comic books and novels. If you want to read my *Sailor Moon* mixup go to http://sailor-ranko.com. You see, I do more than program! Now, I'll go find a burger.

It's burger time!

CHAPTER 4

Tim Cain, Game Designer X

Tim Cain (see Figure 4.1) is best known for producing two seminal computer role-playing games (RPGs): *Fallout* (1997) and *Arcanum* (2001). Considered masterpieces by fans of the genre, these games firmly established Tim's reputation as a superb storyteller and iconoclastic game designer. When I interviewed him on a sunny afternoon in June 2010, he was quite affable and mellow, but with a marked cynicism toward what he considers the failures and hypocrisies of the games industry as well as government and society. I get the impression that for Tim, living an insincere, inauthentic existence is a fate far worse than a nuclear holocaust.

His disillusionment with the status quo is easy to see in *Fallout,* where the scattered survivors of just such a holocaust eke out their existence among the irradiated remnants of an extrapolated '50s-era society. The war was brought on by foolish, self-serving government officials who afterward fled to a secret location, where they continue to plot against "the people" they allegedly are sworn to serve. Despite its more fantastic setting, we also find dark social themes in *Arcanum,* a world where racism is rife and mages are forced to sit in the back of trains. Despite the "open-world" dynamics of these games, players are often left feeling powerless despite their own heroism and tireless self-sacrifice. They remain unloved and unwanted even by their own people, who usually turn out to be no better than the ones they've been fighting against.

Tim has also struggled with publishers, who frequently disagree with him on matters of not only game design but also marketing and packaging. Although nice boxes and full-color, spiral-bound manuals add to the cost—and thus cut into the profits—of games, Tim is well aware how much these "extras" appeal to his core demographic: his fellow members of Generation X who grew up playing *Dungeons & Dragons* and watching movies like *Mad Max* and *Red Dawn.* This is the generation described by author John Ulrich as a "group of young people, seemingly without identity, who face an uncertain, ill-defined (and perhaps hostile) future." It's a fitting description for Tim's characters, fans, and perhaps the man himself.

How long have you been in the industry, Tim?

I started thirty years ago. I was in high school, and a friend of mine who'd recently graduated had gotten a job in a small games company in Virginia where they were making a card game for Electronic Arts—bridge (see Figure 4.2). He asked me to come over and

FIGURE 4.1   Tim is shown here in his office, surrounded by memorabilia from his previous projects.

FIGURE 4.2   Tim got his start in the industry by programming the card-shuffling routines in this otherwise forgettable bridge game.

help them with some card-shuffling routines. One of their programmers didn't know C; he was teaching himself out of a book. I knew C, and I also knew graphics on the Atari 800. Back in 1981, it had the best graphics of any personal computer on the market. Those two skills got me my job. I worked there for four or five years, putting myself through college with that job.

I left the industry and went to graduate school in California. After a few years, I discovered that's not what I wanted to do, so I got my job at Interplay in 1991.

I'm guessing that you played a lot of *Dungeons & Dragons* all during this period.

Yes! I was a big *Dungeons & Dragons* fan from version 1, the original set. I didn't really get into version 2, but got back into it hardcore with version 3.

Did you ever meet Gary Gygax?

I met him twice. Once in 1993 and again when he was doing *Cyborg Commando*. I actually got him to sign my copy of *Bard's Tale Construction Set* and my version 1 DM's guide. I also met him when I did *Temple of Elemental Evil*, when I'd call him on the phone to ask him questions about the module. There were some contradictory elements that I didn't know how to convert into a computer game.

What was it about *D&D* that appealed to you so much?

Well, when I was a kid, it captured my imagination in a way that other games just didn't. But looking back on it as an adult, I realize it was the open-endedness. All of my games have all been very sandbox, open-ended games. We didn't even have the term "sandbox" back when we were making *Fallout*, but that's what we were trying to do. We wanted to make a game that reacted to the way you played, and let you have your own style—to play your character the way you wanted to play it. That appealed to me a lot.

Did you also play lots of computer games?

I did. I played *Bard's Tale* and the *Ultima* series—my favorite is *Ultima III*, because it was the last time they stuck to pure fantasy. In *Ultima IV* you went to Mars, and I liked it better when it was pure fantasy. I played a lot of the games on the Atari 800 that were specific to that system, like *Star Raiders*. I played all of Sid Meier's games like *Hellcat Ace*, the stuff he was doing before he switched to turn-based games like *Civilization*.

You're the first designer I've interviewed who talks so much about the Atari 800. Most of the others got their start on an Apple II. Why the 800?

That machine is why I'm in game development now. I got it when I was in high school, and I kept it all throughout college … it had a really awful word processor, but I used it to do all my papers at the engineering school. I did horrible things to that machine—I opened it up and modded it … I copied EPROMs off it by turning it on when the case was open. I voided the manufacturer's warranty! But that's the kind of thing you do when you're a kid and you want to know how the machine works.

Did you play *Wasteland*?

I did play *Wasteland*, yes. It was very inspirational for *Fallout*. It was an amazing game because, when you died—it had no load and save. When you left the game, it'd just save out to the disk. You were really stuck with the consequences of what you did in the game, and I thought that was really fascinating. The load and save makes people creep through RPGs—and *Wasteland* didn't have that vibe at all. It was a unique RPG. It had a very high level of violence, too.

Do you prefer violent games, Tim?

[*Laughs.*] The game I'm making now is not violent like a lot of games have been. Most of my games have been very violent, M-rated, or at least teen-rated. Lots of drug use and prostitution; very adult themes, I would say. I'm fine with violent videogames as long as you have to deal with the consequences. In *Fallout*, it was often better to go the nonviolent route, but sometimes that just wasn't available.

Wasn't there an optional setting in *Fallout* to ratchet up the blood and gore?

Yes. We had a trait called "bloody mess." If you set that, it gave you the most bloody, violent, grossest death that was available for the creature model. People would actually choose that trait rather than something that would give them more survivability. They'd rather see the bloody mess.

Are you concerned that violent videogames might lead to real-life violence?

Well, I think that there are violent people who are drawn to violent things, but I think that if there weren't violent videogames out there, they'd just be drawn to something else. At least a violent videogame gives you an outlet that lets you express that in a way that's socially acceptable. For most people, I don't think it's an issue. I think we should make videogames across the spectrum.

One of the videogames I'm playing right now is *Braid*. There's violence in that you jump on things, but you don't have a gun, you don't stab people—you solve puzzles and manipulate time. I love this game; I think it's fantastic. People should enjoy a huge spectrum of games, and if some of them are violent, that's fine. But I don't think you should only play violent videogames. That shouldn't be a prerequisite for deciding to play a game.

A lot of people seem to think—wrongly—that all games should be appropriate for all ages.

Oh, I've explored some pretty mature themes in some of my videogames. [These] games should be played by adults and shouldn't be played by children.

Speaking of mature themes in games, what are your thoughts on romantic and sexual relationships between characters in games? One of the things that surprised me about your game *Temple of Elemental Evil* was the option for gay marriage—that was the first time I'd seen that in a game.

When we were putting together *Temple of Elemental Evil*, we'd put together all kinds of ways you could get involved with nonplayer characters. We had a good-looking woman who a male character could get involved with. We also had a really horrible woman whose father would try to convince you to get married to her so he could get her out of the house. We also had some male characters for female characters. It was Tom Decker [producer/designer] who said, "Hey, we don't have any male–male or female–female relationships." And I said, well, write some up! And he did the male character who was a pirate on a ship and a female character who was working at a brothel against her will.

Atari made us take out the brothel, though, so we lost the lesbian relationship—and I thought that was a sweeter relationship, because she didn't want to be working there, and you got to rescue her. The pirate one was kind of sad, because the gay pirate had been kidnapped as a child and forced to work as a cabin boy. It's a hard luck story, and you felt less like his rescuer and more like you won him from his master. It had a very different vibe than the lesbian relationship, but in both you had to work to get them. I remember seeing some people on forums saying, "Hey, I didn't see this in my game." Well, you're not going to see it unless you make it happen. There's a lot of dialog paths you have to go down before Betram is offered to you. It's no accident if your character is married to another man. I like that.

Well, let's talk about *Fallout* (see Figure 4.3). It's one of my favorite games, mostly because it's so unique—with such an interesting setting and aesthetic. Can you talk about its development?

Well, *Fallout* has a gray origin. I'd finished doing *Bard's Tale Construction Set* while I was a contractor for Interplay. Then they hired me on full-time to do a business simulation.

FIGURE 4.3   The hero of *Fallout* was born and raised in "Vault 13," a giant fallout shelter.

The difficult thing about that was that I just didn't know anything about business—and I can say that now after starting and shutting down Troika—I'm not a businessman, I know nothing about business.

But there was another programmer who was working on *Lord of the Rings*. Now, I'd read *Lord of the Rings* as a kid, and I loved it, and I wanted to work on that. But they wouldn't let us switch. So, as soon as my business game came out, I started pitching different ideas for RPGs. At the time, Interplay had picked up the *AD&D* [*Advanced Dungeons & Dragons*] license, and there were a couple of *AD&D* games in development. Brian Fargo was up for doing more RPGs, but he didn't want it to conflict with any of the *D&D* games—if they came out at the same time, he didn't want them to fight for shelf space or for the same audience.

At the time, I was getting people together every Thursday night to play role-playing games. We were playing *GURPS*,* and I really loved *GURPS*. I played it in all the different genres that were available. We did time travel, fantasy, sci-fi. I did one game that used every book I had—I called it *GURPS Everything*. Nobody knew what was going to happen in that game.

I convinced Brian that we really needed to make an RPG based on *GURPS* and started working on a *GURPS* engine. I programmed it up and did a character editor for it. For the first year I was the only one assigned to this project, which would later become *Fallout*. Toward the end, as people were coming off other projects, I'd get them to come in after hours and add to the game. I got some artists, a designer—Scott Campbell. Eventually we decided we wanted to do a postnuclear setting. We thought of a lot of really cool settings, including a time travel one with dinosaurs. We settled on the postnuclear setting, but it was initially very different than what ended up in *Fallout*. We had aliens, and it was all a simulation. We settled on the vault idea, though, and people started getting assigned to the project.

After a couple of years, we started having problems with [Steve Jackson] over the *GURPS* license, and we eventually lost it. But the way I programmed it, *GURPS* was a module within the game itself, so I just took it out, and Chris Taylor and I worked up new roles for combat and character creation. Chris came up with perks … We just came up with all that, and then just plugged it in as a module. It took only about two weeks to replace all that.

By that time, we'd grown to about thirty people. After another year—three and a half years, total—*Fallout* shipped as a fully fledged, SPECIAL-based nuclear game.

Do you think the game would've been better if you'd managed to hold on to the *GURPS* license?

Well, it's hard to say. I'm a huge *GURPS* fan, [and] I really wanted it to be *GURPS*, because the underlying engine was so generic that I was able to envision all of these different RPGs we could make with it afterward—in all kinds of different settings. In hindsight, though, because we made SPECIAL specifically for *Fallout*, after we had two-thirds of the maps and locations already made … We knew what kind of stuff we'd need, like stealth, ranged combat, melee combat—we made a system that was very specific, and it was easier for a casual player to make a character for SPECIAL than it would have been for *GURPS*. Still, I would've loved to see it come with *GURPS* (see Figure 4.4).

---

* GURPS, or Generic Universal Role-Playing System, is a 1986 tabletop role-playing system by Steve Jackson Games.

FIGURE 4.4 Originally intended to be based on a *GURPS* license, *Fallout* instead introduced an original and influential role-playing game mechanic of its own.

Let's turn back for a minute to the postapocalyptic setting of *Fallout*. It's proven very popular not just in games but also in books and movies. Why do you think people like it so much?

I think the idea that you can adventure in this world—your own backyard—but all semblance of civilization has been destroyed—that's really interesting to people. Especially for me with *Fallout 3*, which is set in Washington, D.C. Since I grew up there, I got to experience that firsthand. It was fun to run around D.C. and see the subway stations … It was the sense of, this is the world I'm used to, but it's not my world. That resonates with a lot of people. Also, there's the idea that if civilization was swept away, you'd have a chance to be a hero—your chance to stand on your own two feet and not be constrained by society. I think a lot of people feel that urge very strongly. It's part of the whole role-playing game attraction. You can be somebody you can't be in real life.

Of course, *Fallout*'s postapocalyptic setting isn't set in the present times, though. More like the 1950s.

We cast about for a long time trying to find what we wanted the vibe of the game to be. I forget who said it first, maybe one of our artists—don't set the game in the '50s, but in the future that the '50s thought was going to happen. That gave us a lot of great ideas. Robots would look like they did in *Fantastic Planet*—more like Robbie the Robot than Terminator robots. We'd watch movies. *Mad Max* and *Road Warrior* were on continuous loop in one of the artist's offices. We also watched *City of Lost Children*, because that had really unusual steampunk tech. We watched *A Boy and His Dog, On the Beach* … We tried to get an idea of what people in the '50s thought of the Cold War, because it was a society in which you thought that it was just a matter of time before the bombs fell. Bomb shelters, government agencies that dealt with it—it was just a matter of life back then. What I thought was

FIGURE 4.5   Much of *Fallout*'s tropes are inspired by the bizarre and often surreal civil defense literature of the '50s, such as the famous *Duck and Cover* film of 1951.

interesting was that the government really tried to downplay how horrible the aftermath of nuclear war would be. We actually saw a video where it said, "Kids, just crawl under your desk, and the fallout won't hurt you" (see Figure 4.5). Now we know that you're going to breathe it in; that it's going to be much, much worse than this movie is letting on. So we adopted Fallout Boy as our mascot. He's always smiling, always cheerful, even if his hands are being blown off because his gun backfires—he's happy and smiley taking a bath to get all the radiation off him. In reality, that's just not how it's going to be.

It seems to me that there's a lot of social commentary in *Fallout*; it's not just purely for fun.

We loved putting social commentary in *Fallout*. It's riddled with it. A big part of it is that you don't trust your own government—we made it quite clear that the government is lying to you. There needs to be a check and balance, the military needs to answer to civilians—because the military in *Fallout* took over. Corporations were taking over. You saw that the vault you were living in was made by Vault-Tec, and all the products were built by them, your Pip-Boy, everything was made by one, really invasive company. We even had a page inside the manual that described other manuals you could buy from Vault-Tec. They made light of all the horrible things that can happen to you after nuclear war. This company was making all of its profits off of people's fear of the war—and if war actually happened, they planned to profit off of that as well.

We were trying to comment that while this is all exaggerated, a lot of this is true about our own society. I don't think that anybody doubts that Halliburton profited off the Iraq War. Now it's profiting off the BP oil spill. It wouldn't hurt if that game and other games helped raise the consciousness of the players who played them—made them look at their own governments and society just a little more critically.

One thing I really liked about the game was how the look and feel of the interface matched the aesthetics of the game world.

Our lead artist, Leonard Boyarsky, liked to make everything look like it had a theme to it. Saying everything was made by the same company meant he could use the same textures for everything. You could see exposed bolts and screws on everything. He gave it a very manufactured, '50s look.

What was the atmosphere like at Interplay when you released the game?

We didn't receive a lot of attention leading up to *Fallout* shipping. There wasn't a big advertising campaign. Our team felt like they were making a triple-A product. Outside the team, they saw it as grade B. They figured their *D&D* games would be their big sellers, like *Descent to Undermountain*. That's not what happened [laughs].

We'd never planned to make *Fallout 2*. But suddenly, we were told that we were going be making sequels and keeping the team together.

The last page of the *Fallout* manual had originally been blank. We hastily put together an ad for a *GECK*, the *Garden of Earth Creation Kit*, just as a hook in case we got to use it. We decided that it was going to be our theme for *Fallout 2*.

We were a little surprised by the [positive] reaction to *Fallout*. We did ship it with bugs, which I wasn't happy with, but it got critical acclaim and we were all pretty pleased. Everyone was walking around with big smiles on their faces.

So Interplay was impressed, then. Considering how terribly *Descent to Undermountain* did on the market, I hope you got a serious promotion for making *Fallout*.

[*Laughs.*] Well, I wouldn't exactly say I got a pat on the back. The game shipped late, and since I was the producer, I was held accountable for that. It was never my intention to make *Fallout 2*—I intended to promote my associate producer for that. It didn't work out, so I got pulled back in. By then, it went from being a small team that nobody paid attention to— which was kind of nice—to being considered one of Interplay's big titles, and suddenly we were getting a lot of attention from marketing and sales. We were getting a lot of dictates about what we could do with the box and with the manuals. We were being told what we could and could not do, and it was very different.

It was suddenly less our game and more like this is IP [intellectual property] that Interplay owns. Interplay wanted to handle it now … And you have to remember, when I started at Interplay, I was employee forty-two. By the time I left, they had over five hundred employees. That made a big difference in how it felt to be an employee there.

What kind of disagreements were you having with them over the box?

Well, the original *Fallout* box was oblong. It was wider than it was high, and it had a flap that folded up, so you could see inside. We were told that none of that could be done anymore. They wanted to change the art, too. The original just had the powersuit helmet. We were told that we had to show a face—we had to have a person there instead of a helmeted figure. We were told the manual was too big and too expensive to make, and I thought that the manual was one of the best things about *Fallout*; it was really fun to read! These were things that, to me, worked for *Fallout*. I didn't understand why they were being changed, and I was upset about it. There were talks about adding a multiplayer component … So many different things were going on; it felt that because we had been successful, we were losing part of the game to a larger group that had bigger plans for it. And while Interplay owned the IP, and we did it on work-for-hire, it still felt like our baby and we were losing it … It was going to be raised by other people.

As a videogame collector, I share your passion for quality packaging, manuals, and pack-ins. It seems the current trend is toward digital distribution. It might be cheaper and faster that way, but I often feel like I'm being cheated out of a big part of the thrill.

Especially back in the '90s—way back in the '90s [*laughs*]—when you got a game, it took a long time to install it. So when you opened up a game, you had about thirty minutes to spend with the materials before you'd actually be able to play it, and I wanted it to be fun. I wanted the manual to congratulate you, welcome you to this new world—give you something to read that'd put you in the mindset we want you to be in when you played the game. I wanted the box to look like something that was from the setting of the game.

My lead artist felt very strongly that the manual, the inserts, and the box itself should look like a "found object." So he tried to make the box look rusty and have screws on it, just like the interface. I really liked that idea. It was more than just a tchotchke, like a cloth map or a coin. I wanted it to be something that you could play and interact with for thirty minutes as everything was copied off the stack of eight floppy disks or the brand-new CD-ROM. The CD-ROM had just come out, and that was exciting for us because we had so much room to play with. But it took a long time to copy that, and we felt like we needed to keep the player engaged while they did that.

You mentioned before how during the making of *Fallout*, Interplay had grown from what we'd probably call an "indie" today into a massive company. A big team clearly has its advantages, but it also seems like you lose a lot of creative control in the process.

I think about that a lot because the team I'm on now is one hundred people—and it'll probably be one hundred fifty by the time we ship. That's three times bigger than the size of Interplay when I joined it. My *Bard's Tale Construction Set* was done by three or four people; *Fallout* was just me by myself for a year; so I'm used to a lot more hands-on control of my games. But I've learned that the good thing about these large teams is that [they allow] you to make games you could never make with a small team. So I'm very happy when something like *Braid* comes out, which was only made by one person and an artist, but I want to play some of these big epic games as well. I've played *Dragon Age*, and that game

FIGURE 4.6 Arcanum is set in a "steampunk" universe where magic and science coexist.

is long, and epic, and I had a lot of fun with it—and there's no way ten people could have made it. It's like what I said about violent games—there should be a broad spectrum. I like casual games made by one or two people, but I also like big epic games made by a hundred.

Eventually you decided to leave Interplay and start your own company, Troika. What were your goals with your first game, *Arcanum*? It's a great departure from the standard fantasy tropes (see Figure 4.6).

Yes, I started Troika with Leonard [Boyarsky] and Jason [Anderson] after the *Fallout* games. We really wanted our turn at making a fantasy game, but of course we couldn't make a typical fantasy game. We needed a twist. So instead of setting our game in the fourteenth century, which almost every fantasy game seems to be mired in, with horses and wagons, castles and moats ... We asked, well what if an industrial revolution happened and it was the eighteenth century, and you were getting locomotives and steam-powered engines, and how would that affect orcs and elves? I think it was Leonard who said that the orcs would be the slaves of all the capitalist machinery. We worked out what the orcs would do, what the elves would do, and it sprang to life. Within a month or two, it had morphed into this Victorian society that was this weird mix of eighteenth-century technology and magic. We had a lot of fun with that.

And part of it was that it was just the three of us for about six months, so we could move quickly and be nimble. We put together a prototype for Sierra that had one level done, and we had magic working and moving shadows—I don't think that made it into the game. But a lot of it was working, and that's a testament to how quickly you can move when it's just a small group. I tell people sometimes that there's more of me in *Fallout* and *Arcanum* than in any other game, because they were made with a small group.

And then there's *Temple of Elemental Evil*, another great role-playing game. It's probably the last major role-playing game I played that still featured the turn-based combat I love so much.

I loved making that game. We had such a good time—such a good group, only a dozen people. We were originally given eighteen months, and I'd done a proposal for a game that didn't include all the classes—I'd gotten rid of the druid and the paladin, and maybe the bard, because they were just tough to do. But Atari wanted all the classes in there, and we gave in. But we really shouldn't have done that. We were really stressed to make a triple-A title in eighteen months …

And then, about a year into it, *D&D* version 3.5 came out. That put us in a really bad bind. In a few months we would have put our game out, but it was based on 3.0, and 3.5 was out. We asked Atari for some extra time, and got two months. So we scrambled and pulled out mechanics, replacing them with 3.5 … Atari wanted us to remove other stuff, so we gutted the little town of Nulb because there was a lot of evil, adult-oriented areas that they just wouldn't approve.

In hindsight, while I loved making it, the game didn't end up what I wanted it to be. I was also upset that it got shipped with bugs, because we'd actually fixed some of them, but we weren't allowed to put out a patch because QA had already been disbanded. We couldn't get the patch approved and couldn't release an unauthorized patch … I felt really bad that people were trying to play our game, and we had a patch that we couldn't release.

I think for a twenty-month game, it was phenomenal. But people don't buy a game and think well, for a twenty-month game, it was worth it. What they saw was a game that still needed six months of development time to be a triple-A product.

I loved that I got to talk to Gary Gygax. I'm glad he got to see it before he passed away. But I wished it had turned out differently.

What did Gary think about your work?

He said he loved it. I called him several times with questions about his modules … He loved absolutes. Anybody who's read his modules knows that he likes to say things like, "When this trap goes off, it will release a gas that makes everybody fall asleep, even elves, who are resistant to sleep." But then he puts in an item that "gives you a saving throw against anything, even if it says you don't get one." So we're trying to code this, and we don't know what to do. So I'd just call him up and ask him his intent if someone walked in that room and was wearing that item. Sometimes he'd just say, "I don't know," and asked me what I thought we should do. Sometimes he asked what would be the easier thing for a computer to resolve. It was fun; he really understood that we'd moved the module to a different medium, and some things had to change because of that. We sent him a copy; I hope he got to play it.

Do you think that turn-based games like *Fallout*, *Arcanum*, and *Temple of Elemental Evil* will ever make a comeback? I really prefer that style to the real-time games of today. Are they just dead?

I'm not sure, because it seems like the industry would rather have more genres than less. It's not just turn-based games; adventure games have disappeared, which I find really sad. I think that real-time games appeal more to the younger crowd, and, for whatever reason, if you don't appeal to the demographic of males aged eighteen to twenty-five, you're a more difficult sell.

It may also have to do with the rise of consoles. People who play console games usually play with more than one person, whereas PC games it's just you. If you're playing a console game with two, three people, you don't want to wait for your turn—it's more fun for everyone to jump in and do something together.

As the creator of the original *Fallout*, Tim, I'm curious what you think of Bethesda's *Fallout 3*.

There were a lot of surprises, some of them pleasant. I actually enjoyed playing the game, which I know disappointed a lot of my fans. But I thought they did a good job of understanding the universe and setting a different kind of game in it. It was very much an FPS [first-person shooter] RPG. But they understood SPECIAL, and I think they adapted that well to the first-person, real-time RPG. They got a lot of the lore done well.

The tricky part of *Fallout* was always the humor, and that's what I'm most critical about. But humor is subjective, so I've kept my criticisms of that to myself. You can't slight somebody for not having the same sense of humor that you have.

Bethesda took it and they owned it—in both senses of the word. They own it, but they also owned it. *Fallout 3* fits in their line of products with *Oblivion*, whereas I don't think *Fallout 1* or *2* would have fit in.

What would you have done differently if you had produced it?

I wouldn't have used so many of the same elements. It was a bit of a stretch to have the mutants out there. FEV—the Forced Evolutionary Virus—was supposed to be localized to Southern California, so it's a stretch to have it way out on the East Coast. I would have come up with something completely different. It's a postnuclear world, there are a million stories out there! Let *Fallout 1* and *2* be in one corner of the world, and do something new for this corner of the world.

Having said that, I think *Fallout Vegas* is interesting because it's close enough to the New California Republic that you can do a lot of stuff with that, and it makes sense because it's right next door. But *Fallout 3* should have been different. Maybe they didn't want to do that because they wanted fans to have lots of touchstones from the first game, but I think it could've stood on its own.

Would you think somebody was nuts if they released a turn-based RPG in this market?

I would not look at them like they were nuts. Actually, in this market, if you did release a turn-based RPG, it'd be a differentiating feature. Young people who had never played a turn-based RPG would probably say, "Hey, have you seen that novel new concept where you take your own turn? It's new and wild!"

Now, of course you couldn't do that in MMO [Massively Multiplayer Online]. We jokingly used to talk about a turn-based MMO, where you go, then you wait for 9,999 other people to take their turn. Then you'd go again. That should never be made.

One thing I like about turn-based is that when you cast a spell, like a fireball, and what you catch in the area of effect is really what you catch. When I started playing real-time with pause games, you lost all of that. A lot of those spells were far less useful than the original game expected them to be. I loved *Baldur's Gate,* but I found myself using magic missile a lot more than fireball … By the time I cast the fireball, the units had moved out of the area.

The last Troika game was *Vampire: The Masquerade—Bloodlines*, another cult classic. I know it met with some division among the critics.

Well, that was an unusual development because we started it at the same time as *Temple*. I came over onto *Vampire* after a year and a half as lead programmer, and took over scheduling, meetings, and boss AI. I put in all the end bosses. It was a different experience for me because I was stepping into a game that already had two years of development on it.

I liked it, but we had to ship it the same time as *Half-Life 2*, and we hadn't finished the last few levels, and it shows. The first two-thirds of the game plays really well, and then it just stops and becomes an endless series of warrens. You just fight monsters endlessly until you get to the end boss.

It was the first true 3D game I'd worked on. We used the Source engine. But it was more Leonard and Jason's baby than mine. Out of all the games I've worked on, it has the least of me in it.

What are your thoughts about MMOs, by the way? They sure aren't anything like the role-playing experience you got with tabletop *Dungeons & Dragons* or the story immersion you get with *Fallout*.

I think a lot of MMOs don't provide a lot of ways for people to role-play a characteristic. I know someone who plays a character in *World of Warcraft* who describes her character as an "octogenarian vegan." So she pretended she was eighty years old, she never jumped, she turned off run. She walked everywhere she went, and she refused to eat meat or drink milk, which was really tough as a mage. She'd eat pastries, which she pretended were made without lard. She'd tell people this when she joined a group, and they'd look at her like she was strange. But I *loved* playing with her! She was fun.

Well, a lot of MMOs don't give you opportunities to role-play like that. You don't have many ways to customize yourself, of interacting with NPCs [nonplayer characters]; to do things that have consequences for your character, so you can tell people, "Well, I've decided that I'm a pacifist," or "I'm going to steal everything that's not nailed down." I'm hoping this will change.

One thing I've noticed is that all the top MMOs are set in pretty traditional fantasy universes. There are a few science fiction ones, but I'd love to see more steampunk and

postapocalyptic games out there. I was really excited when _Tabula Rasa_ came out, but of course it didn't last long.

Science fiction is hard to do. Because you have to give people touchstones. If I tell you there's a vampire, you know what it's going to be—no matter what the game is. But if I tell you that an alien is attacking you, you have no idea. You have to be really careful when you do sci-fi, giving them lots of comforting touchstones, and what I call connotations; things that remind them of things they already know about. If you're attacking a vampire, and you see sunlight coming in through the window, maybe you think, I'll attack him there. So if he starts taking damage standing in the light, you feel happy, because something you thought was right actually worked. I think sci-fi games can err on the side of such unusual things that players can't figure out what to do.

Tim, you have a career that most game designers can only dream about. What kind of advice do you give young people who want to follow in your footsteps?

I really have a hard time with this question, because the industry I got into twenty-nine years ago is so different than the one now that I'm not sure what to tell people to do. I can tell you what I look for in résumés. If you're a designer, I want to see that you've actually made a game. You can make a pencil-and-paper game, you can make a board game, but bring it in and let's play it for a half hour. If you're a coder, code something. Code up a little casual game. If you're an artist, of course you have a demo reel, but play some games and know the terminology. Show that you're passionate. I look for signs of passion in people who give me résumés. Do something on your own; get a degree, a BFA … You've showed that you can set a goal for yourself, and you achieved it. You don't have to go to school, but do something to demonstrate that you have the passion.

We're not making accounting software. We're not making an SQL database here. We're making games, and that's as much art as it is engineering, and you have to bring some of that to the interview.

So, Tim, if you were on the other side of that interview, and they wanted to know about your passion, what would you say?

Uhh … [_silence_]. I guess that I'm not afraid to try stuff, and I'll admit that every game I've put out has had some stupid features in it that I couldn't let go of—but I'm not afraid to try things. I love creating things from scratch. I've never really made a sequel. I've made a lot of engines on my own. Coming from an engineering background, I think of things as categories and subtypes, and relationships between things, and balancing. Four years of engineering school really helped me think that way. A lot of designers come from very different backgrounds. I don't meet a lot of ex-engineering designers, though I did hire one.

I'm really curious. What were some of these stupid features you were talking about?

[_Laughs._] Oh, you want me to list some of the stupid features in my games? Let's see. _Fallout 1_ was originally designed without any followers, and one of my scripters convinced me it could be done in-game. I wished at that point I had gone back and done it in code, because Ian would constantly shoot you in the back with his Uzi. He honestly didn't know his shots went out in a cone, because he wasn't tied into the coded AI system in any way.

When I did *Temple of Elemental Evil,* I was a pit bull about the original NPC rules and that they took a share of treasure. So they'd actually roll and take treasure from monsters you killed. So you'd be sitting there, about to die, and look! There's a healing potion. And then one of the NPCs would take it. That was stupid for a lot of reasons. For one, I heard that a lot of people would hire NPCs, go out of town, and kill them to get all their stuff.

About a week after it shipped, one of my artists said, "Why don't you just have them take a share of money instead of treasure?" I looked at him and said, "Why didn't you think of that a week ago, before we shipped?" He just thought of it. But it was just me being stupid, too enamored with the idea of NPCs rolling for treasure.

I need an editor, someone to look at my ideas and say, that one's good, that one's good … but *that* one really stinks.

CHAPTER 5

Brian Fargo, Patron of Wizards

Brian Fargo is a familiar name to fans of computer role-playing games (CRPGs). As the founder of Interplay Entertainment, Brian oversaw many of the genre's greatest releases, including *The Bard's Tale, Wasteland, Baldur's Gate, Planescape: Torment,* and *Fallout.* As of this writing, Brian is back at the forefront of the CRPG scene, leveraging the popular Kickstarter funding platform to develop an official and very long-awaited sequel to *Wasteland.*

I'd like to think my interview with Brian and the enthusiasm from me and my audience about a *Wasteland* sequel had something to do with Brian's decision to go ahead with the project. I asked Brian what he would've done differently if he'd had the rights to the *Wasteland* license back in the '90s. Would *Wasteland 2* have been a different animal than *Fallout*? After some intense thought, he said that he didn't know but that he's "designing it in [his] head right now." This might well be the first time someone has captured the birth of a game design on video!

At any rate, the fact that his project has raised nearly a million dollars—all of it donated by fans rather than publishers—shows just how influential and respected Brian has become as a producer, developer, and designer. Nobody understands the CRPG fan like Brian Fargo, even if he's felt too constrained (until now) to make the games he really wants to.

I have a hard time imagining what my childhood and teenage years would have been like without the many glorious hours spent playing Interplay's CRPGs. Getting to sit down with the man who made them all possible was truly a pleasure. Surrounded by original game boxes and other memorabilia from his most successful projects, Brian told me the amazing story of Interplay's rise and fall (see Figure 5.1).

You must have a lot of incredible stories, especially about computer role-playing games. Let's talk about you and your origins. How did you first get involved with the industry? I hear you got your start with Saber Software and a game called *Demon's Forge*.

FIGURE 5.1　Brian Fargo is responsible for producing many classic computer role-playing games.

Boy, you're really testing my memory banks on a lot of this stuff. Let's hope I can remember all the detail you want me to remember; there's been so much that's gone on over the years. Saber Software … Well, I'll go back a bit further.

I'm a product of all the things that came together to make computer games. I was a huge reader of books, like Michael Moorcock, Tolkien—a lot of classical stuff, heavy metal magazines, comic books. I'd go see a double feature every single weekend. I've always loved entertainment.

I got my Apple II when I was in high school. There really wasn't an industry at that point, so like a lot of people who go into business, you play a lot of other people's products, and you get to a point where you're like, "You know what, I can do better than that." So that's what launches you into the industry.

Saber Software was my first company. I'd just graduated from high school. I did the very cliché stuff: hand duplicating disks, putting them in baggies, and handing them out. I did a lot of the coding myself, and the artwork was done by Michael Cranford, who ended up being the main guy on *Bard's Tale 1* and *2*. I wasn't a particularly great artist, so he'd draw them for me, and I'd put them on a graphic tablet and sketch them dot by dot to get them in there.

Demon's Forge was my first game; it was an old graphic adventure game. That was the first thing I did for the Apple II.

So let's talk about Interplay. I was reading a lot of your previous interviews, and you talked about your ideology at Interplay, a corporate strategy, and [emphasis on] camaraderie. What was it like at Interplay?

In general, my ideology is to focus on the sensibilities of everything. Whether it was the first game at Interplay or all the way up to *Fallout* or *Hunted: The Demon's Forge,* I focus on the sensibilities of what I think is important. What players like, what I like to play. I drill down on those things, and once everybody rallies around and gets the concepts, then the product takes on a life of its own. It becomes bigger than what any one person could ever do. So that's always, consistently been the way I manage product—that's my style. I don't micromanage; I believe in getting people who understand the concept.

[Interplay's] first product came about in a funny way. There was a teacher at University of California, Irvine named Chris Wells, and he was friends with a professor who was getting a contract from *World Book Encyclopedia,* and the professor needed someone to help code it. I got the contract and hired Chris to be my first employee. His job was to get more contracts … That didn't end up working out, but since it was just me and Chris, we were Wells Fargo.

Later on, I started layering on some other employees: Troy Worrell; Jay Patel; Bill Heineman, who's now Rebecca Heineman; and Michael Cranford. [Michael] didn't come on until later [because] he was at Berkeley. But he was a big part of our next level of success. These were the key players early on.

Was Interplay a formal place? A suit-and-tie environment? If we could zip back in time and walk into the office, what would we see?

We always had a great, fun environment. We had *Joust* and *Mario Bros.* [arcade machines], and I always made sure I remained the champ at those machines. Whenever the employees got out of line, I'd lay the smack down on them at *Mario Bros.* and *Joust.* Jay Patel, who's one of the senior engineers at Blizzard—Jay and I would go head-to-head for hours and hours. After Interplay grew to 500 employees, we'd always joke that there was a point when somebody went out to lunch, and we all hid in the closet and jumped out and scared them. You could never fit the [entire] company in a closet again.

But you could dress how you wanted, come in and stay as long as you want there. It was all so new back then. It was our family. You'd come in to work, and you wouldn't go home until eleven o'clock at night. But that was okay, because you'd go to dinner with them, then we'd play *Dungeons & Dragons* together. We were always hanging out as a group of people. There was no differentiation between your business life and your personal life.

So let's get into the hits. Was *Bard's Tale* the first big hit for you guys?

Well, it was our first *big* hit, for sure. But we did a graphic adventure for Activision before that called *Mindshadow* (see Figure 5.2), which was basically *The Bourne Identity.* You woke up on an island, your memory had been erased, and you had to play the game to remember things. When you found a keyword, you'd type THINK, and then the keyword, and your memories would come flooding back. I worked with Michael Cranford on that. We did a three-product adventure series with Activision, which was *Demon's Forge, Mindshadow,* and *Tracer Sanction. Mindshadow* was a middling success—megahit, no, but a solid seller.

Bard's Tale was really the hit. It put us on the map, it earned us significant royalties—so we could grow the company to the next level. It made us in demand. Somebody told me that when EA was selling our *Bard's Tale* and *Bard's Tale II,* we were generating 10% of all of EA's sales.

Were you friends with Michael Cranford before all this?

I've known Michael since high school. In fact, when I had the Apple II, I'd let him take it on weekends and let him program on it. I was constantly letting him use my computer. We played *Dungeons & Dragons* for thousands of hours. He was the best artist out of the group and a very good writer, a bright guy. He ended up being the dungeon master.

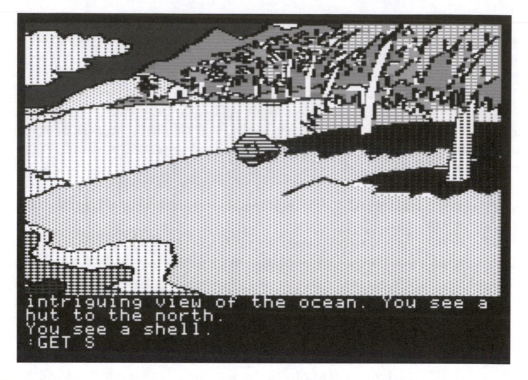
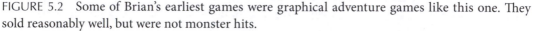

FIGURE 5.2 Some of Brian's earliest games were graphical adventure games like this one. They sold reasonably well, but were not monster hits.

Sometimes with *D&D*, the rules and the statistics—it can become fairly technical in nature. That's part of its fun, but Michael did a great job of layering on a storyline and making it all more interesting. He was great.

What do you think it was about *Bard's Tale* that made it so successful?

Well, at the time *Wizardry* was the big thing. It was the top-seller. It was the de facto standard. You'd look in a computer magazine, and the top three sellers would be *VisiCalc*, a word processor, and *Wizardry*. *Bard's Tale* brought more personality, color, sound, music. It brought a lot of elements that *Wizardry* didn't have. There were subtle nuances, like day and night, and tension-inducing things. Also, we shouldn't forget that it was on the Commodore 64, where *Wizardry* was not.

Once the other machines started coming online, like the Amiga or the IIGS or the Mac, because we were so graphically based, we were really able to shine and take advantage of those new platforms. *Wizardry*, with the black and white, didn't really make that leap.

I've heard so many developers talk about how much they loved *Wizardry*. Maybe we should back up a bit and talk about why people thought it was so compelling.

It was the first to really nail the *D&D* experience on a computer. One, you didn't have to be with a group to play it; two, it took care of all the dice rolling for you. It was a very well balanced game. One thing that both *Wizardry* and *Bard's Tale* did back then that games stopped doing—but I always liked—is that you couldn't save your game in the dungeon.

You'd go into the dungeon, spend an hour, or two, and try to push it. Aw, you're down this far, what's one more door? And then you're being attacked and running for the surface for your dear life. And if you make it back to the top with three hit points left—knowing that if you'd died you would've lost all that work—it was such a great feeling. There's no greater fiction one could write. You'd stand on your chair and cheer. There were some great dynamics to those old games that don't exist now.

Tell me about *The Bard's Tale*, how it came together. What was your role, what was Cranford's role, and what was Becky Heineman's role?

Part one was really all Michael Cranford (see Figure 5.3). I've got to give him credit. He did most of the design, the artwork, and the programming. I helped him with some of the design, but even I shy away from taking too much credit from that. As far as Bill's or Rebecca's contribution—it was minimal. It's unfair that she tries to take credit away from Michael. I think out of the thousands of lines of code, there might have been forty from her—optimized some graphics. What she was very good at was converting code; that was her forte. She's a genius coder and a great storyteller [*laughs*]. Great at porting, but had nothing to do with the design.

After part one, we [Cranford and I] had a big falling out—a contractual thing. But we still kept working together. He made *Bard's Tale II* a bit too punitive to the player. It was too hard. I tried to get more active with the design, but he had his way.

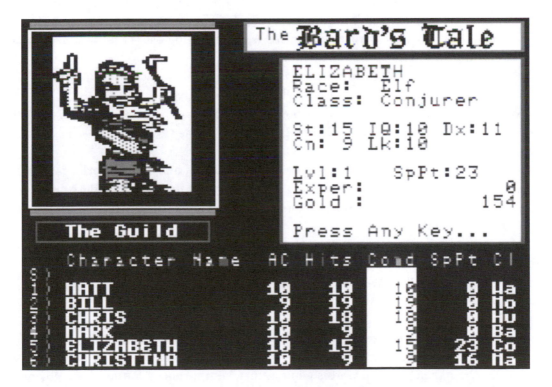

FIGURE 5.3 *The Bard's Tale*, officially known as Tales of the Unknown: Volume I, updated the Wizardry formula with colorful graphics and a detailed town called Scara Brae.

There's a story that Michael literally held *The Bard's Tale II* disk hostage until you backed down on some contractual stuff. Is that true?

That's true. Michael and I are friends again, but that was a big falling out. At that time, nobody in the company got royalties—they got stock options, but I used the royalties for future growth. Toward the end, Michael had a change of heart. I was stuck with Electronic Arts, saying we were done—and I needed the master, and I had to hide from them the fact that Michael had a change of heart on the deal. So I had to negotiate with Michael to pay him royalties instead. Mind you, he'd have been better off taking the stock options at this point.

While we're talking about *The Bard's Tale*, we should talk about the one you designed— the one you did with inXile. Looking back on it, are there things you would've done differently? Rebecca had called it more *Princess Bride* than *Bard's Tale*.

Well, I can see why the diehards weren't happy about it. I think it's important to know that I'd taken a very short break from the industry—five months. I was playing all the different role-playing games, and I'm booting these games—and going right in and killing rats. I'm thinking, "I have been asked to go kill rats for twenty straight years, okay?" It seemed so insane that people hadn't changed it up a bit, you know? So, I thought, "What would it be like to have a character that had himself been playing too many role-playing games?" We thought we'd have some fun with it. We thought maybe the hardcore gamer/player would think it was funny, because we ripped on every convention of role-playing games.

You could say *Princess Bride,* but only because of the humor and parody. The humor and parody were great, but it didn't try to capture *The Bard's Tale* experience. I can see from that perspective why they were disappointed. We were feeling cheeky and wanted to do something off-the-wall, so that's what we did.

Whatever I [end up doing] with *Wasteland,* I would play it straight. I wouldn't do anything funny; just straight-up, give people what they were expecting.

I'm proud of [my] *Bard's Tale,* and anybody who played it with an open mind and wasn't trying to relive their time with *The Bard's Tale* of the '80s, they loved it …

While we're talking about humor, I hope we can talk about one of my favorite games on the Amiga—*Battle Chess*. You said in an earlier interview that you thought what made the game successful was the humor. I know a lot of people probably think, "Man, how humorous is chess?"

I can tell you a couple of fun stories about that one. There were a lot of knockoffs, but they just thought it was about one piece attacking another piece—they would do these really dry combats. Blah. We had really clever stuff, like the rook eating the queen and burping afterward. On the Mac version, the bishop pulls out a scroll that says "New Mac Price List," and the other piece falls over from the pricing. The humor made it work.

When I was having lunch with George Lucas at the Skywalker Ranch, they wanted to find a way to merge LucasArts and Interplay. I was enamored. I still have the book he gave me, which he signed "May our forces join together." But he goes, "*Battle Chess*! Where'd you come up with that?" I said, "Well, I don't know." I cracked up (see Figure 5.4).

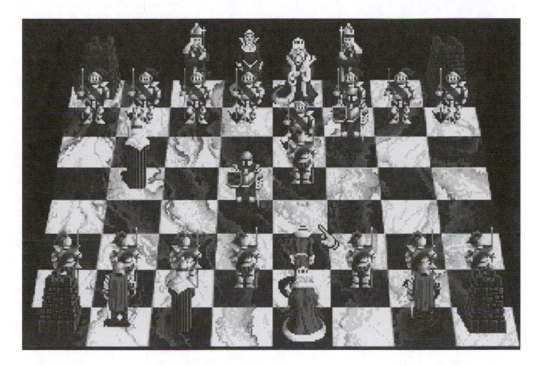

FIGURE 5.4 *Battle Chess* "updated" the classic game of chess with fun and often hilarious animated combat.

Wasteland is a game that anybody who likes role-playing games is familiar with, a cult classic. What's the story behind it, and why do you think its setting resonates with so many different kinds of gamers?

A couple of different things. One thing that made *Wasteland* such a big deal at the time, and why so many people still have a very positive memory of it, is that it was the first sandbox game. It was open world: do anything you want, any order you want, and see ripple effects that could happen one minute or thirty minutes later. There were other open games, like *Ultima*, but things tended to be more compartmentalized—they weren't as rippling as this thing was.

The moral ambiguity also made it so interesting. That was very much what we riffed off [of] when we did *Fallout*. When we did the vision document for *Fallout*, six out of ten things were straight out of *Wasteland*. It was all right there—bang! The only reason there is *Fallout* is that I didn't have the rights to do a *Wasteland 2*.

The postapocalyptic [setting] is something that people could grasp. It was something that could actually happen. It's not like with sci-fi; I don't think I'm going to be flying around in a spaceship anytime soon. But this kind of stuff feels ... it's gritty realism. Women in wheelchairs with machine guns—it's gritty stuff.

And the writing was great. It was Michael Stackpole and Ken St. Andre, and Liz Danforth, Mark O'Green. What people have forgotten is that *Wasteland* took almost five years to do. It was huge because each square was a program.

You mentioned that you couldn't get the rights to *Wasteland 2*. If you had attained the rights, would *Wasteland 2* have been different than *Fallout*?

Hmm ... That's a good question. I think that uh ... I'm kinda designing it in my head right now. I have to really think about that answer, because it wasn't really an option. I think the party-based nature and the way the AI [artificial intelligence] worked in *Wasteland* would've been brought to the forefront more. I found myself in *Wasteland* spending more time managing my NPC [nonplayer character] party in a way that was different, blowing up clips, getting upset with them. The party-based nature of it would have been played up more; the personality of the player would have been the biggest thing.

A lot of people don't realize that *Fallout* was going to be based on Steve Jackson's *GURPS* rulebook. We ended up getting off that because Steve was offended by the content and where it was going. I had strong feelings about the sensibilities of what *Fallout* should be, so we dropped out of the Steve Jackson deal and created our own system.

It's my understanding that he thought it was too violent. Is that right?

Yeah, yeah. He saw the opening—the one most people consider to be one of the greatest cinematics of all time, with the soft music and the violent backdrop, and he just wouldn't approve it. And I told him, "Well, if you don't like that, you ain't seen nothing yet!" So that was the beginning of the end.

I wanted to also ask you about a curious game called *Stonekeep*. I really don't know what to make of this game. On the one hand, the graphics are top-notch, state of the art for the time. But some people felt the game engine was too old, obsolete.

Yeah, another nearly five-year epic of ours. Boy, you can't fault us for trying to be ambitious. At Interplay, we were always trying to be on the cutting edge. That was a product that if it'd just gotten out a year earlier, we would've nailed it. But so much time had passed during the development that by the time it came out, the other dungeon games like *Ultima Underworld* let you look up, down, and side to side like *Doom*. That's not how we started. We went for graphic fidelity; we're going to lock the camera in place, but it's going to look beautiful. But by the time it came out, the scrolling view had become the de facto standard. So right away, we were in the hole coming out of the chute. And that hurt us a lot.

Stonekeep had a lot of personality, singing, puzzles, lots of depth (see Figure 5.5). You know, whenever I've tried to lighten the front end, so that it isn't so heavy and hardcore for new users to get in—it tends to bite you in the butt. You're better off just letting them create the character, get down and dirty. We lightened up the front end [too much], and the hardcore just said, no, it's not for me. Truthfully, there's a ton of gameplay there, a lot of depth ...

I think people look back on it now and say, whoa, what a classic. But it suffered from that front end and the comparison to *Ultima Underworld*.

It does seem like the game *Doom* had a lot to do with the negative reception.

It did, absolutely. There was no *Doom* when we started, but there was after that!

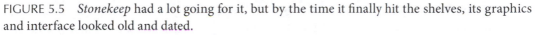

FIGURE 5.5 *Stonekeep* had a lot going for it, but by the time it finally hit the shelves, its graphics and interface looked old and dated.

Let's talk about all of the licensed games you've done: *Star Trek, Lord of the Rings* **… In general, what are the challenges of doing a licensed game? A lot of people seem to think, "Well, it's a licensed game, so it must be crap." There's a lot of crappy licensed games out there. Why is that, and how were you able to buck that trend?**

Hmm … A couple things. It wasn't as bad back then as it is now with the "it's a licensed game, it must be crap." There wasn't as much of that going on. There was a little of that stigma but not much.

When we picked up *Star Trek,* it was a dead license. I think it was twenty-five years old. People weren't excited about that at all. But we did that first adventure game, and we really nailed the sensibilities of *Star Trek,* and it was a big hit, and everybody loved it.

With any license, you've really got to nail it. You've got to nail it for the audience. Take *Shrek.* Apparently, that's based on a children's book—I'd never heard of it before. But they took that movie, and they nailed *Shrek* … We have that same responsibility.

[Considering] games to movies and movies to games, I try to ask, "Would this [game] stand by itself without [the license]?" If it could, it's probably the right thing to be doing.

As a producer, would you rather work on a license or an original property?

I don't have an affinity for one or the other. It depends, right? If you said, "Hey, Brian, would you like to do a *Star Wars* game?" [I'd] be very excited about that. It really depends what they are.

Creatively, we like our own universes. With the *Bard's Tale* remake, there was a lot of work and study done into recreating that universe. There's a lot of Scottish mythology and Celtic stuff … There was a lot to it.

On the other hand, launching a new franchise is more difficult [now] than it's ever been. There are more hurdles to getting a new franchise out there, because there's already enough. I have to think about market conditions.

I want to get your perspective on modern role-playing games. I'm a big fan of the classics like *Bard's Tale* and *Fallout*, but it just seems like I can't get my fix anymore. Maybe we could zero in on *Fallout 3*. Do you think that's just as groundbreaking as the first two?

Well, I think they [Bethesda] did an excellent job. I mean, look. Everything's about trade-offs. No matter what you do, you make a trade-off in development. The first two games weren't console games; they were PC games. The interface and the way you approach a console is different than a PC. You're not going to bring the exact PC experience across. You could make this really vocal minority extremely happy, but you're going to ruin the sales.

We could nitpick [*Fallout 3*]. I would've done an edgier product. But they did a wonderful job, and it's certainly outsold the first two combined times whatever. I didn't have a big problem with what they did. They did a respectable job. They had a great mythos to start from, with the Pip-Boy, and that great '50s look, so they had a lot to go with.

You've said before that you can't deliver an '80s experience, because "nobody wants that in a modern title, so we're trying to take the best of past games that people understand and are familiar with, and mix it with some new experiences." But, you know, I'd love an '80s experience.

It's interesting. We go out and do press tours. The people who play and buy these games now—the great preponderance, even the interviewers—they've never heard of Interplay. They've never heard of *Baldur's Gate*—never heard of it! So, you think I go in, and I have a long track history of stuff … I was doing a press tour in Europe and the guy says, "So what have you done?" He had no idea. I'm like, *Wasteland, Battle Chess, Descent,* and he's looking at me like I'm just making it all up. His eyes are rolling. So the whole rest of the tour, the running joke is, "and then I invented *Pong!*"

If I'm not thinking about the marketplace, and just what I want to play—I love the '80s games, too, trust me. But if I'm not thinking about the marketplace, I won't be able to make games anymore. I can't survive on just the small groups. So what I try to do is bring some of that stuff forward, so that at least the old-school guys will give them a nod but without putting myself in a box where I can't have commercial success.

Even with *Hunted: The Demon's Forge,* we have some old-school puzzle solving and things like that. It is an action game, so if you hate action games, what can I say? But if you get past that—we put those old school elements in, so new players will think it's very innovative, but you'll say, "Ah! I've done that before."

Just being specific, with the old-school games I really loved the turn-based combat. I loved creating an entire party of characters. Why are those two things so rare nowadays?

Those shouldn't be. Those are things that could be relooked at and should be relooked at. I like the parties and the turn-based options. I don't disagree.

You've noted before that modern games seem to lack the creativity that was present in the '80s and '90s. Do you think that might have something to do with the rise of consoles, and the console gamer's comparative lack of tech savvy and patience for slower-paced games?

I think the biggest issue is really the cost of making games. If you go to the mid-'90s, you have a game like *Descent* that was made by a couple of guys. I think the budget on that was three hundred thousand dollars. You could reasonably expect two or three guys to forgo their salaries, put together a pretty good sample, and put something out for six figures … You could do some really innovative stuff. As [the cost of] games started going up higher and higher, that breed of person disappeared. There was nowhere for them to go except to get a job. Now you're just at a job, working on big projects, just pulling tasks off the wall. There was no commerce—no opportunity to sell.

But now, here comes Flash, here comes iTunes. I look at today's environment and [see the] creativity of the '80s and '90s. I think we've come full circle, but there was a gap there where, if you were just a couple of guys, no publisher is going to give you the five million dollars to make a new game. They had established developers, like myself, who are trying to get those same budgets. Or, they bought a lot of other companies, and they have to keep them busy. Now, that's all changed.

I feel sad about Interplay's decline in the late '90s. I can only imagine what it must have been like for you.

There were certainly tough times toward the end; it was frustrating …

There's two schools of thought. The one school says, stick with what you know. The other school says, who moved my cheese? Move with the times, move with the times! [*Snaps fingers.*] We did great on the PC side of the business. There were not many companies who can look back and point to as many franchises that we helped create in a very short period of time, with budgets. We never had the resources that EAs of the world had. We did great stuff—*Redneck Rampage, Kingpin, Descent, Battle Chess, Fallout* … The list goes on and on. We got a lot of great stuff. But the PC business was just being killed by consoles.

So here's the console world, and we were just out of cycle. It takes a couple years to get up to speed, and we couldn't just throw everybody on it. That's why we did the Shiny acquisition—because if we didn't get in the console business to some degree, we were going to be in trouble. So I bought Shiny, and they worked on *Wild 9* for three years—and boom. It wasn't just them; don't get me wrong, but that was supposed to be our big bet to get into the console. So we're the world's tallest midget. The PC business is going [downhill], and here we are at the top five, top six, but we weren't making any money off that.

We made our mistakes, don't get me wrong. But a lot of people's success—you can point at a title that really made it for them. THQ—*Wrestling*. Four- or five-million-hit seller. Activision—*Tony Hawk*. Take-Two, it was *Grand Theft Auto*. EA had sports and other things; they had a lot other stuff. But the remaining players, they had that one big seminal product that kept them alive. We didn't have it.

FIGURE 5.6 *Baldur's Gate* and its sequel are widely regarded as masterpieces, but the heavy royalty obligation to BioWare and TSR reduced their value to Brian's company.

The closest thing we had was *Baldur's Gate,* but there were issues with that (see Figure 5.6). PC hits weren't as big as console hits, and we had a heavy royalty load to BioWare and TSR. If we hadn't had to pay royalties to them, it might have been a different world. That's not a complaint; just a reality. So we didn't have that kind of unfettered console success that would really push us over the top. We couldn't make the transition.

It's easy to see that console technology has improved a lot graphically. But have you noticed a similar evolution in gameplay?

Well, the styles of games are so different. People's attention spans are shorter. They're not willing to put the time in. You'd better have a lot of save points. People don't have a lot of time now, and there are so many distractions. We have to be more cognizant of that.

And this whole *Call of Duty* phenomenon … It's like some games have become like sports. It's like, I do football, I do volleyball, I do *Call of Duty*. They all play it in high school and have a reference point for it. That makes for some interesting dynamics, too.

Is there a specific year or title that you'd call the golden year of computer role-playing games? A point where you thought, "It's not going to get better than this," and it still hasn't?

Interesting. Wow. It's so hard for me to choose. For me, there was a period of time when we had *Fallout 2* and *Icewind Dale*. *Icewind Dale* was one of my absolute favorite RPGs. I loved it more than *Baldur's Gate II* because it wasn't overindulged in spells and things like that. There was a short period of time where I was just absolutely loving those experiences, and I can remember the music as I'm sitting here now—and playing those things all night. For me the late '90s is the golden age. Right around that time there were several products that just haven't gotten any better.

Now you're working on *Hunted: The Demon's Forge*. What has you most excited about it?

The thing about the product is the execution. There aren't a lot of co-op games, and for me that's one of the things that's been missing. How many games can I sit down with my wife, or my friends, or whoever—and play through them completely, start to finish, all together? When you start to think about it, the number gets pretty low pretty quick. With ours … You've heard of co-op before, you've heard of fantasy before, you've heard of action before. But we've put all these elements together and we've executed it really well.

What advice do you have for a young student, maybe in high school, who wants a career in the games industry? What impresses you when you interview people? What do you like to see on their résumé?

What impresses me is certainly anybody who tells me something I don't know. If there's a particular category of games that somebody likes, role-playing games, or strategy games, whatever—*know the category cold*. You can't come in and start talking about game design if you're not even up to speed on the products in the category … Come back when you [are]. You've got to know everything about everything [in the category]. You can't know everything about everything, but you'd better know everything in your category.

The other thing is obviously passion. Passion backed up by knowledge. And know a little bit about a lot of things, [such as] musical scoring, writing, movie pacing. Know something about the psychology of how they score a soundtrack for a film or the way Foley sound effects or motion capture works. Why was *Avatar* innovative? Why do people say that? How do 3D televisions work? What makes stereoscopic different? Know how entertainment works, because you'll find yourself applying those lessons and thinking broadly about what you have to do.

CHAPTER 6

Chris Avellone, the Iconoclast

Chris Avellone is the creative director of Obsidian Entertainment and the senior designer of *Planescape: Torment,* a critically acclaimed role-playing game (RPG) that ranks among the best in the genre. Known by many of his fans simply as "MCA" (Mr. Chris Avellone), Chris is known for his bold, deep narratives and complex characters.

Chris played a key role in the development of several outstanding role-playing games, including *Icewind Dale II* (2002), *Star Wars: Knights of the Old Republic II* (2004), *Neverwinter Nights 2* (2006), and *Fallout: New Vegas* (2010). As of this writing, Chris is working with Brian Fargo on the Kickstarter-funded *Wasteland 2* project, due in 2013.

Of all the developers I've interviewed, Chris seems to have the best understanding of the psychology of role-playing game players. Whereas lesser designers obsess over graphics, special effects, or the drawing power of a big license, Chris zeroes in on the minute details of characters and micromanages their interactions in the game world. He is also adept at taking familiar gameplay concepts, such as the death of a character, and turning them on their head. Chris is never happier than when he is busting clichés and giving players exactly the opposite of what they expected.

When I interviewed Chris back in May 2010, I was instantly impressed with his enthusiasm and obvious passion for his work. Although not all his projects have been successful—*Descent to Undermountain* (1998), *Lionheart: Legacy of the Crusader* (2003) and *Alpha Protocol* (2010) were all widely panned by critics—he has not lost his willingness to take big risks and buck trends in game design. One might use many adjectives to describe Chris Avellone, but "predictable" will never appear on the list (see Figure 6.1).

When did you realize that you wanted to become a professional game designer?

I never actually thought of myself as getting into game development; it was more that I wanted to be a game master and go through made-up adventures with rules. I wanted to play pretend and use my imagination, and the idea that someone had created a rule set for that with *Dungeons & Dragons* totally blew me away. None of my friends would ever game master the games, so I ended up doing all that. After that, I wanted to do more and more game master stuff, and when the opportunity came up to actually make money doing that—which caught me by complete surprise—I went for that full force.

FIGURE 6.1 Chris "MCA" Avellone is known for defying conventions in his game designs, turning familiar stereotypes on their head.

As a game master, I had a lot of pressure from the players to keep on producing new adventures every week. I'd go to school, come home, and start preparing new adventures. It was a lot of work.

I learned a lot about how to balance rewards for each play session. Because we only played once a week, I had to give them enough rewards to keep them interested and stroke their egos enough to make them want to return session after session. One other thing I learned was that it's really important to pay attention not just to the mechanics the players use to build their characters—like, I'm the tank, or I'm the badass spellcaster, or a sneaky thief … You really have to pay attention to why they made their characters that way. I asked them a lot of questions about what they, as players, saw as being heroic. What sort of things did they really want to do? What really fuels their ego? What makes them excited to play as this character? Then, as a game master, I trained myself to consider every angle of a dungeon and look for places where each character could shine and be special. That way, everyone felt like they were contributing to the adventure and had their moment in the sun.

You have to have meaningful choices when creating your character and playing your character once you're in the game. The game world—dungeons and people—have to react in meaningful ways to those choices and how your character is developing. I would even argue that having a strong storyline is absolutely secondary, or even tertiary, to those things. It's the game system that allows players to develop and respond to the consequences of that development. Most RPG players will form a stronger narrative themselves based on the actions they take in the game—they don't care about the NPC [nonplayer character] they talked to or the big "wow" moment you threw at them. What they care about is that time their third-level dwarf fighter was able to fight off those thirty orcs in a corridor with a ballpeen hammer. That's the story that gets them excited, and that's the story they tell. They were able to pull that off with *their* character and *their* character build, and I totally respect that. I'll try to create a good story, but chances are that your experiences are going to trump anything I throw at you.

What are some of your favorite moments playing RPGs?

I think some of the best moments were when I couldn't distinguish between a good versus a bad karma option; I couldn't tell what evil or good was. I just had to make a decision based on the information I had—those decisions would panic me and get me more immersed.

As someone with such a deep background in tabletop RPGs, how would you compare that experience with playing a computer RPG?

I think a lot of computer fantasy RPGs are modeled strongly after *Dungeons & Dragons*, especially the stats they have in their systems, or how their spells work. You can see in many cases how they started in *Dungeons & Dragons*. I think the whole spell book system didn't last very long in computer games, but a lot of the elements have a strong influence on today's games.

How did you transition from being a game master to a computer game designer?

When I first started in computer game development, I didn't actually know that much about programming. I understood the if-then-else series of conditionals, which means that I knew enough about scripting to make the story make sense.

I think that I was the stupidest guy in the computer lab. I went to a magnet school in northern Virginia called the Thomas Jefferson High School for Science and Technology. Let me tell you, nothing makes you feel stupider faster than being with about 900 other kids that are clearly smarter than you. It was a very humbling experience, and I was definitely not the smartest guy in the computer lab. Going to that school did give me exposure to things like CAD [computer-aided design] programs for architecture, so I learned how to lay out levels in 3D. I picked up a lot of good, strong writing skills, and the typical school day at that high school was so brutal; it programmed me to have a strong work ethic for the rest of my life. I sometimes wish I could relax, but that's not going to happen.

I started off as a very junior designer at Interplay Entertainment, working in their Dragon Play Division doing *Dungeons & Dragons* games. Dragon Play got rebranded into a role-playing game subdivision. Feargus Urquhart, who's now our CEO at Obsidian, led the charge in that division. He got a lot of new RPG projects going and finished up the ones that were still going on.

As far as my career goes, it went from junior designer to designer to area designer to lead designer, with all sorts of designers in between. Now I've apparently reached the ceiling, which I'm absolutely happy with, as creative director at Obsidian.

What games have had the most influence on your designs?

There are a few. One is not really a full role-playing game, but it's *System Shock 2* (see Figure 6.2). I thought that game did so many things right that I almost consider it a design doc for computer games. In terms of actual RPGs, the first one that I loved was *Bard's Tale II*. It got me excited because I could play as a player and not have to be a game master—the computer would handle everything, and I could make my own party of adventurers and customize them. I never played *Wizard's Crown*, unfortunately, but I did play *Eternal Dagger*. The amount of customization that SSI [Strategic Simulations, Inc.] allowed was pretty incredible.

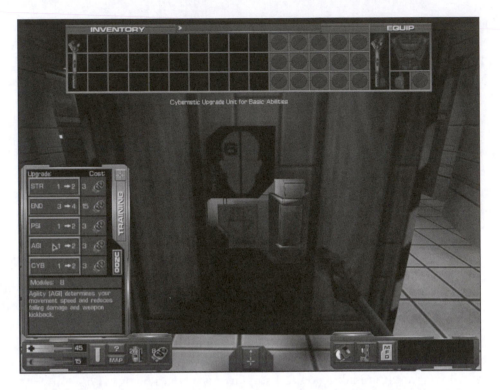

FIGURE 6.2 *System Shock 2* (1999) is an innovative game that combines the first-person shooter with role-playing game elements. Chris cites it as one of his key influences.

It's a little embarrassing, but I handmade some miniatures and put them by my computer keyboard with all the stat sheets for my characters. It's the nerdy stuff you do when you're all alone in your room, and your mom comes knocking on your door for dinner. Otherwise, she doesn't see you for the rest of the day.

Wasteland had a huge influence. It did things with the story and adventure locales that no other game to date has really tried. There are areas in *Wasteland* where you go inside an android's brain and use your intelligence to combat the obstacles there. For a 2D, turn-based game, it was incredible.

I also played lots of console games, such as *Chrono Trigger*. I could go on, but the four games I've mentioned [*System Shock 2, Eternal Dagger, Bard's Tale II,* and *Chrono Trigger*] influenced me the most.

Planescape: Torment is widely considered one of the best computer role-playing games. It stands out sharply compared to other exemplars of the genre. What's the story behind its development?

When I first interviewed at Interplay, Marc O'Green, the division director at the time, said, "So, if you're doing a game set in the *Planescape* universe, how would you start it?" And I said that I'd start from the death screen, and just tell the story of what happens after that. He said, "Ah, that sounds interesting. Do you want a job?" I said, "Sure!"

So I started working at Dragon Play. We had the *Planescape* license, but we weren't doing anything with it. Then Feargus comes to me one day and says that we're doing

Baldur's Gate. We could license the Infinity engine from BioWare. Could I do a game in the *Planescape* universe using the Infinity engine? I said sure.

I was allowed to grab the reins and go; there were really no parameters. So I just wrote a good story set in the *Planescape* universe and tried to think of some really cool characters that would complement the license. I had a really strong lead programmer and artist, really dedicated people, and it was really a lot of fun.

It was under the radar for a while at Interplay. Feargus had input, but overall it was just my small team who understood the game really well. The fact that there wasn't a lot of switchbacks in terms of where the game should go—that helped a lot. I think a lot of this had to do with the way the first *Fallout* turned out. Nobody had thought *Fallout* would be more than a B product—people weren't expecting great things, so they didn't interfere with it. *Planescape* was in a similar situation, though I think *Fallout* turned out a lot better.

There were two strong vision points that we wanted to hit. One was kind of personal to me. Over my years of game mastering, and working on and playing the computer role-playing games at Interplay, I had written out a list of things I hated about RPGs. Just hated them. I wanted to take every one of those clichés and break them, because I was sick of them. I didn't want any elves, I didn't want any dwarves; halflings can go jump off a cliff. I'm sick of those guys. I tended to keep this stuff to myself, since it hurt sales.

The other thing I tried to do was introduce a lot of reversals. You'd start off at the death screen instead of ending on it. You don't find out your name until the end of the game rather than choose it at the first. [Instead of dragons], rats are some of the most dangerous creatures in *Planescape*'s universe. We wanted to take all those clichés and not just break them, but turn them 180 degrees and present them in a new light. [That's why] we intentionally made the undead some of the most sympathetic guys in the game. That was part of our design philosophy—and we were so sick of how they were portrayed in other games. Fall from Grace is a succubus that doesn't have sex. This is when *Diablo* had you going through a ton of dungeons and killing succubi left and right; they were total sexpots. I thought it'd be cool to take Fall from Grace and completely reverse that, making her chaste and celibate, well-spoken and polite. She's one of the nicest people in the game. We thought stuff like that would be interesting, and, in my opinion, it turned out really well.

One of the more intriguing aspects of the game design, to me, is how the game handles death. It's really unlike anything I've played before or since.

In most RPGs, it's very straightforward what death did to you. Death made you reload the game; it wasted your time. In *Planescape* we thought we had an opportunity. The setting lends itself to experimenting with what death really is. We decided to use death as a puzzle tool; another power the player has. When you die in *Planescape,* your body gets transported somewhere else; you can get picked up by the Dust Men. You could also use it to circumvent traps or to figure out what's going on in the game.

Another thing I always noticed in the pen-and-paper format is the alignment system (see Figure 6.3). Players usually pick their alignments before they actually get exposed to the game world and have their actions tested. I always thought this was really weird,

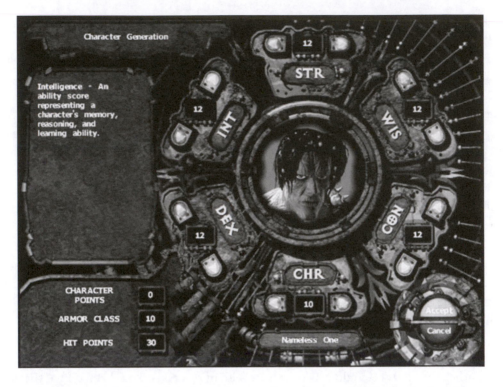

FIGURE 6.3 Instead of simply choosing a name and an alignment at the beginning, *Planescape: Torment* makes these aspects a critical part of the story and gameplay.

because you really can't say what kind of character you are until you're actually thrown into a situation. So, in *Planescape,* we made the character a blank slate. He wakes up with no memory at all, and his personality is there to be shaped based on the actions the player takes and what he's exposed to. We didn't want the player to say, "I'm lawful good," or "I'm chaotic good." We wanted to let the game tell you what alignment you were approaching based on how you react to certain situations. I thought this was a much better way of doing it than determining it beforehand.

Everybody talks about how much they loved the characters and setting. It's definitely one of the deepest and most philosophical CRPGs [computer role-playing games] I've had the pleasure to play.

We were lucky to have two of the *Planescape* pen-and-paper designers come onboard at Interplay. One was Zeb Cook and the other was Colin McComb, who actually worked with us on *Planescape.* A lot of the philosophical approaches for the factions came directly from the *Planescape* universe. We can't take credit for any of those things or the slang they used in the game. Those were things that were already part of the setting and why it is so interesting. We tried to stay true to the faction philosophies. Other philosophical aspects were more player-centric, like how your actions shaped your alignment and how that determines who you are at the end of the game. Those are things that we brought in.

FIGURE 6.4   The character of Ravel shows up in various forms in several of Chris's games, forming part of a metastory that connects them all.

What was the mood at Interplay when the game was launched? Did you know that people would still be playing and talking about this game over a decade later?

Up until the day of release, we didn't know how the game was going to go, and QA [quality assurance] didn't know either. It could be the worst thing that we'd ever put on the shelves. But it wasn't, and I'm thankful for that.

There's so many great characters we could talk about, but one that I'm really curious about is Ravel, a mysterious crone who keeps reappearing throughout the game. What's the story behind her? (See Figure 6.4).

I think the reason her archetype kept perpetuating itself is actually Ravel's fault. When we were designing the character—because of how she exists … Her whole premise is that she's basically a tree that has its branches throughout the planes. She touches all these different souls throughout existence. When we did *Icewind Dale* games, there'd be old women in there that would be blind or couldn't see very well. Those characters were manifestations of Ravel's branches. Whenever I had an opportunity to write one of those characters, I'd always include hooks to Ravel to communicate to players that she exists on multiple levels.

Your latest game is *Alpha Protocol*. How are you handling player choices in that game?

As game developers, we have a responsibility to make sure that the game world is reacting to your choices and how you develop your character. We really tried to make sure we

FIGURE 6.5 *Alpha Protocol* was the first "espionage RPG," a bold attempt at a new subgenre. Unfortunately, it was not a hit for the company.

hit that in *Alpha Protocol,* and even reduced resources in other areas. We reduced the cast of characters to have more interactivity with the environment (see Figure 6.5).

Finally, *Fallout: New Vegas* is due out soon. What would you like your fans and fans of the older *Fallout* games to know about it?

As far as *Vegas* goes … If you liked *Fallout 3,* imagine that with more cool stuff in it. I think folks are going to be pretty happy about it.

CHAPTER 7

Chris Taylor, the Problem Solver

Chris Taylor, founder of Gas Powered Games, is best known for *Dungeon Siege,* an action role-playing game (RPG), and *Total Annihilation* and *Supreme Commander,* two much-loved real-time strategy (RTS) games. Although he certainly has plenty of great ideas for original games, his key strength seems to be identifying problems in existing games and coming up with brilliant solutions for overcoming them (see Figure 7.1).

By the time *Total Annihilation* was released in 1997, the real-time strategy genre was well established, with plenty of great franchises, such as *Command & Conquer* and *Warcraft,* to choose from. Unlike these games, however, *Total Annihilation* made the terrain itself an important tactical element, taking into consideration the height of hills and valleys when moving and firing. It's still played online by hundreds of diehard fans.

Although the first *Supreme Commander* (2007) was well received, it's really the 2010 release of *Supreme Commander 2* where Chris really shines. This game features an innovative control scheme aptly suited for the Xbox 360 game controller, a problem that long stymied the genre's migration from PC to console.

Dungeon Siege, released in 2002, updated the classic *Diablo* formula, correcting two perceived flaws: the need to individually click on each enemy in order to kill it and constantly running back to town to sell one's loot. Chris dealt with this latter issue by adding a pack animal that could also defend itself (and quite possibly the fallen hero) with its powerful kick. Unfortunately, the two sequels have not been as warmly received.

In February 2011, Chris's company took over development of *Age of Empires Online,* seeing the product through to release that August. As the title makes clear, the idea was to adapt the real-time strategy formula for a massively multiplayer online format. As of this writing, it's still going strong, receiving a major "Anniversary Update" on July 11, 2012.

Interviewing Chris was almost as much fun as playing his games. A constant jokester with considerable charm and endless energy, it's hard to imagine him sitting down quietly for endless hours at a computer keyboard. Indeed, out of all the designers and developers I've talked to, he's the only one with his own farm and video blog. Does he ever power

FIGURE 7.1   Chris Taylor is a master of the real-time strategy genre, with such well-known titles as *Supreme Commander* and *Total Annihilation* to his credit.

down? When Chris says there's never a dull moment at Gas Powered Games, you get the feeling he wouldn't—couldn't—have it any other way.

I've met a lot of game developers, Chris, but I think you're the only one who has a farm.

Well, we have an acre and a half. My wife has some gardens, and we had a horse that came with the house. The people who sold us the house had it, and they couldn't take it with them, so they asked if we'd like to have it. I said, sure, why not? So we ended up with a horse and some dogs. Then my wife said she'd love some chickens, so I built a chicken coop. Then we added geese, sheep, and a koi pond. Our parrot died about a month ago. You can fill the back of a pickup truck with feed for all these animals pretty easily, which is what I have the biggest issue with. Having them is no problem; feeding them is another story!

I thought for sure you'd mention a donkey or mule in there somewhere.

Yeah, like a pack mule.

He could help you with all your loot!

Well, I'd like a goat, because they can eat almost anything, and we have a lot of blackberry bushes and things like that. So I think that might be next.

So what are you working on now when you're not farming? I know you're doing *Age of Empires Online* and *Kings and Castles*. You must be an extremely busy man.

Yeah, well, game development is an industry kind of like film. As you get closer and closer to the final release, you get really busy. Our industry has historically been very crunch-oriented. We're getting better at it, but there's no substitute for the kind of excitement that happens just before you release a game. Things come out of the woodwork, and no matter how much experience you have, you can't predict it. There's never a dull moment at Gas Powered Games.

It's my understanding that one of the policies at Gas Powered Games is to try to stick to normal working hours as much as possible. Do you still try to adhere to that?

Yes. When I had my first son, I was acutely aware of the horror stories about how much I'd regret it if I didn't watch them grow up. So I really tried to avoid crunch. We still had crunch. But there's a difference between crunching for the last couple of months and crunching all year long, year after year.

On *Dungeon Siege,* we started the company and worked pretty normalish. Then I met my wife over the summer and got distracted. I told her, look, I have got to finish this game, so I worked on it for the next two and a half years. We worked seven days a week, twelve to fourteen hours a day, to get our first game built.

It's a young man's game in a way. You really can't do that when you have responsibilities, and we've seen that. There's the famous EA widow story and all of that. We all grew up, but we were trying to work the way we did [as teenagers] into our thirties and forties. That was starting to break though, so we had to hit the reset button.

When I had my boy, I said, I'm going to try to work a normal week and really look at the schedule and properly manage the process. It hasn't gone smoothly, but it's been a big improvement.

Let's talk about your history. You first game was *Hardball 2* back in 1989, but how'd you get there? Did you study computer programming at school?

I actually have a lot of my old computer stuff in this office. I've got my original TRS-80 in a box just over there. It was in a garage, though, and you know how electronics don't store well in a garage. They get all corroded. It'll never work again. But I brought it into the office to make sure it doesn't decay any more.

I also have a book here—one of the first I ever bought. It's *How to Program the Z80.* This book is assembly code. Now I was fourteen years old when I bought this book, and I got to tell you—I didn't understand a damn thing in it. It was really intense. It's not all evident how you go from what's written in that book to how you program a videogame. I didn't even know what an assembler was. But I muddled through it and did a bunch of hand-coded assembly games on my Z80.

Why not BASIC? Wouldn't that have been a lot easier?

Assembly was necessary to get a decent frame rate. If you used BASIC, stuff would move around so slowly, it was useless. Nothing good or cool was ever done in BASIC. [*Laughs.*] Ah, there were a few stock market games that were pretty good, but they weren't graphical.

I got my first professional job when I was twenty-one. When I walked in, I told them my history, that I'd written hand-optimized assembly code on a Z80, and I did the same thing on a PC. A friend had loaned me his PC, so I learned 8088. I was writing a 3D editing program in assembly that I could show them, too. I should have written that in C, but they were impressed enough to give me a shot.

I got to work on *Hardball 2,* and of course I was doing it in C, which I technically didn't know. I had lied to them during my interview, claiming to know it, but I really didn't. I went off for a week and learned it quick before my job started. I managed to bullshit my way through it. If you're going to get anywhere in life, you've got to learn how to tell a good story and bullshit your way into something [*laughs*].

Are you a prodigy with mathematics? A brainiac?

That's so nice of you to imagine that. I think I'm really stubborn. These days, we talk about people having super powers—what's your super power? I think mine is being very focused and very stubborn. Math? I've never been great at math like calculus and the more advanced stuff. But once I figured out that you need to know trigonometry to spin things in 3D—geometry and trig—I learned that stuff right away. That was why I learned math.

What kind of games were you playing back then? I know you're a fan of *Wizardry*.

Over the years, people ask me about my favorites back then. I think it's really mean to pick a favorite, because I played *everything*. I started in the arcades back in the '70s, playing *Asteroids, Space Invaders,* and all of that. Then Sears' *Pong* came out. My mom bought us an Intellivision, and I was crazy about that. One of my favorite games for that was *Utopia;* just awesome. Meanwhile, the arcade machines were getting more sophisticated, and I played games like *Sinistar, Roboton, Defender,* and *Stargate.* I've actually got some coin-op games right in my office. I know this is making me seem very eccentric, but I'm really not that eccentric really.

I've got so many favorites. And let's not forget about pinball! Pinball was awesome. I actually managed to get my hands on a *Black Knight 2000,* and I had it in my house. When you have a pinball machine in your house, you get so good it's scary. You can play it forever—you have to quit and walk away, because you're just racking up such a crazy score. I sold that, and I regret it. Never sell your stuff; always keep it. They can break it into bits and throw it in your casket so you can take it with you.

Did you know back then that making games is what you wanted to do for a career? Or did it take a while for you to come to that realization?

No! It took me ten seconds. I was standing in an arcade, and this guy is fixing one of the machines. He's got the back open on it, and it's got wires and circuits and stuff, and that smell of burning electronics in the air! I'm like, I have *got* to do this. But I was born out in Surrey, British Columbia. If you were born there, in the '70s, you'd think that the rest of the world is everywhere but where you are. Everything interesting is happening somewhere else. There is nothing going on in Surrey. I wasn't going to get a chance to go into the business unless I moved. Distinctive Software, in Burnaby, was where the job was. It was founded by Don Mattrick and Jeff Sember. Those guys had to be one of the first software companies in Canada. It was a pretty rare thing to have a videogame company back then.

I got very, very lucky. You cannot discount pure luck. I'd found this ad in the back of a newspaper, the *Vancouver Sun,* a tiny little ad. It was a tiny classified. What possessed me to open that newspaper and find this tiny, tiny little ad? I answered it, and they were recruiting for Distinctive Software. Now, they didn't want to say they were hiring for a videogame company, because they'd have a line of people a mile long. They were looking for young computer geeks who loved videogames—but who could sit and write tight code.

FIGURE 7.2 *Hardball 2* (1989) won Chris an award from the Software Publishers' Association.

I don't want to sound like, "I need to tighten the graphics on level three,'" but that was it [*laughs*]. Looking back, I think my code was very loose. I learned everything I needed on the job from the incredible people who worked here.

The path from being fourteen and getting a computer to getting a job … That was a path filled with randomness and luck.

Everyone must have been really impressed that your first game, *Hardball 2*, won the Software Publishers' Association Sports Game of the Year award. Not bad for your first time at bat!

Well, back then, everything that Distinctive Software did attracted crazy attention. *Test Drive* was super successful, going double platinum. This is going to sound odd, but when *Hardball 2* won the SPA award, it was kind of disappointing, because the sales weren't anywhere near where the other games were. It only sold a few hundred thousand units rather than a million, so it felt like a screw up (see Figure 7.2).

The first *Hardball* was for the Commodore 64, which had a completely different kind of demographic than the PC. The PC just wasn't a baseball gamer's market, but *Hardball 2* was for the PC. So it's kind of a time and place issue. To be quite honest—maybe I can be honest about this now—baseball wasn't really my dream game. I was more into *Total-Annihilation*-style gaming. I wanted tanks, planes, and bombs. Explosions! That's who I was; over-the-top, explosive kind of guy. To make a baseball game, which is a meticulous, plodding game… You can go to a baseball game and maybe something happens, maybe nothing happens—wow, yeah, baseball! [*Laughs.*] The fact is, though, I took the job and did

---

˙ Chris is referring to an infamous 1990s television commercial from Westwood College.

the best I could. But it would've been better if I were a baseball nut and could infuse that passion and energy that I put into *Total Annihilation*. But if you're just doing something for a job, you don't accomplish that.

Was that also the case for *4D Boxing*?

I was a little more into that because it was 3D. I've always been a big fan of 3D—even now, I love 3D. I buy every single game that's 3D. This is going to kill you, but I didn't work on the boxing. I worked on everything but the boxing. I worked on the front end, the code for the ranking system, the training system, the control room stuff. Jay MacDonald was one of the first people I ever partnered with, and he wrote the code for the boxing; hitting and colliding. He wrote this amazing motion capture system.

Neither of us came up with the idea. That was Don and the other management, who were pretty excited about a boxing game. So we said, sure, we'll build it.

In 1997, you joined Cavedog Entertainment and made *Total Annihilation*. How did you get the opportunity to finally make the game you'd been wanting to make for so long? (See Figure 7.3.)

Well, this is going to be a theme—I'm a very lucky guy. When I was doing *Hardball 2*, there was a producer at Accolade named Shelley Day. I stayed in touch with her after she left Accolade. I'm really big on staying in touch with people; networking. Being able to pick up a

FIGURE 7.3 *Total Annihilation*, first published in 1997, introduced terrain elevation as an important tactical consideration.

phone and call someone is important. Shelley went to Taito, then LucasArts, where she met Ron Gilbert. Ron and Shelley decided to start a kids' game company in Woodinville, where I live now. I called Shelley and told her I was leaving Electronic Arts and wanted to start my own game company. She put me in touch with Ron, and after we talked, he asked me what I really wanted to do. I wasn't interested in just doing conversions and pick-up work. What I really wanted to make was a game like *Command & Conquer.* It was so awesome and had so much potential—just an amazing style of game. I don't even think they had the name real-time strategy then. He invited me to come down and join Humungous and build the game.

Ron gave me some unprecedented creative freedom. I tell you what—not only was it unprecedented then, it's unprecedented now. People don't usually get that kind of freedom; you have marketing, executive management, all sorts of people who participate in the design. If Ron didn't quite understand why I liked some part of the game, he said, "I may disagree, but it's your call. You do what you like; you're the creative guy." Ron was amazing.

I'm sure that people who played the game thought it was crazy; that you just couldn't do this. Who would allow someone to do this? That's what happens when creativity runs wild and nothing stops it. That's what I think is going to happen more these days with iPhone and Web apps. It took fifteen years for that to really happen again, and I don't think anybody predicted it.

Was it your idea to have the elevations and terrain that affected troop movement?

Yeah. There's a tremendous amount of *Total Annihilation, Dungeon Siege,* and *Supreme Commander* that's not me. I'm not every creative idea. But that particular idea of an elevated battlefield was mine. My idea started with the idea of a 3D battlefield. I was playing *Command & Conquer,* and thought the pre-rendered units didn't have the fluidity a 3D object would provide. But more than that, I was such a nut about the military and Abrams tanks. I knew they could move and shoot at the same time. When those tanks move, the barrel stays level because of all the sophisticated computer systems. I said, hey, we're making a computer game, we can do that better than anything in real life. If you have high ground, you can shoot a projectile or artillery round much farther if you're on high ground. That brought strategy into play in a much bigger way than just a toe-to-toe fight. I thought it'd be cool if you had five units and I had ten, but you could still beat me with better tactics, rallying around my units and out-gaming me.

Have you played many miniatures-based games like *Warhammer*?

I dabbled a little in *Dungeons & Dragons,* but I didn't have the attention span for the rules. But I played a lot of *Risk.* When I was in that age group, I had a computer, so I played computer games. I played arcade games, Commodore 64 games like *Impossible Mission*—remember that line about "Destroy him, my robots!" [*Laughs.*] That was so awesome. I think my friend pirated every Commodore 64 game—such a crime. I, however, bought all my games on the TRS-80 ... because there was no piracy community. I had to actually spend real money. I bought every game RadioShack ever sold.

I wasn't into board games and miniatures so much because I had computers. It was rare for a kid back then to have computers.

FIGURE 7.4 *Dungeon Siege* introduced elements from real-time strategy into an action role-playing game.

Let's move on to *Dungeon Siege*, one of my favorites. I was looking at some of the contemporary reviews, and they were very positive. What do you think made it so successful? (See Figure 7.4.)

I see something today—a pattern in games. If you can do something fresh; some place you haven't been before, but it plays smooth; does what you want it to do when you click. There are some new ideas, like the continuous world—no loading screen, which was an enormous amount of engineering work. Arguably, it was too much work, and we shouldn't have done it. It came at too high of a price. We had the pack mule, a multicharacter party that made it feel more like an RTS game. It felt like a traditional RPG. We looked at *Baldur's Gate, Neverwinter Nights*. They were an adaption of the pen-and-paper games brought to a computer. What I did was bring an RTS sensibility to the RPG, making the action-RPG a lighter experience. *Diablo* was of course the gold standard, but it was a bit mechanical—and it sold so much more than *Dungeon Siege*. We have to say that [*laughs*]. We had a lot of fun making it, but we were trying to do something different. The million or so people who bought a copy felt that come through; we weren't just throwing a paintjob on somebody else's game. I refused to do that. Even if I were told to do that, I'd end up not doing it. The artistic integrity has to be there; I can't abandon that.

It's a beautiful game, but I think my favorite part is the mule. The first time I saw him I cracked up. What was the rationale behind having pack mules as party characters?

Well, I was playing *Diablo* and always got frustrated because my inventory was always full. I spent all my time going back and forth to town. I needed a bigger inventory. But if I have a multicharacter party, and I sacrifice a fighting character for storage, that's a good trade-off. And what really exacerbated the problem in *Diablo* was the slow loading time. So it was bad enough I had to go back and forth to town, but then I had to look at a loading screen.

It was really nice how the pack mule could also fight.

I can't remember if you could control him in the first one or if he'd just defend himself if he was attacked. But it came in handy in the first one, especially if everyone was unconscious. Sometimes the pack mule would be the only one left, and he'd be kicking, and you'd be saying, "Go, pack mule, go!" Every once in a while he'd save the day, and that was great. That was an emergent behavior. You couldn't have put in the design document, "And every so often the pack mule will save the whole party." It was cool.

I saw an earlier interview with you where you'd said you felt the game was too big, and the quality suffered a bit because of that. Do you still feel that way?

At the time, *Baldur's Gate* was a hundred hours. We felt we had to compete with it, which was just silly. We were shooting for a hundred, and we ended up getting to fifty or sixty. We failed to understand the economics of game development. Our budget was okay, but it wasn't the budget of the products we were competing against. What happens is that the quality of the experience gets thin, and you don't have enough time to do it right. We should have done a shorter game—let them go through it, then say, okay, I'm done, I had a great time. Now I'm ready for the next time. We made the same mistake with *Dungeon Siege 2,* and it was still huge and too long. That's the kind of experience you shouldn't have to get by doing it. You should be able to read this in a book, because it's too many years of your life. It took seven years for me to learn that lesson. Now, a six or seven hour shooter is not uncommon.

It seems like gamers of the older generation might still wish games were longer.

I find that a little hard to believe, because I'm from that generation, and I'm so busy that I find myself enjoying really short games that I can actually get through. I loved playing *Portal 2.* After three nights, I was done—check it off the list. If I had to go on for weeks and weeks, I would've been like, oh, shit, the rest of my life is waiting!

It might be tied to the notion that if you only get a game once every few years, it's got to be long. But now there's a great game out every two weeks, so I can live with these shorter times.

Let's talk about *Supreme Commander*. The reviews were fantastic, and it became a big franchise, but it's my understanding that you had a hard time finding a publisher for it (see Figure 7.5).

Well, games cost a lot of money to make, and it was a PC game at a time when console gaming was really on fire. There was a lot of talk about PC gaming being dead, a lot of prognostication that it was dying. It never really died. There's got to be a song or a poem in there somewhere.

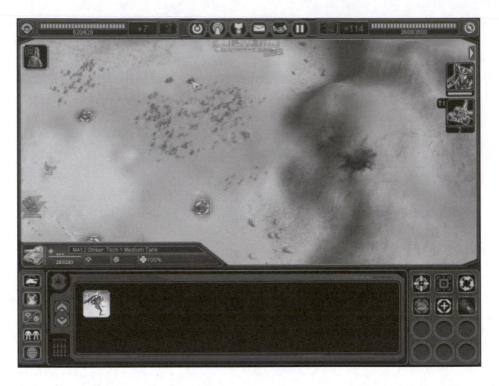
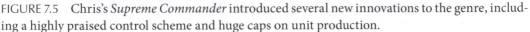

FIGURE 7.5   Chris's *Supreme Commander* introduced several new innovations to the genre, including a highly praised control scheme and huge caps on unit production.

But when you're making a big bet, spending millions of dollars, you need the publishing community to rally around it. They have to all believe they're going to make money, get their bonuses and reach their numbers. If there's a bigger game that's sitting on the table that they could spend that five to ten million on—you're going to get stack ranked to the bottom: "Here's twenty-five games we'd love to publish, but we can only spend money on the first ten." Something's got to give.

Didn't you woo publishers by getting it featured on the cover of a magazine?

Yeah … I think you're right. Believe it or not, I don't remember everything that's happened to me over my career [*laughs*]. Now it's coming back to me … I think it was *PC Gamer* who did the story, and they gave me a wonderful lift. I love those guys, they're great, and I'll never, ever cancel my subscription [*laughs*]. They've treated me so well and helped me get the word out on my games. I believe it was Dan Morris, the editor-in-chief, who did the story on it. I owe Dan an enormous debt of gratitude.

Eventually it ended up on the Xbox 360, which must have been a risky proposition to some people. There are many critics who think that consoles just aren't suitable for RTS games. Obviously, you don't share that opinion.

There was a time when the belief was that first-person shooters wouldn't work on consoles. We know how that story ends. We thought RTS would make a transition to console, and, as it turns out, I believe RTS runs great on a console. I know that's going to surprise people to hear me say that. Buy *Supreme Commander 2* for the 360, and give it four hours to learn the controls. You're going to say—"Holy cow, this plays fine." It plays fine because of strategic zoom, the ability to zoom out and zoom in. Without that, it's a lot harder—a lot clumsier.

But we did some crazy stuff in *Supreme Commander 2* to fix the UI [user interface]. We took an idea from *Halo Wars* called paint select. Evan Pongress came up with the idea of paint attack—click and hold the attack, and swipe around the screen with a big brush to attack. It was so cool that we took it over to the PC version, and it was a huge improvement there, too. Instead of click, click, click, you just click and grab all those units.

Yeah, RTS runs great on a console, we had great ideas that we brought back to PC, and when we finally figured it out—the party hat had moved on. After all that, it was like people didn't care anymore. Why? This was tremendous … But I feel like we cracked the nut; we solved it. Regardless of whether the world cared or not, we solved it.

Let's talk about *Space Siege*, which came out in 2008 for Windows. *Dungeon Siege* in space. How do you feel about that project?

We took the *Dungeon Siege* process—we knew how to build a world and build an RPG, but we failed because we thought we could take that process and build a brand new fictional world and do it in eighteen months instead of three years. If you play the game, you know it doesn't have the magic that *Dungeon Siege* had, and that's largely because we tried to make a very big game in a very short period of time. You know the old saying, nine women can't have a baby in one month—that applies to RPGs!

I have to take a lot of blame. It was my crazy idea; I was the one saying, "We can do this!" The business was getting tougher, PC gaming was under siege, and I was bullish. I said that we could do this game and do it inexpensively, and I was just wrong.

It seems like things are working out much better for *Dungeon Siege 3*.

I haven't seen the reviews, so I'll take your word for it.

What? You don't look at reviews?

Reviews are painful. If they're all good, and you just want to shower yourself in praise, that's fine. But if you get mixed reviews, or get people who are permanently angry and hate everything—I just don't include it in my routine.

The Metacritic score always seems to find its way to me. That drives me crazy, too. You take an average, you have no qualifiers on that number—really? We all have to carry that burden.

I read an interview of yours where you said that you wished we could get back to the days when just anybody could walk past a game like *Pac-Man* and think it was cool. Now we're kind of stuck in this phase where the hardcore is too hardcore and the casual is too casual. You want to do something about that.

Well, *Age of Empires Online* certainly scratches that itch. It's a game of depth, strategy, and tactics—it's a rich game with an incredible world (see Figure 7.6). But it's also a game that the more casual or social gamer can jump into. I think we've got the right thing there,

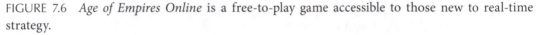

FIGURE 7.6 *Age of Empires Online* is a free-to-play game accessible to those new to real-time strategy.

compliments to the good work by the guys at Robot, Microsoft, and Ensemble. Those guys did the heavy lifting; we're just really excited to be part of it.

The early '90s were a great time. You had a lot of creativity and a lot of innovation, but the costs were low enough that people would take chances—throw stuff at the wall just to see what sticks. Now we're returning to that. Now somebody out in the middle of nowhere can write a game in Flash, Java, Javascript, or Unity, and drum up some excitement for it and maybe even make some money with it. That was unheard of back in the '90s; you couldn't put a product on the shelf if you were an individual who just liked to code on weekends. This is the most exciting time ever. I don't think it gets any better than this.

I don't care if you make soap in your garage; you can put a website up and let the world shop at your soap store. Gaming can be digitally distributed, so it's even better. Before, if you didn't have the infrastructure, you couldn't get into the business. But now innovative, creative people can make their dreams come true. It's not easy, but it's a hell of a lot easier than it was.

Do you prefer working with a smaller team? If I recall correctly, Gas Powered Games has sixty or so employees.

Yeah, at one point we went over seventy, but generally speaking I have no goals for size. This is not an ego contest where seventy is good, but a hundred and forty is better. I'd be perfectly fine with whatever number is the right number to make a game.

You've got to think of it more like a movie production than a traditional business. If you're a director of a movie, and you're shooting a scene with a thousand people coming over a hill screaming, you don't say, "Oh, yeah, I got a thousand people working for me." You go, "That's what it took to make the shot work." In game production, it's the same thing. You hire however many people you need to get the work done, then shrink back down again. No harm, no foul—everybody understood there was three months of work, six months, whatever.

How much have toolkits and modding affected your views on game design?*

After *Total Annihilation,* we were so taken aback by all the great work the modding community had done. Nobody could have predicted just how fabulous and over-the-top it was going to be. We had over a hundred websites dedicated to the game. It was incredible.

We tried to duplicate that completely with *Dungeon Siege* by including tools with the release—at tremendous cost. It was superexpensive. We probably spent twenty percent of our budget on developing tools for the community.

The responsible businessperson says, "How do you monetize it so that it pays for itself, and you're not just giving money away?" The irresponsible, creative-minded designer guy says, "Who gives a shit? I don't even care, woo, woo." But seriously. If you can find a way to monetize that community component, then you really win, because there's real entertainment value there and it's worth something. But it doesn't have to cost a fortune, and nobody has to get rich. I've never been interested in getting rich. I just want to give people an experience and make them happy and pay my own rent.

We've had to cut it because of the economy. We just don't have the dollars to support it anymore. I don't spend money out of my own pocket; I have to go raise the money by pitching a publisher on something. The process of raising money got so much tighter and more controlled. The circle got smaller and smaller, and it got hard to justify cutting out a big chunk of the budget to make tools for the community—and get no return other than goodwill. It was hard to sell.

Now you have to hack the code to do it. We're all for it. Hack away, but don't violate the EULA [end user license agreement].

How do you see the mobile evolution affecting strategy games?†

The mobile revolution is affecting everything, not just strategy games. But it's allowing people to play more strategy games—more than ever. So it's helping. It's also bringing back turn-based games; I never would have believed it. I'm playing *Army Attack* by Digital Chocolate on Facebook. This game has tremendous potential as a turn-based game, and the guys are adding content all the time.

I think we're going to be playing more strategy games than ever, on more devices than ever. Mobile gaming in general has made gaming available to more people. It seems like everyone is playing games now! When was this true before? It was just us geeks before, with gaming consoles or the big PC rigs. You could light a cigarette off the CPU of those things [*laughs*]. It was just stupid. But now everybody is playing games, and I think gaming is going to do even better over the next twenty years.

---

* Question submitted by Chris Anderson.
† Question submitted by Tony McCrary.

CHAPTER 8

Howard Scott Warshaw, the Sad Clown

Howard Scott Warshaw is one of the most controversial figures in the history of the Atari 2600, responsible for both the best (*Yar's Revenge*) and the worst (*E.T.*) games ever released for the platform. Sitting down to chat with him in the summer of 2010, I was immediately impressed with his candor and seemingly infinite supply of hilarious stories about the earliest days of the videogame industry.

Famous for his pranks, jokes, and overall wackiness, Howard might well have been a stand-up comic instead of a hardcore game designer and programmer. So it's all the more surprising that his tenure at Atari began after the departure of its pioneering founder, Nolan Bushnell, who had sold his company to "Big" Warner. Bushnell was an engineer, and he'd run the company like one. The new management, by contrast, was strictly business, with little to no understanding of how games were actually made. The result was completely unrealistic deadlines, massive overspending on popular licenses, and overweening hubris. All of this led, inevitably, to the terrible "Crash Christmas" of 1983.

Howard's story is perhaps the most dramatic in this book, since he literally went from industry darling to industry scapegoat in little more than a year (see Figure 8.1). Although he's clearly maintained his lightheartedness and penchant for humor, it's also clear that he's still stinging from the rejection he received after *E.T.* When he said he wanted a time machine so he could go back to fix it, for the first and only time during our chat he wasn't smiling. Tellingly, he was far more affected by the idea that he'd disappointed his fans than any damage it had done to his career.

When did you become interested in programming?

Well, me getting into programming is an interesting story because I avoided computers like the plague until midway through my college career. I had access to them in high school, but I never wanted to get near them; that wasn't where I was going to go.

I was at Tulane majoring in economics. But everybody kept telling me, if you don't know computers, you aren't going to get anywhere with economics. So I tried a little half-credit

FIGURE 8.1   Howard Scott Warshaw, the best (and worst) game designer on the Atari 2600.

FORTRAN course—and I loved it! I just thought, oh my God, this is it for me. It was all fun, no homework. You just hang out and solve puzzles. It was great! I dove into computers.

My first job programming was at Hewlett-Packard doing distributed systems, some of the first networks. I was one of the first people to work on the "Internet," although back then it was called the Arpanet. I wrote packet switchers and node software back in the late '70s. That was cool, but it was getting kind of dull at Hewlett-Packard. I always thought of it as the software pasture where programmers go to die. I liked microprocessors and real-time controlled programming. I was also a wacky guy, especially for Hewlett-Packard.

One day, one of the people I worked with started telling me about his wife and the cool stuff she was doing at her job. He said it sounded just like what I wanted to do. I asked where she worked, and it was a place called Atari. So I went in and did an interview, but they didn't want to give me an offer because they thought I was too straight. But I begged and pleaded with them. Finally, they gave in, and as it turns out I wasn't too straight to work for Atari [*laughs*].

You worked at Atari after Nolan Bushnell had left and Ray Kassar had taken over. What was Ray like?

Ray was a very interesting guy. He was a classical manager that came from a huge company. He was brought in to run Atari by "Big" Warner. Then, nobody really understood software management. Ray came in to straighten us out and produce products just like he had done at plenty of other companies.

Ray was a very intelligent, sensitive, and interesting guy, but when he put on his CEO coat, he let go of a lot of the things that made him that way and turned into this classical manager. Your position on the org chart determined how you got dealt with. He wouldn't relate to people as people, but only as positions. That was a huge problem when dealing with software people.

Programmers are blue-collar intellectual workers. Blue-collar workers are traditionally not stupid but also not densely intellectual. Programmers are. The idea of a blue-collar worker who's just as smart if not smarter than the managers—that was a relatively new phenomenon. Ray and his staff really weren't prepared to deal with it.

Can you describe a typical day at Atari?*

We had a rule at Atari. You couldn't come in until you wanted to, and you couldn't leave until you felt like it. You'd think that people wouldn't spend much time at work there, but there were people there around the clock. There were some people who'd come in early in the morning and stay until late in the evening. Some would come in during the afternoon and stay until morning. There was always someone there, because what we were doing was so much fun and compelling that you just wanted to be there. The work was fun, and the people were just so interesting.

You'd go there in the morning, and people would be rolling up joints. You could smell the smoke. You'd get stoned and go to lunch.

We had a thing called the MRB. That was the code you'd hear over the intercom: "MRB in so-and-so's office" or on the roof. MRB was the marijuana review board. If someone wanted to get stoned and chat, we'd call an MRB. A lot of games got developed during MRBs.

What did you think about the Atari 2600 as a platform?

The Atari 2600 was a machine with very limited capabilities that ended up getting taken far beyond its original design parameters—through programming (see Figure 8.2).

The 2600 was invented to do *Pong* and *Tank*. That was it. You had two players, two missiles, one ball, and a playfield. That people took it as far as they did is unbelievable.

You have to consider that initially you only had 2K for your whole program, and that was ROM. Then you had 128 bytes of RAM to deal with. People today can't even conceive of that, because people work with RAM in the hundreds of megs to gigs. It's unlimited, and there's no concept of limited resources when you're making a modern game. You couldn't fit the average data structure for one component of a game today in an entire game space back then. 128 bytes of RAM is ridiculous; it's insane.

But what I liked about it was that it really tested your creativity. You had a few chips, a few registers to play with, very little RAM, a little bit of ROM. You really had to think of new ways to use that. To take a machine designed for *Tank* and do *Ms. Pac-Man*—which they did—is astounding. The people who designed the 2600, when they saw the variety and

---

* Howard also tells this story on the *Once Upon Atari* DVD from Scott West Productions, available for order at onceupo-natari.com.

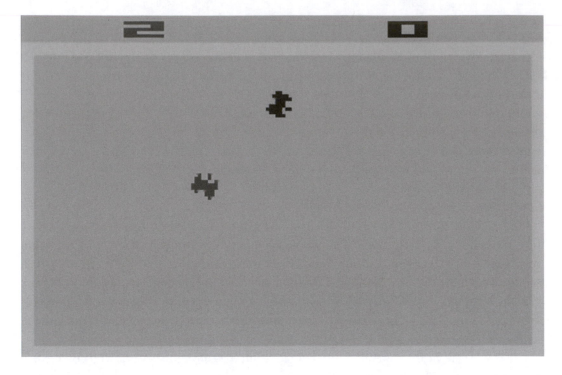

FIGURE 8.2 The Atari 2600 was originally designed to do two games based on successful arcade machines: *Pong* (1972) and *Tank* (1974). *Combat* (1977), shown here, is based on *Tank*.

the style of games that were actually available on it, it blew their minds. It was beyond their imagination. But that's the way really good invention goes. You create capacity and ability. You don't create a device that's an end to itself. You create an ability. What it shows is that even though the designers had a very specific end in mind, they created a system that wasn't limited to that. They had the basic design smarts not to close the system or limit it.

It took a lot of very intelligent and creative people years [to figure it all out], but it's amazing how far they got with it.

What was your first game for Atari?

My first game was *Yar's Revenge*. My goal was just to make a game quickly. When I got there, I got a manual and started working on it. Actually, I was assigned to make *Star Castle*, which was a coin-op game. Even though I'd only been working there for three weeks, I went to the manager and said that *Star Castle* was really going to suck on the 2600 (see Figure 8.3). Even then we knew that some coin-op games just didn't convert well to the 2600. However, I told him I could take the basic components and rework them into something that might be a more viable game. To their credit, they said go ahead. At that time, licenses weren't the be all and end all. This was before that specter of licenses took over.

So I made the game that would become *Yar's*. It was tough and the going was slow, until we had a breakthrough with the controls. Suddenly the game was hot—people were digging it. It was obviously a slick game. Then I started adding features and some ideas from movie making. I wanted *Yar's* to have a lot of firsts. It was the first to have a pause mode,

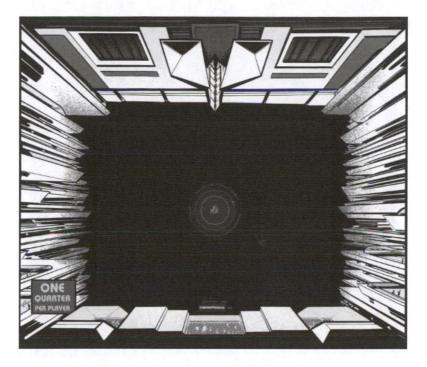

FIGURE 8.3 Howard decided that *Star Castle*, shown here, was simply too technologically demanding to run properly on the 2600. A successful conversion was finally completed by D. Scott Williamson in 2012.

the first full-screen explosion, the first game to display its code on screen—the ion zone is actually generated by the code on the card. It was also the first to be published with a backstory and a comic book. I wrote it because I wanted to name the game.

I'd always dreamed of adding a word to the English language. I thought it'd be very cool. If the game got popular, I could effectively add a word to the language. The ideas for names from marketing were very lame, though, and I wanted something special.

I actually pulled a little marketing stunt on marketing. I found out they were about to name the game, and the marketing rep told me there was just a few days left before the decision. So I asked if I could suggest a title. So later that night I came up with Yar, which was Ray spelled backward. Ray Kassar was the CEO, right? It takes place in the Razak solar system, too, which is Kassar spelled backward. So I made up this story about flies on a spaceship, mutating and taking over their own solar system. I wrote this whole sci-fi backstory just to make the name more likely to get in.

So I talked to them the next morning and gave them my submission. The next day, I told the product manager I had a little secret. I'd tell him, but I didn't want it to get out. I made him promise not to tell. I made him swear three times just so I'd be sure he *would* tell everyone. I told him that Yar spelled backward was Ray. Right. He figured it out and said, "You mean this game is named for Ray Kassar?" I said, "Yeah. That's why I don't want you to tell anyone, because I don't want it to bias the process." Then he asked if Ray knew about it, and I said, of course Ray knows about it. I wouldn't do anything like that without clearing it with Ray!

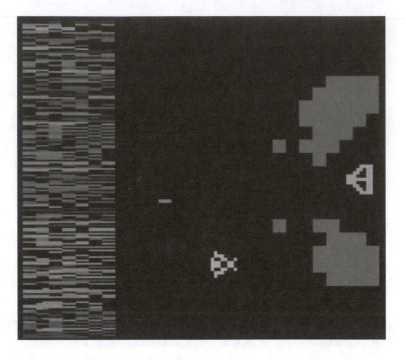

FIGURE 8.4   *Yar's Revenge* is widely considered the best game for the Atari 2600.

I knew two things at this point. One, Ray Kassar knew absolutely nothing about this. I also knew that the product manager was going to run and tell everyone right away. Two, I knew that nobody in marketing had the stones to go talk to Ray about this; they'd just assume it was all there. So about a day later, he told me they were going to go with *Yar's,* and were even going to create a comic book to go along with the game based on my story.

This was the first time a programmer got credited, because they were going to credit the storybook. Then they figured since they gave me credit for that, they also had to give me credit for programming. So I got credited as the programmer.

Months later, we were at a media event, and Ray Kassar was there. I was playing *Yar's Revenge* for the press, and Ray comes up to me. He told me he'd heard about my stunt. I asked him what he thought about it. He just said, "Just make more games, Howard." That was Ray. But he did have a smirk.

Yar's Revenge became one of the first original games to sell over a million. I was very proud of it and happy it was my first game (see Figure 8.4).

After scoring such a huge hit with *Yar's Revenge*, it must have been doubly troubling that *E.T.* had such a negative reception.

E.T., the five-week wonder. There's a lot of speculation about that game, a lot of talk. For me it was a challenge. Until then, I believe that no one had done a game in under six months. I had to do a game in five weeks. That challenge alone was worth it to me. And I wrote fresh code, fresh graphics—it was all new. I wrote a one-line res kernel because I did want it to have a better graphics capacity, because I wanted some kind of hook. But the key to making a game in five weeks is to do a game that you can do in five weeks. If I'd had

FIGURE 8.5   Atari spent a fortune acquiring the rights to make a game based on *E.T.: The Extra-Terrestrial*, but only gave Howard five weeks to make the entire game from scratch—all by himself.

another week, that'd be another 20% of the schedule. Nowadays a game takes a year and half or two years. In retrospect, I could've made a very different game if I'd had that week. But I made a full, complete game, and even tried to make something new. I wanted each of my games to make a real contribution. It was on a 3D world; this cube that you played on. It made sense.

Now the pits were the pits. It was a big mistake to make it so easy to fall into the pits, and it was tricky getting out. There were some real mistakes I made with *E.T.* But it's a full, complete game, and even after returns it still sold over a million (see Figure 8.5).

People frequently rate *E.T.* as the worst game of all time. Realistically, is it even the worst game on the 2600?

Probably not. There's a lot of games that nobody talks about anymore that may be worse. But I like it when people make it the worst. I support the idea that *E.T.* is the worst game ever done. The reason I do that is that *Yar's Revenge* is often considered one of the best games ever done. So the way I look at it, between *Yar's* and *E.T.*, I have the greatest range of any developer in history. I'm always looking for the upside.

Some people will take criticism too far. The gameplay does get monotonous. That bothers some people a little, others a lot. I rarely argue with players, though. If they're just trying to be mean—that's different. But, for the most part, I never argue with players about their feedback, because that's what they feel. If that's what they're getting from the game, it's pretty silly for a designer or creator to argue about that. I know a lot of people didn't like it.

There is another factor with *E.T.*, and that's the movie tie-in. *E.T.* is one of the most beloved movies of all time. That's bringing an emotional tone to the expectation. When people complain about my game, they're not just complaining about the game. They're

104 ■ Honoring the Code: Conversations with Great Game Designers

complaining because they didn't get an experience that compares to the emotional ride they got from the movie, which is huge. I'm not going to get there with a game; a game on the 2600 is not going to take you to the kind of emotional place that E.T. touching Elliot's finger is going to get you to in the movie. A lot of the criticism of the game is valid, and I'd love to go back and change that. But some of it is just disappointment that it wasn't the same experience they got with the movie, and I can empathize with that … but I can't fix it.

What did you do after *E.T.*?

Well, after it came out, I was just really satisfied with the work. I felt I had done what I set out to do. When the reactions came back, I was in a pretty whacked out place. I had really thrown myself into Atari for years … At first, it was hard. It hurt to feel this hated thing coming back. Between *E.T.* and *Pac-Man* together, there was a lot of unmet expectations from consumers … Those two games created a one-two punch that was very tough on the industry. But with time, as I got a little more perspective, I realized that the points people were making are valid. These were things that if I'd had a little more time to let other people try it out, I would've changed.

It felt bad at first … It felt really bad. But you can't argue with people. If I ever get a time machine, and go back, I promise you that *E.T.* will be a much better game.

CHAPTER 9

Jon Hare, the Rock 'n' Roller

Jon Hare, founder of Sensible Software, is one of Britain's most eminent game developers, responsible for the terrifically successful *Sensible Software* series as well as *Cannon Fodder* and dozens of other classics for the Commodore 64 and Amiga platforms.

Before I interviewed Jon, I'd assumed—quite wrongly—that game development was a similar process on both sides of the Atlantic. After only a few minutes, though, I realized there was (and likely remains) a stark contrast, at least for those of Jon's generation. In short, American developers are much less concerned and impressed with "tight coding," that is, doing the most with the least possible amount of memory and processor power. Jon sets the bar high for programmers; they're either geniuses or they've got no business in the industry. More shocking, perhaps, is his obvious regret that gaming became a mainstream hobby; it was much better for him when only nerds played videogames. And don't even get him started on big publishers like EA and Activision!

But how much of Jon's antipathy toward the status quo is merely sour grapes? After all, his last truly epic project, *Sex 'n' Drugs 'n' Rock 'n' Roll*, was eventually canceled when the team found itself simply overwhelmed with the demands of 3D programming. Likewise, his popular *Sensible Soccer* game was eclipsed on consoles by products from rival companies, a fact Jon attributes to shady double-dealing on the part of Sega.

John Romero has described his team as functioning like a rock band, but Jon Hare's team literally was a rock band (see Figure 9.1). Simultaneously playing gigs while making games, Jon and his friends only became full-time game developers when it became clear there was a lot more money to be made with their keyboards than their guitars—it was just the sensible thing to do. Nevertheless, his connection to the music industry gives Jon a unique perspective, and in many ways I strongly agree that games would be much better if their developers had the same sort of close camaraderie enjoyed by so many successful rock bands.

You seem to be a man of many talents, including art and music … but where are the sports? I expected to see "football champion" on your bio somewhere.

Well, I do play football, though I'm not the best. I do still play. After forty-five years, I run slower than an elephant on Prozac, but there you go.

FIGURE 9.1   Jon Hare is a musician who later found himself making games for a living. He still keeps a guitar close at hand, tuned up, and ready to play whenever the mood strikes him.

And a little cricket with the Amstrad?

Yeah, we played cricket with the Amstrad, and some golf until my back went. But I do enjoy competitive sports. I play a bit of snooker, darts … can you call them sports? Bowling? No, football is my main game. I play all sorts of football, whenever I can.

So what game development have you been doing lately? I've heard something about a game called *Word Explorer.*

Brilliant! For me, *Word Explorer* is a really big deal. We can talk about what's been going on for the last few years, but making original games has been really hard. For the past fifteen years, it's been hard to get them into the market without committing financial suicide. *Word Explorer* is a game that I first started looking at about four or five years ago as a PC game, but I translated it into a game for iPhone, Android, Symbian, whatever. We're looking at a whole bunch of different platforms, and we've gotten quite a bit of interest from multiple platform holders, which is great for us.

The game is basically a twenty-first century crossword … The point of the game is that you're a traveling photographer, and as you travel, you find key words related to cities, landmarks, animals. We've done an amazing amount of research. We've got two hundred thousand photo opportunities in this game from across the world. So you travel the world, doing words, solving anagrams, taking photographs, collecting them, and finding certain cities. If you unlock Boston, for instance, you can take a ship to Norway and explore Europe.

For me, it's fun because it's original, innovative, and a different kind of area. I do tend to get tired of being pigeonholed as something from the past. At Sensible, we were making new games all the time. Look at *Wizball, Parallax, Microprose Software, Shoot'em Construction Kit, Mega-Lo-Mania, Cannon Fodder*—we were jumping around all over the place. Then, suddenly, we got to a point where the whole industry seized up creatively because more money was put into the budgets because of 3D. Because of that, the people who were backing us to do whatever we wanted just stopped like the brakes came on. It's only recently, since we entered this iPhone-led era of smartphones and casual games, that we've got platforms again that we can innovate on without financially destroying ourselves. It's fun for me because I get to make new stuff; I hate doing the same thing again and again.

All the time, people expect you to just do new versions of *Sensible Soccer* or *Cannon Fodder*. Fair enough, but to be honest, I did it twenty years ago. It's not like you'd ask Neil

Young to go do the music he was doing twenty years ago. That's like my personality—I like to work on new things, with different people, and ride whatever seems interesting at the time. If you're good at it, you can make money from it. I think this premeditated, accountancy-led mentality of running media doesn't accommodate that.

It's like alchemy. You have an idea, you turn over your idea with somebody else, and suddenly this energy happens that has its own life. It's like giving birth to this new thing that takes on its own life. That's how you create things. Musicians know that. If you write a song, and the first time you play it with a band it just clicks and it works—it's a better-than-sex moment. Everyone is being selfish, but everyone is enjoying the moment. I guess that's like very good sex [laughs]. The same applies to making games or anything. It can't be written down in documents. Not all of it. Bits of it need to be written, but not all of it.

When I did the design for *Cannon Fodder 3*, it was 270 pages. The game never came out. I did the design for *Sex 'n' Drugs 'n' Rock 'n' Roll*, it was a 1,500-page document that never came out. *That* needed to be done, because there was a lot of organization there. But at the end of the day, all of our hit games weren't document-based games. They were based around what was happening on the screen—and we were modifying that, and writing documentation and little plans to support it, charts. A lot of detailed planning but not a lot upfront. That doesn't give you any room for the musical equivalent of arrangement; you don't know how you're going to need to arrange it. You do the first bit, see how it runs, make modifications, adjustments—this fear of not quantifying everything upfront is incredibly stifling for games, and film, and other areas of media.

A bit of fresh air about the iPhone and smartphone markets is that there is room for change. The problem is that all the guys running the business are so used to overmanaging and fearing creative people—not just artists and designers, but also technically creative people like producers, brilliant marketers, or businessmen. There's creativity in all these areas, but there's a whole bunch of people sitting in the background who are fearful of the unknown. They don't understand that publishing is about educated gambling, not about surefire hits. If you want surefire hits, go work at Wal-Mart selling toilet rolls. They're never going to go out of fashion [*laughs*]!

You talk about these new markets opening up creative options, but the most popular games are really simplistic—like *Tiny Wings*. The first time you saw that game, would you have assumed it would be such a monster hit?

I've got a theory about *Tiny Wings*. Let's start at the beginning. In 1985, I started making games and set up Sensible Software in 1986. During that period, up until about 1993, in general, the game-playing public had picked up computers as an extension of a home electronics hobby. Then when the ZX Spectrum and a few other machines came out, the people who used those machines were those kind of guys—people interested in electronics. Almost exclusively male, I might add. The quiet, intelligent, nerdy guys at school, you know?

Guys like us, you mean?

[*Laughs.*] Yeah, like us. So, in general, when these guys were playing games, you tended to have a higher intelligence than the average person—more interest in innovation and open to new ideas. They were much less inclined to say, "You can't do that, because it works like this." They were more inclined to say, "That's interesting, let's see where this is going." And build on it. That kind of spirit—intelligent people open to new ideas—allowed us as innovators to pour whatever we wanted into the machines, and they accepted it without challenging it. They weren't fearful of something beyond them.

When people who are intelligent see something they don't understand, if it's done well, they want to master it and want to understand it. They don't reject it out of fear of being made to feel stupid. They try to overcome it.

But when you go to a big mass-market thing, and a good example here is the Sega Megadrive or the Genesis, that and the Sony PlayStation was the turning point. Suddenly, the average intelligence of the gamer nosedived. We were making games for the not-so-clever kids in school, the ones who didn't want to have to struggle to master something and who just wanted to play a game to follow a pack. "Oh, my friend said it was cool, so it must be cool. Am I allowed to say it's cool?" You know these guys? This happened when 3D came out. So suddenly you had massive production increases, all of the media companies sniffing around to control you by accounting—Warner, Sony, all these guys—they all moved in as a pack in the mid-'90s. At the same time, your audience was less able to deal with challenging content. So you just got a massive sea change in gaming from the massive innovation that was happening throughout the '80s and early '90s to this very stifling, very safe way of making games that were very similar to other games—so you got licenses and sequels and me-too games.

Sensible Software had ten number one games that I designed. And yet no one would sign my games from 1995 onward. That's madness, right? So just having the chance to make *Word Explorer* is a big deal. I'm self-publishing it, some brilliant guys in Poland to work with. But it's been very frustrating to me to have to stop my creativity to make commercial sense. It gets so boring.

Well, Jon, you might be frustrated as a designer, but old-school guys like me are even more frustrated as gamers. I'm so tired of seeing the same old first-person shooter come out year after year.

[*Laughs.*] I remember being on game committees and sitting down to play ten games to give out awards. I was on the Gameplay Jury; the year before I was on the Sports Jury. To be honest, I don't play first-person shooters. But I sat down and played four first-person shooters this year. They were so similar to each other! There are some differences, but it's like different levels of the same game. You get different art; a few little tweaks.

Do you remember which ones you played?

It was *Call of Duty, Halo, Bioshock,* and *Mass Effect 2.* I understand *Mass Effect 1* was more complicated, but *Mass Effect 2* was just a not-so-well executed first-person shooter. I actually got to understand from this exercise why *Call of Duty* is so popular, because what the game is good at is flow. It's got really good flow; you can go and be mindless for half an hour, and it's really enjoyable. That's my take on it. It's not something I would seriously get into, but for a bit of mindless fun, it's enjoyable.

I've been a designer now for thirteen years, so I'm very quick at looking at a game and analyzing its strengths and weaknesses. I thought *Call of Duty* had great flow—you just pick up a gun and run for it. It's like, "Run, Forrest, run." That's what the whole game was like [*laughs*]. It was a like a chase movie. But is it worth sinking half the budget of the entire games industry into games like this? I don't think so. Is it innovative? Not at all.

It's like level designers trying to be designers. I get that all the time. They might have a good idea for a mod for their favorite FPS (first-person shooter), and maybe have done a couple levels. That's not game design. That's like me saying I want to be a cook because I can make good soup. I like cooking, but I'm not a cook. I consider myself a songwriter. I've written a few songs, but I'm not professional enough to do it properly. And certainly with football; I love playing but am not fit enough and have never been good enough to be professional. I just enjoy it.

I know this is incredibly insulting to people—and it's aimed directly at *Tiny Wings* ... *Tiny Wings* is an insult to professional game designers. This game that could have been made in half an hour with a decent team has sold so many copies. That shows the depths to which the intelligence of the average gamer has sunk. Not just intelligence—the experience.

On the iPhone, there are a lot of people who've never played games before. I have to say, a lot of these are women. We know that women have made up more than 50% of the audience on PC casual games. On the iPhone, action games have not had a female market. It's like going to a foreign country and trying to teach someone French, and they're talking like a four-year-old. It's really that basic.

When you play *Tiny Wings,* all you do is push your finger on the screen to decide if gravity is turned on or off. That's all you do for the entire game. But now you get everybody trying to make money by making really simplistic games, so you get all these games with cute birds in them.

The problem with *Tiny Wings* is that it ignores the past twenty-five years of gaming. It's a bit like a really sophisticated composer would feel when suddenly they see the most terrible punk band, with very limited musical skill, getting the hit records, after they've spent thirty years training to be classically brilliant. But what we have to do is embrace it and unwind some of our sophistication.

We've been challenged to relearn in this market. If I observe what's happened with *Speedball*, which really is the best version since the Amiga—it's too complicated for a lot of iPhone gamers. *Speedball* had three target markets: guys who knew the original—a very easy sell, predominantly in Europe. The second was people in the States who like sports but maybe had never heard of *Speedball*. Those guys have been pretty hard for us to reach; I still have to find a way to do it, since I'm sure a lot of guys would love it if they could just find it. I don't have any doubt that sophisticated gamers would love it in the States. Third, you have the guys who are totally new to it. I think that some of these kids who just like console games will like *Speedball*. Some of your newer iPhone crowds, though, who like *Tiny Wings*—I doubt they're ever going to like it.

It's also unlikely that it's going to appeal to women. It's a sports game—a brutal sports game. It's got very little that would appeal to women, which are half our market. *Word*

Explorer is more tailored to women than it is to guys. I think that action games for the iPhone can't be that demanding of people's reflexes and hand-eye coordination. *Angry Birds,* which I think is quite brilliant—it's very simple, you've got plenty of time, and it's not that difficult. Not being overdemanding is very important in these games. If you notice, all the successful games either limit what you can do at once, or they give you all the time in the world to consider simple actions.

Cut the Rope is actually quite demanding for one of these games. It's the most demanding of them. You have the most different actions you can do, and you have to do them very quickly, one after the other. It's great—another great game for the platform. *Angry Birds* and *Cut the Rope* I have a lot of respect for. *Tiny Wings* is the bottom of the barrel. Sorry, Mr. *Tiny Wings.* It's only a young Russian guy, and it's been great for him. But really, it's like *X-Factor* gaming to me.

It seems like the iOS is a bit of a paradox. People who have iPhones and iPads like to think of themselves as intelligent, sophisticated people, but you're not really seeing that in any of the popular games for the system.

The problem is that those of us who've been playing games for twenty years plus have developed a very good sense and internal back catalog of game concepts, game ideas, the way games work, what appeals to us and what doesn't. People who encounter games for the first time on an iPhone or on Facebook—all that's just happening now. We have to understand where those people are. It's a different market.

Right now you have a split market. On the one hand, there's a huge demand for really visually sophisticated stuff on consoles. Really on the top end. The latest *God of War* game has absolutely stunning art. It's one of the best games I've ever seen artistically. The benchmark is so high to reach that. The gameplay itself is simplistic. It reminds me of *Call of Duty,* kind of a chase game that looks nice.

World of Warcraft is a really sophisticated game (see Figure 9.2). Just think about how mature that game is in gaming terms. Brilliantly executed; probably the best executed game we've seen in the last twenty years. Really, brutally addictive. That's because the achievement settings of the game are so well tuned. It's like cricket. It goes on for five days, and you sit there waiting for one guy to get fifty runs and another guy to get a wicket, a record to be broken. Basically, every ten minutes something important is going to happen, so you just sit back on your couch and watch it more and more. It's the same in *World of Warcraft;* there's always something dangling over your nose to keep you playing for the next half hour. It's a perfect paced, never-ending game.

But all this is so far beyond what casual users on an iPhone want. It's so far beyond it. There's an interesting observation going on at the moment. I'm working with this Polish team called Vivid Games. We can support about nine different platforms, covering all the main mobile platforms, Sony, PC, Mac, Flash games—all kinds of different things. But if you have ideas like *Word Explorer* and *Speedball,* the way you monetize those games—the way you make money—is different for every platform. Some of them only work if you sell them for free—giving them away. So you need the internal currency. Some of them you can

FIGURE 9.2 *World of Warcraft* is one of the few modern games Jon greatly admires. It has flourished despite its considerable complexity and sophistication.

sell at different price points. If you try to sell them and then use internal currency, people don't like it because they have to pay twice.

Then you have socialization differences. With Facebook games, people have to be able to share and gift things to each other. Here's this thing I've made, and I'm going to give it to you. What I've found is that this doesn't really work. People don't really do gifting on iPhone. It's more about, if anything, comparative scoring. I've scored this much on this level, see if you can beat me.

What we have to do is bring a game to eighty-five percent complete, and then finish it off for my target platform, figuring out how to tweak it for a platform. Do you use Game Center? Score Loop? Some other new thing at the moment? It's not ideal; it's fragmented and irritating as hell. But there are opportunities. Those opportunities haven't been there for so many years. The console and other mobile platforms have been so license heavy.

It's easy for me to keep harking back to the old ideas, but the reason that the Amiga was the good old days was that this stuff wasn't an issue. You could make original games. Publishers wanted them, the public liked them, everyone was happy. Suddenly, everything slowed to a grinding halt. And I know it's not just games. I've heard Bruce Willis about five or six years ago talk about the scripts he's going through, and how it's the same bloody film again and again and again. It's very familiar, right [*laughs*]? He just wasn't interested in the scripts. So it's great that we have this opportunity, and I really hope the public embraces this spirit of buying games.

The generation that's a bit younger than me has fallen hook, line, and sinker for consumerism. I see that my sixteen-year-old daughter's generation is slightly different, not quite so sold on consumerism. They've had it since they were zero. I think there will be a cynicism coming through as people start making less money, their pensions run out. A new energy will come through, and the complacency of shopping mall culture—and the economic abyss that it's going to drop us into—will change the mentality. It might take fifteen years.

Great creativity takes social change to stimulate new energy. We've not really had games around in a time when expression, in a way you look at Bob Dylan and what he did in the '60s—software as a medium hasn't been around when that need for expression has been strong. But in ten or fifteen years, it could be totally different. We might find totally different means of expression happening in software. Now we see games as entertainment, but there are many different ways we could be making products that stimulate people; not just by playing, but by playing and thinking—that combination. I hope that we've opened a new door. It's not just you shoot someone, or you do an RPG [role-playing game], or a platform game.

I'm sick of hearing people say that there are no new game ideas. There are thousands. I've got eleven good ideas sitting in my drawer. It's just that nobody is willing to put money into them; that's all.

What you saw in the '80s and '90s is that when you innovate, it encourages other people to innovate on top of your innovation. You got this rapid growth and expansion of ideas. You've got to keep on encouraging that. Obviously, you don't want to lose money—not losing money is the first rule of business for me. So you need the smaller platforms to make it happen, because on the bigger platforms, you can never be risk-free. You need to be risk-free to be expressive. If you've got an artist, and he's worried that he's got no house, food, and his wife is about to walk out on him—he's not going to make his best art. It might inspire tragic art a few years later, but during that time when his life is falling apart, he's not going to make his best art. It's when you'll be watching the bottom line, doing the work for hire again instead of doing your thing. That's the reality of what happens.

Too many guys in our industry see games as purely technical or purely business or purely license driven, and completely forget the creative, artistic side, which isn't just about pictures, it's about ideas, direction, sounds, good teams of people fusing together to make great products.

Generally, in that kind of creative team, you can't get more than five or six people before it becomes about politics rather than dynamics.

What you're talking about now was the genesis of Sensible Software, right? The philosophy behind it?

Absolutely! When we set up Sensible, Chris and I were at school together. We first met on a tube train to see a Rush gig. We didn't know each other, but we had mutual friends at school, so that's how we met. Chris and I started up in a band and played for four years before we made a single game. Our mentality was that band mentality—you make stuff together, you make it good, and you try to sell it. We were making games and music in tandem. Eventually, the games started making more money, so we focused on them more. We added Martin Galway, a great games musician. He did *Wizball* and *Parallax* and a lot of great Ocean tunes on the Commodore 64. We signed Chris Chapman, who was the programmer for *Mega-Lo-Mania* and *Sensible Soccer*. We added Stoo Cambridge, the artist on *Cannon Fodder*. There was Judy Jameson, Dave Korn, Richard Joseph … There was about six of us, a little team, and it felt like a band. If you see the *Cannon Fodder* video, that's what it expresses. We were a bunch of guys making something happen together. It's a fantastic process.

It only really changed in 1995 when we signed a three-product deal with Warner. We needed more employees because we'd signed up to do three 3D games, and we'd become the masters of 2D. I would say that we were the best Commodore 64 team, the best Amiga team in Europe. We moved to 3D extremely late, and we needed all these extra people, and the dynamic changed. You went from one of the leaders of a band to being the conductor of an orchestra. It was out of our depth. Now you had the guys who weren't any good, but you didn't get to suss them out until it was too late. They could hide in the mass of the team. We hadn't had anyone like that before. All the guys before were brilliant. Now it wasn't so hands-on, not so direct, not intense. You got the odd guy who didn't do his part, so now someone else is wondering why he should work late when that guy didn't. But before, you worked late because it was great—we were making great products and making a lot of money. It was a lot of fun.

We tried to keep the spirit alive, but it required a lot of focus on your work and a lot of skill, as well as the fun. At one time we experimented with putting beer in our drinks machine at work. That was a mistake [*laughs*].

Was that around the time of *Twister: Mother of Charlotte*?

No, that was around the time of *Cannon Fodder 2*. We tried the beer. We had a little game room with a television, pool table, some consoles, a fruit machine. In fact, one of the traditions at Sensible stems back to using an Amstrad for a cricket bat and a roll of tape for the ball. If a key fell off the Amstrad you scored. That was good fun. We had a history of equipment-breaking as part of the ritual for Sensible.

We did a photo shoot for *Mega-Lo-Mania*, and we had a bunch of broken monitors and computers. It was our first commercial shoot and inviting in a magazine. We destroyed all the computers with rocks. It was so much fun! We worked next to this old station yard where you could do all this stuff.

Chris Chapman used to work extremely hard; he was a brilliant programmer. We allowed him to get his frustration out with the old Koenig joysticks. We played conkers with the broken ones—you know, where you throw the thing to smash it.

The very worst thing we did was with this old fruit machine that broke. Somebody had brought in some dumbbells to keep himself fit while he was at work. Then someone decided to smash the fruit machine with this great big weight bar. It was like one of those competitions where they smash up a piano to stick it through a tiny hole. After that we just Hoovered it up. It was that kind of spirit in the office; everybody worked hard, worked late … The place had its own atmosphere.

Sounds like some good advice for anyone working for you would be to wear a hard hat.

[*Laughs.*] No, the hardest thing about working for me is being told to do something again because it's not good enough. I'm quite a perfectionist. I have more stamina for waiting until it's right than most people I know. Mike Montgomery, who runs Bitmap Brothers, is worse. I've seen him go three days without sleep. I can do two. But it becomes a way of life, and you just get used to it.

Sensible Software has a great catalog of very diverse games, and each one has its fans. Let's talk about some of them, starting with _Parallax_ (see Figure 9.3). I was just listening to the music in this one, which is just fantastic.

It's amazing. That music, even now, gives me goosebumps. Martin was a genius on that machine, on making the SID [sound interface device] machine sound like its own instrument. He was a massive Tangerine Dream fan. All of his music is inspired by that kind of sound.

I did all the art for _Parallax_ and all our games, right up to _Sensible Soccer_. Really, _Parallax_ was more about Chris Yates, my partner, who did all the programming. He was an absolutely brilliant C-64 programmer; a genius. It allowed me as a creative person to work with someone who was technically brilliant. Chris was creative himself; we co-designed the games on the C-64. We were a creative partnership. I don't know if we were Lennon–McCartney or Chas & Dave—but we were like a songwriting partnership.

Parallax was Chris showing what he could do on the Commodore 64 in terms of movement. I was doing level design and metagame design. The part where the guy gets out of the spaceship and walks around; it's a bit basic and not quite what we initially had in mind. But it was a good start.

We got some humor in the game as well. Chris and I have a similar sense of humor. When we finished doing _Parallax_, we were on the edge of memory, but we needed a message to tell you that you'd won the game. We had no reward. Chris came up with this message in ten bytes that just said "system off" in a tiny little screen. That was your reward for getting through the whole game. It was very anticlimactical.

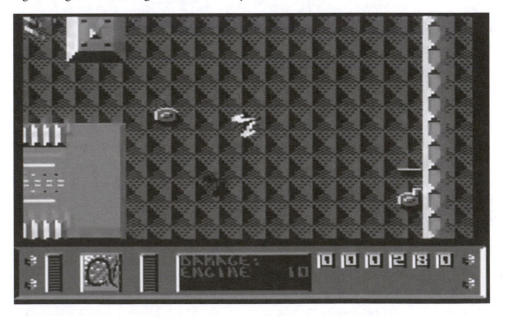

FIGURE 9.3   Jon did the graphics for _Parallax_, a 1986 game for the Commodore 64.

Parallax was a great start, and we got a lucky break. We went to Ocean in 1986 on a train. That was a fair trip for us; we were teenagers. Our first ever business meeting—here's a check, here's a contract. We were very lucky.

Did they give you a good deal or did they try to screw you over?

Oh! They screwed us over big time! We didn't know. We got a check for a thousand pounds. On the way back, we were smoking cigars in the dinner car. I think the whole deal was five thousand pounds, a thousand up front. We never saw a penny of royalties. But it was our lucky break. I can't complain. Everyone needs their start, and that was ours, and I've always been thankful to Ocean for that.

Then you made one of my favorites, *Wizball*. What a fun and original game! I don't even know how you'd get that past the first wave of publisher rejections nowadays. How in the world did you come up with *Wizball*?

We signed it with Ocean; it was our follow-up to *Parallax*. In those days, they didn't want a huge document before they signed a game. I don't even think we had a document. It was a bit like signing a music artist; you didn't say, "What's going to be on your next album, Bowie?" before they signed it. They just said, "Okay, mate, you're pretty good. We'll have your next one, please." We were coming at it as musicians, and it was like that back then—and it was better when it was like that. The good old days.

At the time, we were playing lots of arcade machines. Chris was a big fan of *Nemesis* and *Salamander* and these kind of Japanese space shooters. *Wizball* was inspired by *Nemesis* (see Figure 9.4). If you look at *Nemesis* and the way some of the waveforms and weapons work, it's clear. The bouncing ball was something Chris developed. He had this mechanism with a thing bouncing. I think I drew the green ball face as an idea, which showed the rotation off quite nicely. Then we had the idea for the Catelite. I love the cooperative mode in *Wizball*, it's pretty good. I think it's one of the first games that had that kind of cooperative mode.

Coloring the landscape was more my area. Do you remember *Wizkid*? It's by far the most far out game we've ever managed to get out. It's truly eccentric. *Wizkid* is *Wizball*'s son. There's a very twisted story I can tell you later. But in *Wizkid*, you play a head, bouncing

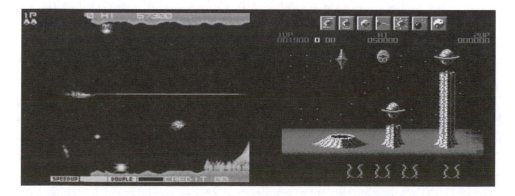

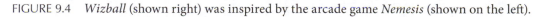

FIGURE 9.4   *Wizball* (shown right) was inspired by the arcade game *Nemesis* (shown on the left).

bricks to clear out the level. But there's another bit where you can grow a body and explore the background. It's like a small adventure game where you can pick up objects. If you want to understand the full expression of me and Chris working together, play *Wizkid*. It's alchemy. Let's put a crossword in; hey, that works. It's very bizarre, but it works. You might think it's more of a Japanese game with all the quirkiness.

Often you find that the best games come from the process Chris and I used. You don't write everything out from the start. We weren't expected to do that from our publishing obligation. Gary Bracer, the producer at Ocean, was open to whatever we wanted to do. He loved it; he thought it was funny. He got our sense of humor and encouraged us to express ourselves, which is fantastic. It's what you need.

With *Wizball*, we managed to have interesting ideas, nice looking art for the time, very good controls. My one criticism playing it back again is that it's too hard at the very start. It really is demanding. That's why it wouldn't work in the current market. The learning curve at the start is too steep. I guess we could retune it.

Nah! I was wondering if you could make a version for the iPhone that used the accelerometer.
Yeah, I think we could. The thing is, people are always asking me for new versions of *Cannon Fodder, Sensible Soccer* … I am always looking at those and turning them into new formats. Or they ask about *Sex 'n' Drugs 'n' Rock 'n' Roll*. But I think the truth is that every game has its time in which it works. Within the frame of when *Wizball* came out—it was great for the time. Now? It's a retro-remake. I look at *Speedball*; I'm very happy with our remake. But this is a game that came out in 1989. If we took some music from 1989 and put it out there and pretended it was new—people would know it wasn't new; they'd know it was from 1989. It's old '80s music.

Sex 'n' Drugs 'n' Rock 'n' Roll is a good case in point. Highly innovative. To me it was the next stage up from *Wizkid* (see Figure 9.5). At Sensible, we had two kinds of games. We had our safe games—*Sensible Soccer* was our safe game. *Microprose Soccer* was a safe game. *Shoot'em Up Construction Kit* was safe. Then we had our out-there games: *Wizball, Wizkid* … *Sex 'n' Drugs 'n' Rock 'n' Roll* would have been one of those. We tried to have a balance, in the same way that people now have a balance between work-for-hire and original games.

You mentioned *Shoot 'em Up Construction Kit*. I remember playing a lot of the games that people made with it, especially one called *Smurf Hunt*. Have you played it?
[*Laughs.*] I've not played it, no.

I don't think it was an officially licensed product.
Shoot 'em Up Construction Kit was actually pretty simple. Chris was trying to come up with a tool for me to use to design levels and make the art on. I started using what he'd done, and I said that it was good enough to release as a product. Chris finished up the utility as a commercial product, and I made four demo games. It was good for me to learn more about level design and wave design. It taught me quite a lot.

I like some of the games for it. There was one called *Celebrity Squares*, which was appalling. But I liked *Slap 'n' Tickle*. I like the name.

FIGURE 9.5 *Wizkid* is the wacky, surrealistic sequel to *Wizball*. It's one of Jon's proudest achievements.

Shoot 'em Up Construction Kit is an attack on U.S. coding. In those days, there was a difference between the U.S. and U.K. approach to coding. The U.K. approach was minimal; try to do everything with minimal memory. U.S. coding was not quite as tight. I think we see that amply demonstrated in every version of Windows. *Shoot 'em Up Construction Kit* loaded in one load, all at once.

However, Commodore had just released that big blocky brick of a disk drive. When we did the NTSC [National Television System Committee] version, they complained that the disk drive light wasn't flashing when they played the game, because they expected to see it loading. Chris had to fake the light coming on and off to pretend it was loading—to get it approved. [*Laughs.*] That was our first number-one game. Very fondly remembered for that reason.

Why did you prefer the Commodore 64 and the Amiga over the Atari STs and other machines that were out there?

The Atari ST was popular in France and Europe, but not in the U.K. We used to refer to it as a door wedge, because of the shape. It was known for a better sound chip but not much else. I guess we'd just had Commodore always, so we were used to it. It was our prime format. We did conversions, but when we did that I just switched to doing another game.

Commodore was the label we fell in love with until it blew up.

It must have been a disaster for you guy when the Amiga died.

We were so heavily in bed with those machines. We were the top developer on the Commodore 64 when the Amiga came out, and we were very slow to adopt the Amiga.

When the Amiga ended—we were the top developer in Europe when it stopped. We really got caught with our trousers down. We hadn't had any real need to do 3D programming, large team sizes. We'd gone from being top developers to novices at 3D and large team management. The only reason we moved was that we were offered four times more money to move on to these other machines.

The market forces refuse to part with money unless you do what they want—it's their choice, it's their money. We'd never pushed PC, and, in retrospect, had we pushed it more we would have had more of a profile in the U.S. That would've helped us more in the long term. It's frustrating and boring to me to tell people that I've had ten number one games and you've never heard of any of them. And the biggest one was a soccer game. It just doesn't work in the States [*laughs*].

Sensible Soccer made Sensible Software worth more money, to be honest (see Figure 9.6). We nearly signed it with Virgin, but they wanted to call it *Virgin Soccer*. Renegade was a great company; they worked like an indie record label. They were happy to let us call it *Sensible Soccer*. They gave us the best royalty deal we'd ever had, and it was our biggest hit.

Why call it soccer instead of football?

I don't know, actually. I don't know why. No idea. For me, *Sensible Soccer* just went together better. The term football is a different sport in the U.S., so it'd be confusing to just use the word football.

Sensible Soccer is the one that worked, and I wouldn't change a thing.

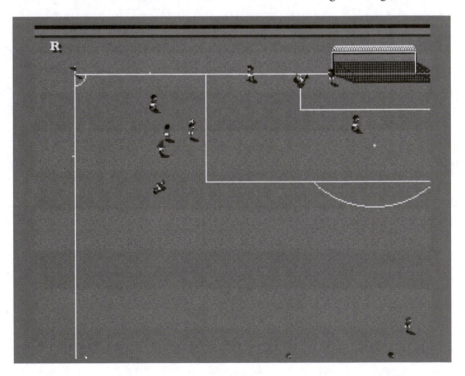

FIGURE 9.6 *Sensible Soccer* was a huge hit for Sensible Software, making it the superstar of Europe's gaming industry.

Was it the biggest hit ever for Sensible?

Oh, my God! *Sensible Soccer* was the top football game in the world for about two and a half years. Until the first version of *FIFA* came out on the Megadrive, we were number one. *FIFA* stole our crown. We remember it.

There's a particular point, which I've never forgiven myself for, that's led me to wonder. We submitted to Sega the Megadrive version of *Sensible Soccer,* and it was due to come out a couple weeks before *FIFA*. I'd taken a bit of artistic license. I noticed the Italian and French flags were the same; they were just red, white, blue; red, white, green. When you went in between them, they looked very similar, so what I did was flip the Italian flag 'round to green, white, red. They rejected our build on this basis. The flag was the wrong way 'round.

By the time we went through the whole submission process again, we came out after *FIFA* instead of before it. How much that dented our impact on consoles, I have no idea. We never really had the same impact on consoles.

I'm not even a sports guy, but I love *Sensible Soccer*. You don't really need to know a lot about soccer to enjoy the game.

I think what was really good about *Sensible Soccer* was that it was instantaneous and very fast. The speed of decision making when you're playing real soccer—you're under real pressure, making quick decisions about making a pass, putting a curve on the ball, or going in for a tackle. I think *Sensible Soccer* replicates that a lot better than the modern games. They give you the role of an armchair watcher; the television viewer perspective, not the player perspective. What we did was put you in the pitch like a player. The angle always lets you see everything you can interact with, and you're under time pressure to execute, which is much more like real soccer.

The other games give you the TV angle; you're sitting on your couch at home. More people can relate to being a player. A lot of people have said they're not into sports but enjoy *Sensible Soccer*.

Really, our game *Sensible World of Soccer* is our best game. The depth of data accuracy was unparalleled for many years, until we got *Football Manager* and *Championship Manager*. In 1995, we had 27,000 players from around the world, 1500 teams—every professional league in the world, including El Salvador down to division three. Player names, positions, values. Anyone who loved soccer as a sport—as I do—the depth of detail was amazing. I think what we did right, though, was that it worked even if you didn't care about that. It wasn't in your face; it didn't alienate the non-soccer fan, but it was sufficiently near the surface to appeal to the real soccer fan. We got that balance right.

What I struggle with now making games—when you sit down with junior programmers who have only been working for a year or two, and they're learning … It's fun if you think you're taking on the role as a teacher. But if you're trying to express your own creative stuff, and you're dealing with someone who's trying to learn a lesson you learned over twenty years ago—when you keep on repeatedly doing it, it's very frustrating. I think I've found that to be the most difficult thing to deal with since 1995, when we got a whole bunch of people in who were not strong. It's people who are not brilliant. When you're used to dealing with people who are brilliant, people who are not brilliant are very frustrating.

I'm a guy who has ideas and can draw a bit of art and knock up tables and talk. I can't make a computer do anything; I can barely make the bloody printer work. So you're relying on all the technical guys to be brilliant at what they do. I'm sure I'm not the only one who thinks like this; it's immensely hard to keep your optimism up when in your heart you know it's not good enough—it's not that 98% game that you had before. You have to let your standards decline with reality. Unless someone happens to give you twenty million dollars, a great group of guys, and says, go ahead and do what you want. That's my dream. I understand that's not going to happen.

Do you have a short list of star developers you'd like to work with?

I think I could stitch together the perfect team of guys, but different formats require different skills. One thing I learned watching Chris on the Commodore 64 and the Amiga, it took him until his third or fourth game on the Commodore 64 before he was a brilliant Commodore 64 programmer. You need a bunch of different products all on the same machine to become a maestro on an instrument. When you shift from machine to machine, as the fashion changes and the uncoordinated, sprawling advance in technology—with no plan—I find that a massive frustration. It demands that people constantly diverge their attention to a new medium. It's like saying to an artist, "I know you like charcoal, but charcoal is out now. You've got to use oil paints." That's what is happening to programmers especially.

You'll notice toward the final phase of a machine's life you'll get the odd product that's brilliant, but it's coming out too late. The machine is no longer sold in stores and they're pushing for the next version of it. But that game could be technically brilliant for that platform. That's the kind of time programmers need to really become masters.

One thing I think everyone forgets in our horrifically overcommercialized world. After fifty years, people only remember the really massively important groundbreaking pieces of art in the different media. Everything else is forgotten in the dustbin of forgotten stuff. I find it very depressing that over 95% of people in the games industry don't seem to care. I wish they'd think more with their ego and less with their bank account. We should be trying to make the next brilliant thing, but that takes publishers to back people to take educated gambles and not just go for the safe bet. It takes developers who can acknowledge when they're just *X-Factor* singers; they're not geniuses. I really hope that we can get out of this overcommercialized cycle that's just sucking out the energy of all the great people in the creative media world. To make money, we're forced to play dull games. History will remember how many games from each decade? One, maybe two? How many great novels can you name from the eighteenth century?

A lot. [I am an English professor, after all!]

I don't know if I know any.

Robinson Crusoe?

[*Laughs.*]. Okay, well, the point is that that's what it boils down to. That's what our vision should be. I don't think I've done it yet. The best game I've made is *Sensible Soccer*. I'm not convinced it's innovative, original, or creative enough.

I don't know, Jon, what about *Cannon Fodder*? That's a fun game with a profundity to it, a political statement.

Cannon Fodder did turn out to be a really nice combination. It's so nice how it fell into place politically. It wasn't planned to be like that; it evolved like that. We didn't plan to have people thinking about dead soldiers.

The start was a control system with four guys running around and firing bullets. Group combat! Now that's something interesting that hasn't happened before. Then some level design, rank progression, and this big empty screen with a hill and guys queuing up but nothing happening. What can we fill the hill with? Graves. Maybe the guys with bigger ranks should have bigger graves. Okay, that sounds like fun. Then we thought we'd show the names of guys whose rank went up—that's cool, that's what Nintendo would do. And then let's show the guys who died as well; show their names because they died. And when we did that, we realized how many people were dying. We didn't realize how many people were dying until we put the numbers up ourselves to test it.

We called the game *Lemmings with Weapons* when we were making it—the internal name. Obviously the name *Cannon Fodder* made sense with all the war dead. And of course the music added to it, the poppy we tried to put on the cover—that got banned.

Yeah, what's up with that poppy?

We put the poppy on, and it was spot-on. It's what the game was about. Do people in the United States wear poppies?

It's not something I've often seen.

All right. Well, this comes from the First World War. They wear them in the U.K. and in France. A lot of people died in the fields in France and Belgium in World War One. A lot of them died when the poppies were up, so people died in fields full of poppies. So once a year, when there's a remembrance of all the soldiers who died in the wars, everyone in the U.K. wears these plastic poppies with paper petals. They put them in their lapel. We just stuck one of those on the front of the box to remember those who had died in the war.

Unfortunately, the Royal British Legion, the official body who represents these soldiers, reacted to this by saying it was disrespectful to the war dead to put their poppy on a computer game. Obviously, they hadn't played the game, didn't understand it, and we're talking about a massively different generation of people—not gamers by any stretch of the imagination.

The reason I didn't like it was initially they said we couldn't do it because it was morally bad. Then they asked us to pay them money because we breached their copyright—the poppy was their copyright. This plastic poppy. So we had to pay them five hundred pounds, and we changed it back. I've never bought a poppy since because I bought five hundred in 1993. I was quite disappointed in their attitude; I thought it was poor.

Everybody that plays *Cannon Fodder* always talks about the song. Did you help write it?

I wrote it. Me and Richard Joseph worked on it together. But the war song is mine; that's actually me singing.

Wow! It's too bad you don't have an instrument handy, I'd love to hear you perform it.

I do. I can perform it if you want.

Sure! Go for it.

[*Plays the Cannon Fodder war song.*]

That was brilliant!

Yeah, my guitar is always there, because when I'm working, and my computer is busy or downloading something, I pick it up. It's always two inches from my hand.

We had talked earlier about how Westwood's *Dune II* gets all the accolades for being the first real-time strategy game despite the brilliance of *Cannon Fodder*.

Yeah, well, *Dune II* was a little bit earlier, and I remember it being in development at the time. But certainly *Command & Conquer* got massive backing from Virgin, and they didn't pay attention to the fact that in Europe there was already a game causing quite a stir. It wasn't picked up in the States. I never understood why. I understand why *Sensible Soccer* wasn't a big hit in the States, but not *Cannon Fodder*. I think it's just a bit of—I don't know, just not backing the guys from other countries. I think there's always been a bit of that in the U.S., to be honest, with the exception of a few Japanese guys.

You know, I've heard a lot of American developers complain that the Japanese developers and publishers get a lot more attention and publicity.

Really? Well, as Europeans, we barely get any at all. There's not many European-developed games that people will pay attention to.

I want to talk now about *Mega-Lo-Mania*. It's one of the first in its genre. People talk all the time about *Populous*, but seem unaware that this game even exists.

It's the first game that I really burnt the candle at both ends. It was really a lot of work. I worked on it with Chris Chapman. It was the first game we worked on together (see Figure 9.7).

It started off as a space game, flying around and shooting others ships, landing on planets, mining them, developing them—space war. Just before we released it, we realized two things. Firstly, it was bloody hard to fly the spaceship and manage all the resources at the same time. It was very difficult physically to do the two things at once. Secondly, it was graphically lacking something.

Populous had come out six months earlier, and we saw the little cavemen and thought it was a nice look. So we changed the technology. It started off as a space game starting in 2100 A.D., and we just ramped it back and started it in 10,000 B.C. Instead of going from spaceship A to spaceship B, we went from cavemen to warriors in biblical times to Romans and Normans, all the way through the Victorian era, world wars, and nuclear weapons. It was a fun game. I'm pleased with *Mega-Lo-Mania*. It's a nice little cameo.

You used some of the tech from *Mega-Lo-Mania* in *Sensible Soccer*, right? Cave men in football kits?

FIGURE 9.7 *Mega-Lo-Mania* is a real-time strategy game comparable to *Populous*. It was based on the *Sensible Soccer* engine.

Chris and I had been working very late nights. We'd been playing a lot of *Kick-Off*, the big soccer game at the time. We played it whenever we could. But there were a few things about *Kick-Off* that really annoyed us. By the time we finished, we knew we wanted to do a football game, like *Kick-Off* but with some changes.

The first step was to take the *Mega-Lo-Mania* guys and dress them up in football kits. One day when we were waiting for a build to burn, I did some art. I changed the caveman into my team, Norwich City, playing football—running around in the *Mega-Lo-Mania* world. If you look at the title of *Sensible Soccer*, it's identical to *Mega-Lo-Mania*. We changed it to a football pitch, and it just worked.

We then went on to *Cannon Fodder* and *Sensible Golf*. It became our trademark look. As it happens with many of these things, it was an accident that just evolved.

Let's talk about the fall of Sensible Software. I saw where you said that you thought the problem was that you'd gotten greedy, recycling some engines too much.

What happened was that we wrote a few hit games. Everybody wants your games, and you're a ready commodity. We were aware of this, and we got offers to do *Sensible Golf* and *Cannon Fodder 2* and various other things. We said yes to too much. So the same guy who was the lead programmer of *Cannon Fodder* was also the lead programmer of *Sensible Golf*. In order to save himself time, he was using the same engine—a golf game written on the *Cannon Fodder* engine, which was weird, obviously. It created technical problems and limitations. He came to me after six months of development and said he could only animate one sprite on the screen at one time. That was just crippling dull. Golf isn't the most interesting game as it sits, and we wanted the banter between players to be like you get in *Mario Golf*. We couldn't get it.

Sensible Golf is a disappointment to me; I'm not happy with it. As you said, we bit off more than we could chew. We were greedy. We diluted our quality. To be honest, I was focusing on *Sex 'n' Drugs 'n' Rock 'n' Roll* at that time, and it was such a massive game. Between that and *Sensible World of Soccer*, I didn't have time for *Sensible Golf*, and it just slid.

Sex 'n' Drugs 'n' Rock 'n' Roll is kind of a point-and-click adventure. It was a great engine. Well, the idea was great; the execution was awful. The game looked like a cartoon, and you only had one semitransparent cursor. You could click, talk, and listen, and the story was that you are the lead singer in a band—just a nobody band that gets signed by accident (they were mistaken for another band). A lazy record executive just wants to go home and signs the first band he can sign up. You fly to L.A., you get your hit records, go through various phases. You start with punk and move on to a Hawkwind kind of band; they find Eastern religion and go through a Beatles stage (see Figure 9.8). Then they go acoustic, disco, going from different styles of music. All the time, the guy is meeting women, shagging them, snorting cocaine. It's very hedonistic but very humorous.

In the U.K. we have a tradition of postcard humor. It's offensive, but it's done tongue-in-cheek. Graphically, the game wasn't offensive, inferring something offensive rather than being offensive.

Unfortunately, the problem with the game was the technicality. We just hadn't mastered 3D. This was our 1995 being behind the curve on 3D problem. We weren't up to it, and we didn't find out until it was too late. We lost a year and half of development. Then we signed the game with Warner, who put a million pounds into it. We signed a three million dollar deal for that and two other games. We had the money to make it, and it wasn't a stupid idea.

FIGURE 9.8   This *Beatles*-esque photo of the Sensible Software team illustrates the bandlike spirit of the team.

We didn't lose money from it; in the end we made money from it. There was no financial loss. Really, the problem was that Warner got bought from GT—those guys have something to do with Wal-Mart. They're a Bible-Belt driven company. *Sex 'n' Drugs 'n' Rock 'n' Roll* was about shagging women and snorting cocaine.

Sex 'n' Drugs 'n' Rock 'n' Roll.

[*Laughs.*] Whether it was humorous or not, they weren't interested. We had a couple million pounds of advances at that point, and we just didn't know how to get out of this contract. They obviously didn't want the game to come out. We wanted it to come out, and we certainly didn't want to give the money back. We were stuck, really.

We soldiered on, finishing the game off without being paid for six months. Luckily, we had good cash reserves from our royalties for *Sensible Soccer*. We had to wait for them to tell us they didn't want the game, because we couldn't pull out ourselves. Eventually they did. We didn't have to pay any money back. We had a game called *Have a Nice Day* that also had some technical problems. That came out of the contract. *Sensible Soccer 3D* stayed, but we also had problems with that—another 3D problem. We kept on with *Sex 'n' Drugs 'n' Rock 'n' Roll* for about four months, but it required a big team—a ten-man art team. It was going to be on sixteen disks, and then it went down to four, then two. It was technically not managed well. Loads of art—75% of the art was finished, about 80% of the speech, 90% of the script that I wrote. Unfortunately, technically the engine just couldn't run it. We had nothing to demo that worked—just the videos.

The timing was just wrong. If it had been five years after, and *GTA* [*Grand Theft Auto*] was out, people would be falling out of their chairs to grab it from us. People have asked me to resurrect it, and I say, look at the graphics—they look really dated. I've still got the script. But we'd have to start from the ground up. But it's had its time, and it's gone. It's an opportunity missed. I put four years of my creative life in that game. It took me four or five more to get over it. It's like an old relationship that went wrong, and you got upset, but you're over it. I'm pleased with the soundtrack, I'm pleased I made it … But the chance is gone.

Have you thought about resurrecting it as a *Rock-Band*-style game? With playable instruments?

I possibly could, but it's more of a *Leisure Suit Larry* or *Monkey Island* style game. Only the subject matter was different; you were a rock band. As you know, all the point-and-click adventures are gone; no one wanted them for ten years. I have no idea why they went out of fashion; I loved those games.

It was a mixture of psychedelic spirit of *Wizball* and *Wizkid* with *Leisure Suit Larry* and *Monkey Island*. It should have worked. It was funny. It was childish, schoolboy humor.

Have you played *A Rockstar Ate My Hamster*?

Yeah. Maybe some of that. I wanted to push the boat out there, so we had some irreligious jokes. We showed it to a lawyer, and he objected to the irreverence to religion content. But I thought, why not? I'm not religious; it doesn't offend me.

So they told you you couldn't be irreverent toward religion?

We asked them if we'd have legal trouble with this game. They said no. The only thing is, you've got a picture of a guy on a cross, floating around in space, naked and having sex. "Change the cross." So we changed it to a star.

What about the cocaine? They didn't ask you to change that to star dust?

Actually, GT asked us about that. They requested that we change it. We could, but it really wasn't the point. We used drugs as a game mechanic. If the guy was doing certain drugs, his conversation options changed because he'd think of different things to say. That kind of stuff. Drugs are really good game mechanics.

The game was really toned down from what it originally was—we called it *Drugged Out Hippie*. This was a guy in a band who borrowed two thousand pounds from the Hell's Angels to start up his band. He had seven different drug habits to support; speed, dope, heroin. Each drug had a different effect. Speed would speed things up, LSD would make him see weird stuff. That was a fun idea. He could make money by dragging women into a van and pimping them on the side of the road. All sorts of ideas. We really toned it down.

It sounds like all the stuff that *Rock Star* is doing now. You guys had that in your game?

Well … I think we did it in a lot of our games at Sensible. It's the kind of humor that you use with your friends in a bar. Nobody gets offended because everyone understands it; you're a decent guy saying something funny because he wants to make his friends laugh. That's how we approached our work. We weren't particularly trying to be anything.

Do you still have the *Sensible Soccer* code?

Yes, I think we do. I'm sure it can be dug up.

Are you interested in releasing it as an open source project?

I don't own Sensible Software. We sold it to Codemasters in 1999, and they got all the old games. That's why they bought it [*laughs*]. *Speedball* I have more control over.

We haven't talked much about *Speedball 2: Evolution,* which is a fantastic version of *Speedball.* It's been about on iOS for about two months. It's on Mac, Symbian, Android. It's really good. A lot of the *Speedball* engine is just *Sensible Soccer.* There's hope yet.

It's been a great hit game for us. We've been number one on the iPad in Germany, New Zealand, number 2 on iPhone and iPad in U.K. As usual, the U.S. hasn't been there.

Do you prefer Apple's approach with its App Store or the Android Marketplace?

I'm a professional game maker. I don't like my games being given away for free. It's bad enough that our back catalog dies because the technology changes.

One of my biggest bugbears is that I've had lots of hit games … If you talked to a musician who'd had ten number one hits in the past, he would be earning so much money from the royalties on that, all the years subsequently. What happens to us is that after two or three years, nobody buys the games anymore because the technology moves on. The lack of legacy from an artistic point of view is a big deal. It means that you certainly can't afford for a game to be free when it comes out, because you've only got two or three years to make money from it before you're not going to make any money at all.

Obviously the creativity in the games is important but not losing money is important. I resent the fact that technology companies have not prioritized the software developers in terms of making sure their product has long-term legacy and some money-earning ability. I think we've been pretty much shafted by every single hardware company for the last twenty years. They've not taken the care to make their machines backward compatible and for some money to be made.

It's cost us quite a lot to do the *Speedball* conversion. People are very used to free entertainment now, and that's because there's a lot of shoddy entertainment out there that deserves to be free. To be fair. But some people take a lot of care, do things very professionally, but they can't do that for free. So I prefer iOS, in short.

I think it's ridiculous to say here's a model where the product is totally free. It's okay for hobbyists to think like that. I don't think they've really thought about it. If you look at the history of mobile platforms, they treat games as the second rate. Actually, the applications are second rate, and games are a small part of that. They're almost an afterthought. That's why I've got time for Apple—they treat us with respect. The other mobile companies have treated developers like dirt.

Do you get pissed off at all the abandonware sites and all the pirates?

Pirates are okay as long as it's going on in tandem with sales. When *Speedball* and *Cannon Fodder* were at their peak, we were getting a ten-to-one piracy rate. For every copy sold, ten were pirated. But we knew those guys weren't going to buy the games, and we were still selling millions of copies. But when you're not selling millions of copies—and you're selling tens of thousands of copies—if the piracy rate is ten-to-one, that annoys you.

I think there's just too much content in the world at the moment, which has bred a lack of respect for content. There's not enough discrimination about quality. Discrimination is not a bad word; it's calculating whether something is worth it or not, whether it's different or not. I think the quality has dropped in a lot of cases.

One last question, Jon. You were talking earlier about how you had to work with some people who weren't the best. So what do you tell the kid or teenager today who wants to become one of the highly skilled experts you actually want to hire?

Okay, I'll be very brief. The first thing you have to understand is that it's very hard to make games on your own. You need a team. You need three or four guys. Pick a small platform. iPhone is ideal or a small Flash game. iPhone is great because you get all the way to the end, making a game and publishing it.

Make it small and unambitious. As much as I've criticized *Tiny Wings*, it's what you want. It's not an ambitious game, and for what it is, it's executed well. Pick something small and within your ability, and execute it as well as you can. Really, really push the quality. You don't know anything about games until you've gone through the complete development cycle, starting it, going through all the problems, and coming out the other end. Once you've done that two or three times, you'll be good enough.

I'm actually working with a bunch of different universities at the moment, going through their programs, and trying to come up with a real game development project in the courses. It's quite fun for me.

Be realistic about what your skills are. Do you know what being a game developer means? It means loads and loads of detail. Every single detail about the game, you're going to need to know the answer to. Anyone involved on the team—if they have a question, you need the answer. That's what being a game designer is. If you want to be a programmer … I'm not sure anyone really wants to be a programmer nowadays, because they don't understand what it entails. It's about making everything work. If it's an artist, it's got to be a commercially slanted artist, but keep your creativity. I always say to people, your best ambition should be to keep your head in the stars and your feet on the ground. You need to stretch yourself both ways. Find your most realistic dream and aspire to it.

And don't just talk about it, do it! All the talk in the world never did anything. A game that is 99% finished was a waste of time. That's what I feel about *Sex 'n' Drugs 'n' Rock 'n' Roll*—it was a waste of time. *Cannon Fodder 3* was a waste of two years. The same with every single demo. If you don't finish it, no one is ever going to see it; you've not proved yourself and wasted your time. If you're on a team, you wasted their time, too. So stick to it. Get to the end. That's the hard bit.

CHAPTER 10

Ralph Baer, the Father of Videogames

In 2006, Ralph Baer received the National Medal of Technology for his pioneering work in the videogame industry (see Figure 10.1). Specifically, he's responsible for the "Brown Box," a prototype he built in 1966 that would eventually become the Magnavox Odyssey, the first game console. In short, without Ralph's work, we wouldn't have videogames in our homes today.

Or would we? Well, that depends on who you ask. Nolan Bushnell, founder of Atari, would almost certainly disagree, as he did back in a series of court cases fought with Baer over *Pong*. According to Baer, *Pong* was a rip-off that infringed on his patents, and he had proof that showed Bushnell was at a trade show where he'd demonstrated his work. The case was eventually settled in Baer's favor, but, ultimately it was Bushnell and Atari, not Baer and Magnavox, that most of us remember today.

Indeed, Ralph's electronic game *Simon* is much better known and loved today than his breakthrough Odyssey console.

In any case, I was thrilled to have the opportunity to chat with Ralph, who was just shy of ninety at the time of our interview. Age has done little to dull either his mind or his passion for inventing. He still maintains a fully functional workshop and spends the better part of his days there.

You're probably best known in the videogames industry for your pioneering work on the Magnavox Odyssey. However, you also did a lot of very important work for Coleco. Can you talk about that?

Let me give you a little background. In about 1975, I was still at Sanders, and I was still an engineering associate. I didn't have a responsibility for a division anymore and could do pretty much whatever I wanted. I was already doing toys and games in my lab at home on nights and weekends.

Next thing I know, I've become the outside electronics capability for Marvin Glass and Associates—one of the largest independent toy and game designers in the country. They were in Chicago. On my various trips there, which were almost weekly, I met Arnold

FIGURE 10.1   Ralph Baer receiving the National Medal of Technology from President George W. Bush. (With permission of Ralph Baer.)

Greenberg, the president of Coleco. Coleco was a big toy and game manufacturer, so I got to know Arnold. Somewhere along the line, Arnold had expressed an interest in going into the videogame business.

I got invited to a demonstration at General Instruments in Hicksville, Long Island, to see a single-chip production of a ping-pong game. I go to Hicksville, I see this device, which became the AY-3-8500 chip, made by TI, which had become the microcomputer company in Arizona. I called up Coleco and told them they had to put in an order for this thing. They got to be at the top of the order list at a time when the yields for the AY-3-8500 were still pretty low. So they built a game.

Next thing I know, the phone rings in my lab; my office was my lab at the time. The chief engineer of Coleco at the time was on the phone. At the same time, Arnold was on the phone with one of the vice presidents of Sanders. They both have the same story. They took a videogame down to the FCC in Maryland, and we're stuck. Can you help us?

As it turns out, in my division we'd developed a radio frequency interference capability quite a few years before that, which had grown big enough to be the biggest in the northeast. So we had the capability of making the measurements we needed to find the trouble. I said, yes, we can come up tomorrow morning, but you got to do one thing, you got to sign the license agreement, which they hadn't done, because Arnold was never in a hurry to spend money on licensing agreements. He parted with money very reluctantly.

Next morning they show up, sign the license agreement, and we go out to this partial roof we had on the fifth floor of the Canal Street Building in Nassau, and we do all the usual things engineering students are pressed [indecipherable] by Piezo capacitor, grounding some things on the board, nothing worked. So I go home and don't sleep well that night, trying to figure out what the hell to do the next morning.

I come up to the lab the next morning—the other guys aren't there yet, and I see a couple of pieces of equipment on the bench; military stuff. I [noticed] there was a coaxial [cable?] between the two pieces of hardware, two boxes … The ends of the coaxial were looped through two ferrite rings, and they weren't engineered wrong. By coincidence, he actually knew what was going on. I asked him, what are these ferrite rings for? He said, well, we had some television signals being picked up by the other cable, like an antenna, and we suppressed them with these two ferrite rings as RF chokes on the end. They killed the signal.

I ran around the lab, opened up all the cabinet drawers, until I found some ferrite rings. When the crew came up to do the interference testing, I said I want you to put one of these rings on the output coaxial, right on the inside of the case, make it look like a strain release so when you pull it the cable doesn't pull out. We did that and we were in spec immediately. It suppressed the [indecipherable], channel three, channel four, of the ColecoVision game. That's what the problem was. It went down to Maryland, passed the FCC test, and I was a hero at Coleco. Thirty million dollars' worth of hardware, sitting in a warehouse—finished ColecoVision games were ready to ship. That's my Coleco story.

As a result of that, when Arnold decided to improve the line next year, he gave me a contract that had no dollar limitations. I think that's the only one he ever signed that way. It required that we help him with technology problems. We helped him with that machine that was triangular with a gun on one side and hand controls for ping-pong on the other side. What was that other thing? Oh, a steering wheel on the third side.* This was 1974 or 1975. It was very neat—it had a triangular cartridge that plugged in on top to change from car steering for racing to ping-pong controls.

The next year after that we helped with another series of games. The biggest problem was how to book the stuff with Sanders. All the business at Sanders … It was a large company, the biggest company in New Hampshire at the time, upwards of ten thousand people. How do we book this stuff? We're a military company [laughs]. That was the most creative part of the whole thing; how do we collect money? We had the same problem with doing outside RFI work for other companies. How do we book this stuff?

Even though you filed the first patents on videogames and are known for being meticulous with documentation, you still had to fight battle after battle in court to defend those patents against the likes of Atari and Nolan Bushnell. Some people like Larry Lessig have criticized the entire intellectual property system. I know this is a huge topic, but what are your views on patents and copyrights?

Well, I won't give you a long lecture, but I know enough about the subject. I don't know if you can see in the background, but right above my head—that large, white framed thing? That proclaims me an honorary doctor of laws from Pierce Law Center because I spent ten years in court, off and on, have written dozens of patents myself … The bottom line is

---

* Ralph is referring to the Telstar Arcade.

that patents aren't worth the [paper they're printed on?] unless they're in the hands of very strong companies who have the money to assert them.

I just found out that a patent I have on recordable talking books is being infringed by a very large company whose name I shall not mention. There is no way in the world I can assert that patent against that company. They have in-house lawyers on the payroll. It would cost me tens of thousands, eventually hundreds of thousands of dollars. Oh, yes, I can get law firms to work for me on a contingency basis. But if we lose, I owe them their expenses, and that could be millions.

On the one hand, patents leave a lot to be desired. On the other hand, they are a bargaining point if you're in a licensing business like I was. They are very important. Magnavox probably wouldn't have gone into the videogame business if they hadn't have had patents that gave them the rights to sue others who might want to take their market share away from them.

Copyrights? Copyrights … Nowadays, nobody seems to respect anything. A copyright is good as a seal by Congress that nobody will infringe your book or story. But today, people don't seem to have any compunction about copying stuff, putting it on YouTube or anywhere. This is a very, very dicey period we're in.

I don't want to get into philosophy, but take a look at Google. [Imagine] Google run by the government [and] out of control. I think that's how you can describe our current government. You've got the beginnings of a really bad scenario. Video cameras on every street corner, thank you very much.

You're a great inventor, Ralph, with lots of great products under your belt (see Figure 10.2). How hard is it nowadays for someone with a new invention to get it patented and into production? I know that historically, many brilliant inventors have been ripped off and never received a dime despite their products making millions for a company.

Well, the same thing was true and still is true for the toy and game business. I don't want to say lots of negative things, but it is customary for an individual inventor to bring your stuff to a company. If you're introduced, otherwise you can't even get through the door. You go in there and demonstrate your stuff. And who are the clients nowadays? Mattel, Hasbro, a half of a dozen others. They all know you, they all know each other for ten, twenty, thirty years. The problem is that they've seen it all, they've heard it all. They're jaundiced. It's a real uphill fight. A business related to some license thing has got to be the hardest thing since trips to the moon.

Then you've got a new product—now you've got something they want to keep (see Figure 10.3). Then you're stuck with endless committee meetings and have no options to go anywhere else, and they really aren't going to make it. Are they going to tell you? They really should. No, they forget, right? Conveniently forget until next toy fair. But you can't go to anybody else. All this goes on, all the time. Worse yet, they see stuff, and two or three years later, someone inside decides they're going to do something. It's really based on something you showed them two or three years before. Well, they've long since forgotten where the idea came from. So they think they came up with something original.

Can you take them to court? I tried it once. I won't say against whom. Unfortunately, I didn't win, because their lawyers were a lot better than mine. It's a tough business. I can commiserate with the guys who spent weeks, months, working all kinds of crazy hours,

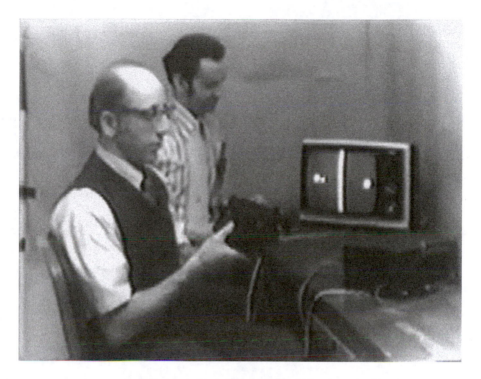

FIGURE 10.2   Ralph demonstrating his "Brown Box" prototype in 1969.

FIGURE 10.3   The Magnavox Odyssey.

without getting a lot of money, creating really good stuff—they all got ripped off. It's just too easy for people to get ripped off.

I see my stuff on YouTube all the time. Did anybody ask me? Worse than that, captions and annotations that come along are usually full of bologna. Somebody used the s-word because people are too damned lazy to research anything. It's so easy to find out the facts today. In seconds, you go to Google, and bingo, you get the story. Does anybody read? No. People are too gosh darned lazy to actually inform themselves on the stuff that they hold forth on. I mean recurrent nonsense on videogames comes along that I had five hundred people working on the development of videogames. Yeah, I had five hundred people in my division, but they didn't have anything to do with that. That was between me, Bill Rush, and Bill Harrison. And we all worked part time on it because we had tons of other stuff to do. We didn't put in more than half a man year total, between the three of us. All this nonsense comes along.

And this nonsense about videogames having a basis in military activity? The bottom line is bullshit. It just ain't so. People have a real problem with acquainting themselves on the subjects of which they hold forth at great length.

I've heard that story about games coming from military applications many times even in academic circles, where you'd think the people would be a lot more critical. How does this misinformation get spread so thickly?

Well, they repeat each other's nonsense. They look at two or three stories on the Web, all of which are ridiculous, right? Then they extemporize on that and add some more nonsense to it, and portray it as factual. I can't respond to it anymore because every day I get a dump by Google, and almost every day there's nonsense up there.

Can you imagine? I'm just one person. There are millions of people being quoted, who are described, whose activities are being quoted, by trillions of people out there. Can you imagine how much garbage is floating around out there? It's just unbelievable. It gets regurgitated, edited, and spread by nincompoops—especially large numbers of people who cannot spell, cannot punctuate, who have no grasp of the English language; too damn lazy to look up anything that might inform themselves on the subject they're dealing with. That's enough venting on that subject.

Let's talk then about making games. What's your advice to aspiring game designers who want to do something really creative or innovative?

Make games! Never mind the graphics and all this jazz. Look at the Wii. The Wii graphics aren't PS3 graphics, but they're plenty good enough. And you'll find the interactive stuff is what we did in 1960. As a matter of fact, let me wax on that a bit.

In 1989, 1990, my sidekick and I came up with a whole number of different ways to use a Nintendo machine—the early NES. We did things like using the floor mat that hooked into the NES to play any game in the NES repertoire with your feet, sitting down or standing up. That was very neat. Then I had a helmet with a gun sight on it and a microphone, so you could shoot at airplanes going by and yell at the mic to fire missiles. I had some other things that I won't talk about because there's still the possibility of reviving them again. The name of the game is interactivity, between the person and the object on the screen. Like moving around. You look at the Wii. I showed this stuff to the VP of Konami, who came with three Chinese manufacturing testers. They went around my lab's display area, taking photographs of everything in sight. He ripped me off on that helmet.

Here we are, twenty years later, and finally the Wii gets around to doing what I proposed to do: interact physically with the screen. I'm happy to see it. It brings a whole new group of people, especially old people who have no patience to push forty thousand different buttons and learn forty thousand different rules, remember twenty thousand sequences so they can go on to the next level. Who wants to do this? Obviously, billions of people want to do it, but there are quite a few billion people who don't want to do it.

Think about anybody over sixty-five. As I remember, there's something like sixteen million females and another sixteen million males in the U.S. alone who are over sixty-five. I bet you seventy-five percent of them are computer-averse, wouldn't touch a computer with a ten-foot pole. So they certainly aren't going to play games on a computer, and they're not going to play videogames, because they're even more complicated than a computer keyboard. Why aren't they involved? Well, they do get involved. You see grandmothers playing with their grandkids when it comes to playing tennis or bowling on the Wii. It's great. We're back to finally putting the emphasis on game. Family games.

I just reproduced an article—it's in German—which was written for the game developers in Berlin this summer. Very, very nice article. It describes what we did without recognizing it. What we did was create family games. Was it a conscious objective in the beginning? I don't think so. The objective was to make interesting games. I started off with steering a car from side to side as a roadway snaked—simple. It was definitely a one-player game. But we fell into multiplayer games once we had a moving spot up there. Put a second one up there, and what could be more obvious than having one chase the other? A two-player game. Then take a light gun, and what's more obvious than having one guy move the target and the other guy shooting it? We were doing two-player games. Now that we have two spots up there, why not a third spot controlled by the machine? That's the ball. Now we're in the ballgame business. That was definitely a two-player, family game. At that point we had something and knew we were in the family game business.

It's refreshing to hear somebody talking about family games. It seems like every time you hear someone from outside the industry talking about videogames, it's just to criticize the violence and sexual content in them. I'm sure you never envisioned anything like that when you were putting spots up on a screen. Do you think there's a relationship between the games kids play and their behavior?

It's ridiculous. When you look at anything on cable—I'm talking about the movies, situation comedies, everything. They're full of sex, full of violence. A lot of it, by '50s stances, is abhorrent. It's just awful. It's become our culture. And the people who are selling this culture out there—are they complaining about videogames? Videogames are tamer than our culture. Besides that, videogames take place in a hypothetical environments. Very few kids get so involved that it screws up their psyche. Kids get screwed up for lots of other reasons. It's easy to blame things. Of course there's a relationship. But there's a relationship with everything. You see a mine blowing up a bunch of Marines on screen—that's not going to upset my psyche? If the Army comes calling and wants me to enlist, of course it's going to affect me. Of course there's a relationship.

There's always a group that has to complain about something. I don't want to go into politics, but there are always huge numbers of people who seem to live in a world that's separated from the world I live in. There's no way you can fight that.

I wish we could get back some of the way we lived fifty years ago, when politeness counted, when you dressed halfway decent. I don't like to go the movie theater and see everybody dressed like they just came out of the garage having just fixed the rear axle of a car. Or worse yet, go to a concert—of course, going to a concert means something different now. It means going out to an open-air affair where a bunch of guys jump up and down, make raucous noises, growl, and yell, and scream—that's what passes for music. It's another degenerate thing I have very little patience for. But then I'm eighty-seven; I'm going to be eighty-eight in a couple months. It's a very different perspective.

It's often remarked that as an engineer, you're very meticulous about your notes and very detailed. Do you think that trait has helped you as an inventor?

You've got to remember one thing. I'm different than most of the other guys. I'm German born, and I carry one of the German traits, which is to be well organized. I never throw a document away no matter how hastily it was scratched. You go to the Smithsonian website and there are five hundred documents, complete with the lawyer scans and even the fingerprints where you can see what they had for lunch. It's all there. You can trace the whole history from day one. How many other people do this?

So many people assert that they've done things, and what's worse is not giving credit to the ones who actually did the work. Here's one thing I believe in: give credit to the people who do the work. I was invited to the Smithsonian to hold forth for a bunch of kids and parents. I brought Bill Harrison up from Florida, he joined me, and we both held forth. He did very important work. For example, would our game have been able to sell if it'd had more parts than it did? Who knows? But he found a way to create a spot, move it vertically and horizontally across the screen, with half the number of parts that a typical engineer would use. That meant six or seven transistors and resistors, which was probably half a buck worth of parts. You multiply that out, and you come out with an extra two or three bucks out of the door. These things are important. There's creativity in the box, and it came from him. So why in the hell wouldn't you want to give him credit? But there are people who have to get their face in front of a camera, and nobody else counts.

What would your history of the videogames industry look like, Ralph? Seems like you'd be the perfect person to write such a book! I'd love to see a feature-length documentary about you. I think it'd be a great contribution to history—a lot better than the film they're planning to make about Atari. Have you heard of that? I want to see *Baer: The Movie*.

A whole lot of people out there would have a different sense of history, because they've been snowed all these years. So it wouldn't be so much a plus as a minus. Think about what would happen if [Leonardo] DiCaprio actually produces that film of our mutual friend, that president of Atari who invented videogames and all this bullshit. How would I be as competition? There will be millions of people who will believe the bullshit because it's done with a flair. I hope that that movie never gets made. A lot of people have voiced their apprehension about what it's going to be like.

Well, there will always be some people like us who will want to know the facts.

Well, you better get moving. I've got problems; I'm not going to be around forever.

CHAPTER 11

David Fox, the Mindbender

David Fox (see Figure 11.1) was one of the first programmers and designers hired at Lucasfilm Games, the George Lucas company that later changed its name to LucasArts. Probably best known for designing the graphical adventure game *Zak McKracken and the Alien Mindbenders*, David is also responsible for *Rescue on Fractalus!*, an innovative action game that used fractals to generate its landscape. David is also credited on several other adventure games, including *Labyrinth, Loom, Indiana Jones and The Last Crusade: The Graphic Adventure*, and *Maniac Mansion*.

David's conception of electronic entertainment goes beyond traditional videogames. His Mirage project was an ingenious cross between a videogame and an amusement park ride that was sadly ahead of its time.

David has also frequently used his skills and knowledge to promote better citizenship and political awareness, and now works with his wife Annie on projects intended to help children and teenagers deal with difficult family and social issues. David and Annie are, in short, good people.

It was a real treat for me to get to chat with David. I wasn't quite sure what to expect; *Zak McKracken* is a pretty weird game, to say the least. I half expected him to show up in a pair of Groucho Marx comedy glasses, and he didn't disappoint. But despite the occasional hint of zaniness, David is actually a quiet, mild-mannered guy who could make Fred Rogers look like a bully. Indeed, it's hard to believe it was David's idea to let players blow up hamsters in *Maniac Mansion* by nuking them in the microwave …

You're latest project is a Rube Goldberg-inspired project. I know a lot of it is still under wraps, but can you tell me anything about it?

I've always been interested in those types of machines; Rube Goldberg is well known for the crazy contraptions that he did. A lot of people know the word as an adjective for crazy devices that are overly complicated for doing very simple things. Rube Goldberg was a cartoonist who died in 1971. He was famous for decades, from the '20s and '30s all the way through to the '60s and '70s. I remember as a kid, loving his cartoons—the humor and the irreverence. More recently, I've seen games that call themselves Rube Goldberg

FIGURE 11.1 David Fox designed the cult classic games *Zak McKracken and the Alien Mindbenders* and *Rescue on Fractalus!*.

games—*Incredible Machines* is one, and there are several more on iOS. I'd like to do one of those myself. I did some Internet searches, and saw that, for whatever reason, no one ever did an official Rube Goldberg game. So I found their website, sent them an e-mail, and got a phone call from Rube Goldberg's granddaughter. Now I have the rights to do it, and we're in the early design stages now.

You mentioned *Incredible Machines*. Do you have a unique spin you're going to take with the project?

I think what's missing from many of the ones I've seen is humor. If you think back to the adventure games that we used to do, humor was one of the earmarks of the Lucasfilm adventure games—wacky, irreverent humor. In fact, if you think about those games, they were like really large Rube Goldberg devices, where you had to pick up strange objects from one place and do things to convert or combine them, and make stuff happen. The whole game was essentially a Rube Goldberg device with a story in the middle of it.

I want to take that quality of humor and Easter eggs, things you didn't expect to happen, and experiment. Of course, Rube Goldberg stuff usually has animals—cats and parrots—and tiny little people. It's not really a physics simulator like a lot of the current ones, but there are those elements. This is going to be very true to his work. We want to replicate his style in his '30s and '40s cartoons, but in color.

I think out of all the developers in the world, you're the one to do this!

Well, I think that's what they figured out. I said, look at my background, this is why I want to do it. And I'm very passionate about it, so it should be a lot of fun.

Let's talk about your early days. Your biography pages mention that you found some discarded cels from *The Flintstones* and were able to make a cartoon out of it.

Yes. I used to love animation. I grew up in Los Angeles—now I live in northern California, but grew up there. Part of my life was in Studio City, where a lot of film studios were, and

Hanna-Barbera studios were a bike ride away. For some reason, they just dumped their cels in a big dumpster. I'd go dumpster diving and come back with boxes full of cels. They were in sequence and numbered, so I'd get a whole series from a scene, and usually it was *Flintstones*. I'd go home, take my 8 mm camera, put it on a tripod, and single-step through it. I experimented with it, like I did with games later on. How did they do it? How can you do animation?

I did my own stop motion, but one thing I didn't like about it was how tedious it was. I was twelve or thirteen years old.

My mother didn't realize they were prized possessions and ended up throwing away whole boxes of them. Now I walk into art galleries and see a single cel selling for thousands of dollars. I had stacks and stacks of them a foot thick. Maybe I'd be independently wealthy and wouldn't have gone into games if that hadn't happened …

Maybe some other kid found them and was inspired, too.

Maybe so!

Let's talk about your early days as a programmer. You and your wife founded the Marin Computer Center in 1977, the first public-access microcomputer center. That sounds amazing. What was the agenda and purpose of the center?

The story goes back a little further—the year before that, I had been looking for something to do next. I ended up realizing that I needed to learn how to do games. I wasn't a programmer at the time. I had taken a couple programming classes in high school and college but not to the point that I'd consider myself a programmer. I was always envisioning some kind of immersive environment, like a Disneyland, where you could go and be immersed in adventure-like games—and learn something about yourself. It wasn't just for fun; it was actually a self-improvement, personal awareness, enlightenment type of process.

After having this vision, I read Orson Scott Card's book *Ender's Game*, and there's this whole subplot with a computer game that the main character plays. It's very much like that—the computer is sentient enough to know what Ender's blindspots were and would devise adventure game puzzles that it knew he couldn't figure out until he overcame the way he was used to thinking. It was a way to enlarge his viewpoint and view of the world. I thought that was great and was what I was looking for.

I thought that if I wanted to make games and theme park stuff, the place to start might be to learn how to program. So we put together a public access, nonprofit organization where we could invite the public in to play with computers, take classes, bring the computers out to the schools where kids could use them there. We did field trips where kids could come in and play the different games that we had. We did that for about five years, and during that process we started with Sol computers. We chose those over the Apple II, because they could do upper and lower case. When we bought them, we thought people would be coming in a lot more for word processing, and we didn't realize the degree to which people would be coming in to play games.

I actually remember in 1977—must have been in spring. I heard about this small company launching a computer. I drove down to Cupertino, went into this office, and there were all these beige-colored cases all over the place. These two men were pitching to me that I should get the Apple II. It turns out they were the two Steves. I watched the demos, and I liked the sound and color, but what about upper and lower case? They thought nobody wanted that.

So it came down to that and the fact that my wife liked the walnut sides that the Sol 20s had. They looked less like computers, maybe. Of course, we ended up with a mix of over forty computers, with Apple IIs, Ataris, and got a bunch of grants for outreach and teaching.

One thing we did a lot was that our volunteer kids would come in and play games that weren't being sold, such as the Adventure International games. We'd rate these games, write reviews for them, and ended up getting the opportunity to do some conversions. We converted some of Scott Adams' early games to Apple II and CP/M machines, and in the process wrote this conversion software that we called Apple Spice. Adventure International sold it for us. It was an assembly-based extension to the BASIC that came with the Apple IIs. It gave them the same functionality as the RadioShack computers had that Scott's original code used. Rather than rewrite all the code, we added to the language.

Doing that let me take apart other people's games, learn about them, and find bugs and suggestions to improve them. It was tough being self-taught by looking at other people's work. I ended up doing some books on programming.

The second book, which was on animation, let me go to a local company doing some amazing stuff with high-end animation—the Lucasfilm computer division. They had just finished doing some work on *Star Trek II: The Wrath of Khan's* "Genesis Effect." A whole planet was being terraformed. I got to use images from that in the book and got to interview people. I was able to hang out with some of the computer division people at SIGGRAPH.

I made a friend at Industrial Light & Magic, which was just starting up a new games group. I contacted the head of the computer games division. I was the second outside person hired into the games group—after Peter Langston, the guy hired to manage it. I was there at the beginning. I used my book on computer animation to show them what I had done.

It happened that Atari had paid Lucasfilm a million dollars to start this games group. They had the right of first refusal for any games we produced for Atari computers. The fact that I had background in Atari animation and games [helped]. Also, Peter was looking for people who were not typical game industry people. He wanted to start from scratch and come up with new methodologies, break into new territory. A lot of the hires were not well-known game designers, but he took a chance on us. I think we did some really good stuff.

I'm interested in the partnership between Lucasfilm Games and Atari. That must have been an amazing time. What was the first game?

Well, we did two concurrently. There was the one I worked on called *Rescue on Fractalus!* (see Figure 11.2). The other one was *Ball Blazer*, with David Levine as the designer.

When I first started working there, we didn't have a separate space for the games folks, so we ended up sharing offices with people from the computer division. I somehow ended up in the office with Loren Carpenter, who I'd met earlier while working on my book. Loren was known for doing fractals and creating animated fractal landscapes. He is a brilliant programmer and coder. Loren and the rest of the computer division was later purchased by Steve Jobs and became Pixar. Loren is now the chief scientist there.

FIGURE 11.2 *Rescue on Fractalus!* used fractal geometry to create the mountainous landscapes. Atari 400/800 version shown.

I asked Loren if it were possible to do a rotating fractal game on an 8-bit computer, such as the Atari 800 or the Atari 5200, which was the gaming system. His first reaction was no. But then it was, well, maybe. Then he comes back a year or so later, borrowed an Atari 800, went home, learned 6502 assembly language. A few days later he had a prototype of flying over a fractal landscape. He proved it was possible.

He worked on the 3D fractal stuff. We had other great people, like Charlie Kellner, who came over from Apple. I'd met him at the computer center. It was a really fun game.

I can't take credit for the part of the game that people remember the most. The original version of the game was more of a pacifist game; you didn't have any rockets or fire buttons. The only thing you could do was go through the mountains really fast, outrunning the enemy saucers. They couldn't steer as well, so you'd have them crash into the mountains.

We had an early beta test with George Lucas, who spent about twenty minutes with the game. He asked, "Where's the fire button?" There isn't one. He said, "Well, is that a game-play decision or a philosophical decision?" I said … more philosophical. He had us add a fire button.

He also came up with the idea of creating tension by having aliens down on the planet. What you thought was a pilot running toward you turns out to be an alien.

That part used to scare me to death!

I still hear stories about when people first have that happen. We had Atari not disclose anything about that in the packaging. You play four, maybe eight levels without any of them popping up. You think it's easy. Then you land and here comes a pilot—he does have a green helmet. Then he pops up. There's stories of people falling out of chairs, and kids screaming to their mom that's there's a monster in their computer. It was especially bad for people playing at night with their speakers turned really loud.

Why wasn't *Rescue on Fractalus!* based in the *Star Wars* universe?

Well, that was in my original design document—let's put this in the *Star Wars* universe. I'll be honest; the reason I was at Lucas was that I fell in love with *Star Wars*. My wife and I considered moving out of the Bay Area and up to Oregon, and I refused because I wanted to work at Lucasfilm one day. That was about 1978, and four years later I had the job.

At the time, Lucasfilm could get a lot more money by licensing *Star Wars* out to other companies. They'd get a guaranteed fee, maybe a million dollars plus royalties. If we did it in-house, there'd be a risk. If the games didn't sell, they'd get nothing. They had an edict the whole time I was there, all during the '80s, that we couldn't do *Star Wars* titles. That totally tuned around in the '90s when they started doing pretty much all *Star Wars* titles.

After the initial disappointment, I still wanted the feeling to be like a *Star Wars* game but without using those characters. We found photographs of a real *X-Wing* cockpit, which I used for inspiration. Because we weren't allowed to fall back on *Star Wars*, we had to be original, coming up with our own stuff. I think that was a good thing, because we didn't have that crutch. We had our own stories and ideas. The other positive was that we were pretty much left alone since we weren't messing with the family jewels. We could experiment and do what we wanted to do.

Originally, we were a very experimental group. Our first two games were considered throwaways. We just wanted to see if we could do something that was fun, and if not, we'd just go on to do something else. I don't know if we would've had that much freedom [with a *Star Wars* setting]. Also, the company wasn't surviving on us. We could take money from the company and get it done right.

You could afford to take risks.

Yes. And there was no marketing; no one to say, "No, that's not going to work." We came up with our own design docs, passed them around to other game designers. We'd polish the ideas. But it was all without the marketing department. It was left completely up to the designers.

I know a lot of designers who'd love to be in that situation!

Games weren't as expensive to make back then. In 1980 dollars, games were a hundred to a hundred and fifty thousand dollars for the game, marketing, the whole thing. Now they could go up to tens, twenties, thirties of millions. Like with a big movie, you want to be sure it's going to be successful before you stick your money in it. With us, we knew it wasn't going to be that much of a loss.

Let's talk about the setup at Lucasfilm Games. I was reading about a UNIX system that you used to write the code, then ported it to Atari and Commodore machines.

Peter's background was in UNIX along with the computer division. We already had VAX computers running—probably Berkeley UNIX. At the time, the computers weren't that powerful, so it was hard to get a good compiler or cross-assembler on the target machines. So we ended up writing our own cross-assembler, first, using LISP. We were coding on a CRT terminal in EMACS as the editor. We wrote LISP code. Then you'd push a button, and it'd compile it down to the binary. There was a serial connection to the target computer, so it'd download it over a serial port and boot it up so you could test it. It wasn't terribly difficult, but there wasn't a lot of great debugging. Eventually, we ended up with Sun microcomputers on our desktops. We could download directly from the Sun to our target computer. When we did Commodore 64 work, we used a routine that would download it to a floppy disk attached to the Commodore, then you'd boot up off the floppy to play the game. The Atari went directly into RAM. When we went to PCs, you didn't have to do that anymore since they were powerful enough to compile their own code. By then, we were using SCUMM for graphical adventures.

Did you have a preference for Commodore or Atari machines?

I was always a fan of Atari machines. Partly because I started on it and wrote a book on it—I knew the systems so much better. I thought it was a better computer, and I was really disappointed when the Commodore 64 became the standard.

Did you do any work on *Koronis Rift*?

Probably none. After the first two games, we had two other games that also used fractals. They took the *Rescue on Fractalus!* code and enhanced it. One was *Koronis Rift,* which Noah Falstein designed, and the other was *Eidolon,* which Charlie Kellner designed. That was the way it was at Lucasfilm—the project leader was also a coder, lead designer, and producer. One person wore all the hats.

I was in conversion hell at the time [those games were being made]. You'd do a game, and then you were stuck for a year or two supervising or working with people converting it to other platforms. There were no translations, but you had all these European machines to convert for, like the Spectrum, Amstrad, and two or three other ones. That was really tedious. I'd much rather have been on a different project.

Was it really that hellish? There wasn't anything creative about the conversion process?

It is a creative process, but more often than not … [sigh]. There's a lot of compromises. If the original platform was the Atari 800 and took advantage of all its unique features, you got stuck with a version that wasn't as good. The Commodore 64 had a slower CPU than the Atari 800, which was 60% faster. That gave you faster frame rates. So instead of six frames per second, you'd get four. That changes the whole way the game feels. The sound was really good, but a lot of other things weren't as good. Then when you went to other platforms, they didn't even have the power the Commodore 64 had. The Apple II or Spectrum Sinclair—it was like, oh, God. It was like taking my baby and dressing it up in rags. They did a miraculous job given what they had to work

FIGURE 11.3 *Labyrinth*, released in 1986, was an early movie-to-game adaptation. David Bowie's likeness is shown here in all its 8-bit glory.

with—contractors or companies in Europe licensed to do conversions for us. They did their best, but it was painful.

Pain aside, was there any advantage to having all those different platforms?

We're better off with fewer. Even when we were doing the adventure games on the PC, we had to support various resolutions and graphics modes—CGA, EGA, and five different sound cards—and what if they didn't have a sound card? Then CPU speeds … All these things had to be checked. That was not the fun part.

The fun part was designing and implementing the original game, not all the other versions. I just want the best one, only. I guess we're always going to have that to some degree. Even with the iOS, you're going to end up with faster and faster CPUs on the subsequent generations of iPhones and iPads. While the code might be the same, if you design something for an upcoming iPhone 3, will it still work on an older iPhone?

What was your involvement with the game *Labyrinth*? (See Figure 11.3.) To me, it's always been a fascinating game because you can see that the interface was the genesis of what would come later.

I was the project lead. I shared a bunch of stuff with Charlie Kellner, who was the technical designer on it. There were parts of that project that were really fun and some that weren't. It was the first game we did based on a license. Even though it was a Lucasfilm production, it meant that it wasn't going to be original, from-scratch content. That frees you up in some ways and restricts you, too.

We got to go to London for a bit and brainstorm with Douglas Adams and Christopher Serf, who was good friends with Jim Henson, the director of the film. That was amazing. I was taking notes and participating in the brainstorming, and it was my job to take all that stuff back and figure out what worked and what didn't for the game design.

When you have some really funny people in the room with wit way beyond my own, sometimes it felt like I was hanging on by my fingernails trying to follow the conversation and all the jokes.

One of the ideas that I wished we hadn't kept was from Douglas Adams, who wanted a nod to *Wizard of Oz*, where it starts off in black and white and becomes full color. So I came up with the idea of starting off as a text adventure, in black and white, and once you enter the world it becomes a full color animated graphic adventure. We did that, and it did give people experience with the "slot machine" interface we came up with. We had verbs and nouns on vertically scrolling like wheels like the date changer on the iPhone. But we went overboard with it; it was tedious.

We advertised this as a graphics adventure, and I wonder how many people bought the game and gave up—"Hey, this is a text adventure, I wanted a graphics adventure!" They might have stopped before they ever got to it. So in retrospect, it sounded really fun, but it wasn't.

Really? I always thought that part was brilliant. You mean people didn't like that?

Well, I hated it because I was playtesting it all the time. I don't know if people gave up or got pissed at the game. It was kind of clever, but I would've changed it.

Were you involved with the *Habitat* project?

I wasn't involved at all. That was Randy Farmer, Chip Morningstar, and Aric Wilmunder. That was an amazing experiment—trying to take a Commodore 64 with a 300 baud modem and do a massively multiplayer environment. And it worked. They crashed the server a few times because there were so many people on it. But they killed the project. I believe Quantum Link was the company, the forerunner of AOL. It was brilliant and ahead of its time.

Okay, well let's talk about the game I'm sure everybody wants to hear about, *Zak McKracken and the Alien Mindbenders*. How did you pitch it?

You have to go back earlier, to *Maniac Mansion,* which was the first SCUMM game (see Figure 11.4). It was designed by Ron Gilbert and Gary Winnick. Between games, I was pitching games that didn't get picked up. This was before we were self-publishing, so we had to get picked up by other companies to do these games. Ron said he had a game that

FIGURE 11.4 *Maniac Mansion* was extremely influential, establishing design paradigms that are still being used in adventure games today.

he'd designed and wanted to know if I could script it—probably wouldn't take more than a month or two. I said sure, sounds like fun. So I learned SCUMM as they were building the backend, so it was like working with a moving target. I believe it was six months later that I had most of my part done, so I went off to do something else. But that experience taught me the language and the system, and I knew that the next game I wanted to do would build on top of what Ron did with *Maniac Mansion*.

I told you earlier that the reason I wanted to do the computer center is that I wanted to find games that would make a difference in people's lives. I was into this New Age stuff. I wondered if there was some way I could pull all those New Age ideas into a comedy—into a game, and make it all real in that game. I spent a few days brainstorming with a friend of the general manager of the games division, David Spangler. He was a spiritualist and an author; I guess he was a psychic. He was immersed in all the New Age stuff a lot more than I was, and he had a great sense of humor. So we spent several days at his house up in Seattle, and we came up with exhaustive lists of all the elements we could toss into the game—everything from ancient alien civilizations to Stonehenge. Also, we were near the place in Seattle where one of the first UFOs was sighted in 1947. The whole idea of telepathy and teleportation, mind-linking—we could toss it all in.

When I came back in, I had to take all these pages and pages of ideas and turn them into a cohesive game, and I did. But when I presented the first version of the game to the team, Ron—rightly so—asked for a meeting to go over this. His feeling was that it wasn't funny or wacky enough. I had a surface level of humor, but it wasn't enough. We changed the character's name from Jason—who was a regular reporter—and he became Zak McKracken, names we pulled out off the phonebook. He became a tabloid reporter, which opened it up to a whole new level of wackiness. Now we could pretend all these tabloid stories were real—Elvis, spaceships, everything else. That was it; it was pretty much set.

I couldn't do this by myself. I had Matthew Kane, one of our sound and music guys. He offered to help and became a coscripter with me. Because we had a lot of leeway with the text, we could look at the artwork coming up and get new ideas. It gets a lot more complicated, and you get lots of ways to weave it all together.

[*David dons a pair of Groucho Marx glasses. Hilarious!*]

So it was Ron's idea to make Zak a tabloid reporter?

I don't know if it was his idea, but it was definitely from that meeting. When you're brainstorming with six or seven different people, it's hard to tell who thought of what and when.

Especially with all those psychics in the room! (See Figure 11.5.)

[*Laughs.*]

One of my favorite aspects of the game is the newspaper that came with it, *The National Inquisitor*. Games nowadays have nothing in the box.

Well, that had two purposes. One was that we were providing backstory and a bunch of hints. The other was for piracy prevention. The idea was that if you got the game without the included material, it'd be useless or much harder to play. In *Zak*, you're going to different airports across the planet, and when you go out of the country you had to type in a

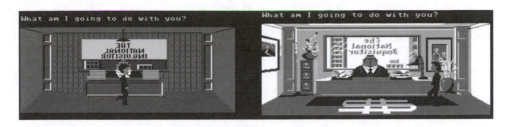

FIGURE 11.5 *Zak McKracken and the Alien Mindbenders* was ported to several platforms. Shown on the left is the Commodore 64 version; the MS-DOS version is on the right.

special code on a Visa sheet. It was a code sheet printed on dark red paper that was close to impossible to Xerox. We were all very sensitive to piracy because our first two games were pirated even before they were published. Apparently, a preview version of *Ball Blazer* and *Rescue* were pirated—before they had their final titles. They were leaked to the BBSs [Bulletin Board Systems].

There's a famous Tim Schafer story. When he came to interview for a position of Scummlet, a beginning SCUMM programmer, I was the person he interviewed with first. I asked him if he'd played any of our games, and he said, oh, yeah, I really like *Ball Blaster*. I said, *Ball Blaster*? He didn't realize that *Ball Blaster* was the pirated version of that game.

Busted!

He thought he'd blown the interview at that point. But I was just ribbing him. That was good.

As I recall, if you answer the question wrong in *Zak*, he gives you a speech about piracy.

That's right.

Why do you think people pirate so much?

Part of it is the challenge. The more copy protection you put onto it, the more of a challenge it is for a hacker to break the code. It becomes a metagame. Once they do, part of the pride is posting it and allowing others to download it.

I figure now that piracy is here to stay, so you just have to live with it. You expect it. A better solution is to use it as a way to promote a game. Hopefully some people will buy the add-ons or the upgrades, expansion packs, or whatever it is.

Once you've had the experience of having something you've worked on so hard pirated like that, it changes your perspective quite a bit. You'll think twice about taking someone else's pirated stuff.

How do you feel now about all the abandonware sites and people downloading games like *Zak* for free?

Well, that's fun for me now. Of course, what I'd like to see is LucasArts go back to some of the old games, like they did with *Monkey Island,* and re-imagine them or do sequels. I think they were going in that direction a few years ago, but I guess the costs were still too high and went back to their *Star Wars* roots.

I'm very happy to hear what happened with Tim Schafer's *Kickstarter* project. It's an amazing miracle. It shows how strong the fanbase is and how much people really want that kind of game.

I think it's evident that marketing thinks people want one thing, when they really want something else.

Right.

What do you think of the fan remakes of *Zak*?

There are several. I can't bless it because it's not really my property, but I am honored when I hear that people are doing it. I've talked to someone before, but since I'm a Mac guy I haven't played them. I've seen some screens. Anytime someone likes something enough to put months and years of work into it because they want to expand the story and live in your universe, that's a huge honor.

I have no idea what LucasArts thinks about it. I think there was a point where they were stopping some sites that were trying to do stuff like that. I assume that if anyone made a lot of money off of that, they'd be hearing from LucasArts' lawyers.

Have you thought about doing a *Kickstarter* project for a new *Zak* game? I know you don't own the rights, but surely if you raised enough money you could do anything.

That's true. If I had enough money to make it worth LucasArts' time to invest in the legal stuff…I don't know what the number was. A few million dollars? Oh, a few million and they'd work with you. Check back with me when I'm a millionaire [*laughs*].

I read some commentary that claimed *Zak* was the closest thing to a non-LucasArts game that the company ever made. They were referring to the difficulty of the puzzles and the possibility of getting the game into an unwinnable state. Was that by design?

I don't think it was by design. We tried to catch stuff where you'd end up at a dead end. This was before we had the edict not to put them in a dead-end situation. If we went back and did the same game, we'd find more of those and find other solutions. I think there were a few that were really well telegraphed—like jumping out of an airplane without a parachute. Even if you did that, if you had a yellow crystal you could still teleport away. But we weren't totally stopping you if you wanted to do that.

At that time, it wasn't that you couldn't die, but that you couldn't die arbitrarily. If you walked off a cliff, you have to expect not to survive. We allowed that. There were a couple places in *Maniac Mansion* where you could die, and we warned you—don't put the radioactive water in the microwave and turn it on. If you do, you die from radioactive steam. It wasn't arbitrary, like you open a door with no signage and a monster just eats you. That didn't happen.

Sometimes a fun death can be a lot of fun as an Easter egg.

I agree 100%. I think one fun thing about *Zak* is the story about the stupidity epidemic. Do you think later adventure games just got dumbed down to the point where they just weren't challenging to hardcore adventure game fans?

I know that Brian Moriarty got a flack over *Loom* because it is a much shorter game than most of the games we'd done before. People could finish that in two to six hours depending on how good you were. There was an expectation that for your thirty or forty dollars, you should get thirty or forty hours. So we had to find ways to extend the games.

One of the ways we extended *Zak*—and I wish we hadn't—was the mazes. Some people liked them, but most people hated it—"Oh, no, another maze!" Now I realize that if I'm playtesting the game, and I dread the mazes, it's likely that players aren't going to have fun with it either. I would've changed that. But that was one of the ways to make the world feel larger. It reused one set of art and mapped it into a large environment—it's just one scrolling background with objects and doorways you can turn on and off. We call them "pseudo-rooms." There was a jungle maze that a lot of people had trouble with. It was one of the more nasty things I did, because there was no way to solve it. You just had to walk through any two doors without backtracking. It was unmappable; I was just counting doors. A lot of people got stuck.

Evil, evil.

We tried not to be too evil. One thing I remember is that when you're in the airplane, you're supposed to pick up the fire extinguisher. The only way to do that is to open up the overheads after you've distracted the stewardess. People probably felt that they were very unlucky, because no matter what order they did them in, it was always the last one.

You didn't get put on any no-fly lists because of that scene did you?

No, but it was my retribution for nasty stewardesses. I've been on enough airplanes with snappy stewardesses, and this was my catharsis.

There are lot of different versions of the game. Do you have a favorite? I played the FM Towns version in one of the emulators, though I don't think I've ever seen an FM Towns system. (See Figure 11.6.)

FIGURE 11.6   The FM Towns version of *Zak* has excellent graphics. Note the *Indiana Jones* poster on the left.

There weren't a whole lot of them.

Fortunately, on *Zak* I was able to avoid conversion hell. By that time, we were big enough to assign that to other people. I looked at the art as it was being made. I remember that the artists who had been stuck doing Commodore 64 and 16-color art were really excited when they got to go to 256 color. It opened up a whole new palette. They did go overboard a few times and got garish. I think the Atari or Amiga versions, with good sounds, are probably my favorite. The FM Towns had this nice music that was streamed off a CD. Otherwise, they're pretty much the same.

There was never a NES version, so we didn't have to worry about changing anything to follow their rules. I remember there were major changes to *Maniac Mansion*. There's a statue of Venus that had to be clothed or removed, a pinup of a mummy wrapped in bandages—like a Playboy poster. They had to remove that. They had to tone down a lot of the irreverent humor.

They missed the hamster. Probably because it wasn't required to complete the game. That was mine, by the way.

Wait a minute—you're the hamster guy?

Yes. I saw that there was a hamster, I saw there was a microwave. I thought, no, should I do this?

Were any actual hamsters harmed in the making of the game?

No, I didn't test it. But I did ask Gary for a blood splat. We thought only a certain kind of kid would be willing to do it—the ones who were more deranged. We called Ron over and had him try it. Heaven forbid, there was a splat after the ding. He thought it was funny.

These games are famous for all the internal references to other games, like the chainsaw in one and the chainsaw fuel in the other. Was all that planned from the beginning?

No. Those were just little ideas you'd get as you were doing it. What should I put in this locker? I know, let's put the gas in there that was missing in the other game. So when Zak goes to Mars, there's a can of gasoline that was for *Maniac Mansion*, which had a totally useless chainsaw—just a red herring. Whenever you tried to use it, it'd say there's no gas for it. There was no gas in the game. It was probably a mean thing for us to do.

That sort of thing became one of the earmarks of a LucasArts game. In *Zak* we had a rotofoil sitting on top of a cabinet in the alien's bunker. There are posters from other games. In *Indiana Jones*, there's a room with objects from all the other games. In the Nazi castle there's a picture that's a screen grab from *Loom*. When people see it, they feel like they're part of the inner sanctum of gamers who recognize those things. We liked doing it.

The game did much better in Germany than it did in the United States. Why do you think that happened?

I don't know. At the time we were doing these early games, the big adventure game developer in the United States was Sierra On-Line. They had the market share. We felt like they were our competitors, but they probably didn't even know we existed. We looked at their games, took them apart, and talked a lot about what we liked and didn't like about them. But they didn't have much of a presence or distribution in Europe. We didn't have their competition in Europe, so our games were a lot more popular there.

As far as *Zak* is concerned, I think the humor just matches the humor in Germany. That's where all the sequels were being done.

Did you play any of Sierra On-Line's *King's Quest* games?

No. I was too busy coding. We had designated people who played their games and did a walkthrough. Often it was Ron Gilbert. He'd take them apart and do a postmortem. Here's an important scene; here's what they did here.

I remember working on an *Indiana Jones* game when we saw a new game from Sierra. This must have been 1989 or 1990. They had way more animation than we'd been using. We said, oh, my God. Ours looks antiquated compared to it. So we cooked up a new animation tool. We added a lot to the puzzle solutions to give you more of a payoff.

We were always watching them. I always felt that ours were better crafted because we weren't doing things to just kill you off for no reason. The one I remember is one that had you walking up stairs, and you'd die just by falling off.

I think that's in all of them.

Yeah. Hey, I can walk up stairs without dying.

There's another one that there's a little piece of glass, and you can cut yourself and die. Come on. I've picked up glass. I might cut myself occasionally but not enough to kill myself. It was like they were looking for ways to kill you any way they could.

We didn't look for ways to kill you. We looked for ways you could advance.

We had ways you could die, but there were lots of warnings. "You sure you want to do that? Okay, well save your game first!"

Well, Darwin Awards are awards too, right? I also wanted us to talk about another of your games, *Cadillacs & Dinosaurs*.

Oh, no! [*Laughs.*]

I'm sensing a story here.

In 1992—I actually spent two years at Lucasfilm working on a cool location-based entertainment project called Mirage. It was the closest thing to my original dream; a theme park experience. It was a *Star Wars* simulator, with two people sitting inside a wraparound, 120-degree field of view looking out over a landscape. There were multiple pods connected together. What we came up with was essentially *Rescue on Fractalus!* on steroids. You were flying through a mountainous terrain with *X-wings and TIE Fighters* fighting against each other. We used a collimating mirror, which meant that the projectors were on top bouncing off the mirror. That made it look like you were focusing on infinity. Instead of looking at a screen a few feet in front of you, it looked like you were looking at something hundreds of feet away. It felt like a vast landscape. That was a blast.

To actually implement these in theme parks would have been more expensive than the market could bear. I think it would have been a million dollars per pod. Now you could do it for it way less; even ten years ago you could have done it for way less with off-the-shelf parts. But we were using professional quality Evans & Sutherland flight simulator technology ... It was really heavily engineered.

When that project closed down in 1992, I didn't just want to go back to doing ordinary games again. So I went freelance for a few years. I figured I could get enough jobs just doing virtual reality stuff. After a couple years of that, I'd had enough. I heard about a new company called Rocket Science Games that was just starting up, and Brian Moriarty was one of the first people they hired. I called them to see if I could join.

They looked great on paper. They had some really strong people, engineers—some of the people who had invented some of the best codecs for compression. They had some amazing ILM [Industrial Light & Magic] matte painters, modelers. It was an all-star team. But what we ended up producing was really heavily art-driven instead of game-driven, and there really wasn't anyone in the company who were gamers other than Brian and myself. Whenever there were trade-offs, they went toward better-looking art.

I was working in a genre that really wasn't my type. It was an action shoot 'em up game. We had to use pre-rendered video instead of graphics rendered on the fly like in *Rescue*. The idea was that you could take this new CD-ROM, put a bunch of video on there, and have it stream off. You'd get to a junction and you could move left or right, and it'd show a transition scene based on the choice.

They got that all to work, but it was taking too long to do all the scenes, computer graphics and the pre-rendering. I ended up taking what was originally a ten- or twelve-level game—with each level offering different gameplay—and converting it to ten or twelve levels of the same game, with only slight tweaks. It was a huge compromise.

I liked the story we came up with, but the game [*Cadillacs & Dinosaurs*] was not one of my favorites.

You mentioned CD-ROM. I saw in an earlier interview that you were really impressed with the game *Myst*. A lot of the other adventure game designers seem to really despise it. Why did you like it?

The part I liked was feeling like I was inside an environment. It goes back to what I was trying to do; to be transported into a new world. The location-based entertainment stuff was designed to transport you to somebody's universe and be able to explore it. *Myst* was one of the first ones to give me photorealistic environments that were imaginative. There were some really fun puzzles; some that were not so fun.

What I disliked was that you were always in a wasteland. Nobody else was there; it was very lonely. You weren't interacting with anyone else. It worked with the story; it really matched what they were going for. But compared to our games, which were character driven, with lots of character interactions, it was a big difference. But they broke new ground, and the art design was really well done. I always loved CG [computer generated] stuff, and they did a great job with that.

In 1992, you founded Electric Eggplant with your wife Annie. Can you tell me about it?

We wanted something like Industrial Light & Magic, taking several different concepts and squeezing them together. The idea was to do multimedia games. We ended up working on projects; sometimes it was me, sometimes it was Annie, sometimes both of us. We did some fun Disney stuff for their theme park, so my dream of designing a theme park attraction actually happened.

Most recently, we've been doing apps. The first step was to work with some of Annie's books for middle school kids, partnering with her publisher. She took the art from her graphic novels and turn it into iPad apps. That gave me the exposure to coding [for iOS] using the Corona SDK. I suggest you check that out; it's a good solution for implementing game ideas with less frustration. I love the environment; it opened up iOS in a way that I couldn't have gotten to with objective C. I'm having a blast.

CHAPTER 12

George Sanger, "The Fat Man"

George Sanger, better known as "The Fat Man," is a unique figure in the games industry and also one of its greatest pioneers. Famous for his crazy cowboy suits, big cigars, swagger, and wit, it's impossible to fit him into a category. Even his chosen epithet doesn't fit him—he's not even fat! (And thank you very much.) I tend to think of him as game audio's version of a Frank Zappa or Captain Beefheart.

I don't need to tell you George's story; he's already done that quite well in his book *The Fat Man on Game Audio: Tasty Morsels of Sonic Goodness*, which I heartily recommend to anyone who can read. It's about as practical and straightforward as the author, who is pictured on the cover in a purple cowboy suit making gang signs (see Figure 12.1). There might even be something in there about game audio, tucked somewhere between the philosophical wanderings, cartoons, vintage photographs, and hilarious anecdotes about seemingly all of the people George has ever worked with. In the introduction George writes, "Almost everything in this book is absolutely true, except the jokes." There are a lot of jokes in this book.

Despite the zaniness of his Fat Man persona, George is one of the hardest working people in the games industry. Along with his company, Team Fat, George has produced audio for hundreds of games. Some of his best-known compositions are *Wing Commander* (1990), *The 7th Guest* (1992), and the *Maniac Mansion* themes for the NES version (1991). Perhaps even more important than his composition work, though, is his tireless advocacy for dedicated standards for game audio hardware.

What are your most recent projects?

Mostly slot machines. I just got through a string of slot machines where I was doing an Australian themed one, a Brat Pack jazz themed one, an American Indian themed one, and what was the other one? I can't remember.

I also just threw out my first extended abstract for a white paper for a conference inspired by Marvin Minsky. He's the artificial intelligence guy, and he wrote a paper about music, mind, and invention. My paper didn't make the cut, but I think I have to throw down with some academics and see what kind of dirt I can stir up.

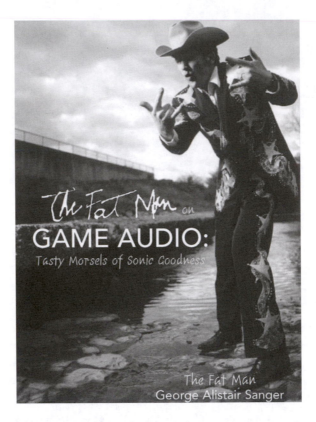

FIGURE 12.1 George "The Fat Man" Sanger is, in addition to his many other talents, also a noted author. Yes, that's actually him on the cover.

Slot machines tend to be side by side in lines of ten or twelve, right? Do you have to factor that in when you're making music for them, making sure they harmonize?

Well, for a long time it seemed like a lot of people thought of it as a solo. But it's really an ensemble, and it's C major for crying out loud. If you do something in C sharp, everything is going to sound bad. So the first part is, keep it in C major. Beyond that, the next step has been companies trying to climb over each other, finding ways to be louder and attract more attention.

The way it's headed now is something I considered getting patented but decided I don't really want patents. I'm working toward getting our slot machines to be networked to all the machines next to us. I want the sounds from one machine to come out from the machines next to it, and create pieces that use all the speakers in the room to create a single sonic landscape. If each slot machine is playing a single orchestra instrument, you could get a sound that you couldn't get anywhere else in the world.

It's tricky, because I have to be subversive about it. You know how these skunkworks projects go. I have to sneak it into something that the company realizes is necessary.

Are you afraid somebody might try to steal the idea?

I'm just not really worried about that. I realize that for everything I think I came up with, somebody else came up with it, too. We're simultaneously enlightened. If an idea is ready to be had, everybody has it. You can read about that in the history of any science or art. But this is one that I've been harping on for over ten years, and I think we're ready to do it. I'm pretty excited.

I've seen in some of your posts and interviews that you like to compare yourself to Walt Disney. Why do you identify so much with him?

The main thing that I admire about him—the thing that glares to me—Disneyland is just the greatest thing. How can one human being be responsible for so much happiness throughout the world? That was my younger view of it. As it's matured, I've seen that the emphasis on design, without stopping the imagination—that's what I admire. That puts him in a category with The Beatles. Yeah, he designed a theme park. But it's not Hanna-Barbera. It doesn't stop with Yogi Bear and the ranger. It's magic and princesses, and adventures that go beyond what's visible. Your imagination fills things in. There's a certain amount of chaos that you can stare into and see what you need to see in your life.

There's a way that good engineers communicate, and it's very close to how bad engineers communicate. But it's way far from the way salesmen communicate. I always think about Bill Volk. One day he said to me, "Oh, oh, I did drag 'n' drop splines on the Z80. You don't want to know how I'm doing it. Don't ask me how I'm doing it. Okay, here's how I'm doing it." That's passion. You can get a sense of what someone's after. A good engineer, a good game designer, isn't going to talk to you about fourth quarter sales and cross promotions.

Amen.

Yeah. Or even the demo that's going to blow the money people away. That's where it starts to go wrong—where they're going to blow them away with some demo, rather than making an awesome game.

I've really noticed that in the people I've interviewed. I talk to a lot of game designers. Some of them will talk about how much they love games and how they're playing stuff all the time. Then you get others that talk a lot about sales and have not sat down to actually play a game in years.

Some people transcend it. You can't run out there and say, that guy's not a gamer, he's not going to put out good games. Some people progress beyond pure nerdiness and develop an ornate nerdiness that allows them to function on all kinds of levels. Richard Garriott is one; Ralph is another. These guys really care about games, but they understand so much about so many other things that it's breathtaking.

You've composed over 200 videogame soundtracks, including *Wing Commander*, the *7th Guest*, *Hard Nova*, *Maniac Mansion*.

Well, I share credit for *Maniac Mansion* with others. I had Team Fat, with Dave Govett, who was my main composer for *Wing Commander*, too. Dave Hayes did the other third of it. We all worked for Dave Warhol.

Sometimes we get credited for *Day of the Tentacle*, but I don't recall doing any of that. But with *Maniac Mansion*, I did the surfer guy's theme, and the team even performs it on surf guitars occasionally. Nobody ever knows what the heck we're doing. Nobody ever put it together that we're actually doing the music from *Maniac Mansion*.

I love surf music. I looked up your old mentor, Bob Demmon, your high school band director and former member of the band Astronauts.

You did? Oh, man. Bob Demmon taught me about showmanship and cowboy outfits. He was the music man in this town—Coronado, California. He walked into this town with cowboy outfits and five buttons up his sleeve, an Elvis collar, and James Dean hair. He took this place by storm. That was 1970.

Some people tagged him as a bullshitter, but we saw it as a way of life. We gathered around his feet and soaked up all the stories. He meant a lot to me. He passed on a couple of years ago, and I bought about four guitars from his estate sale. That's my little piece of Bob for history.

If I drop any Demmon-isms, I'll try to identify them. Like: "Professionalism is being in the right place at the right time." He brought a whole generation of us school kids up that way.

I definitely want to mention your book, of course, *The Fat Man on Game Audio: Tasty Morsels of Sonic Goodness*. Great stuff.

It's been out of print for ages, but it just came out in e-form, just a couple months ago.

***Tasty Morsels.* I remember getting that book from my university's interlibrary loan service, and the girl at the reception desk looked at the cover and was like, "What is this?"**

[*Laughs.*] Yeah, that's been a problem. How old are you, Matt?

Thirty-four.

Well, you carry yourself like a proper hippie.

In the '60s and '70s, it seemed like things could be a little more abstract, and still be handled by the creative public. I've run into a lot of situations lately where you have to spell things out literally. To have a game musician wearing a cowboy hat and a rhinestone suit, standing in a river, and carrying a coat hanger with nothing on it—doing gang signs … In the '70s that would have been accepted as a proper album cover, right?

Yeah, Captain Beefheart, Frank Zappa, and so on.

I'm saying! You don't want to hem yourself in too much with these literal meanings. Life is not about "we've come a long ways from the bleeps and bloops of yesteryear." That's what I'm about. I want to see people listen to music and say—wow, that's really fun. I saw God! Or, at least I saw John Phillip Sousa.

Have you seen *Moog*, the documentary about the inventor of the Moog synthesizer?

I haven't seen it. But I'll tell you, the only time I hung out with him, I was nervous as hell, because I was trying to play a theremin. He was watching over my shoulder. That's the only time I ever played a theremin, and I'll tell you, that's not the instrument you want to play when you're nervous.

George, quick question. What are the biggest problems facing the industry, and what are the solutions?

[*Laughs.*] Well, I think the first thing to realize is that everything is wonderful everywhere, and for every time that you or I see an ad on TV and think that ain't gaming, that's just exploitation, that's just people making money … We've got to remember, if that's not gaming, then it's not us. If I'm a legitimate stage actor, and I'm watching *Gilligan's Island*, I don't need to feel horrible that the art of theater is being dragged through the mud. It's not what I do.

What I see when I look out there—the most important thing is that it is not a bunch of excited nerds. To the extent that it is, though—doing what's exciting to them—which is entertaining each other, well, that's art, and I love it. To the extent that people are putting love into it, that's beautiful, and it's elevating, and I'm proud to be part of it.

But when it becomes trying to impress an investor, or when the marketing person says, "You don't know who your audience is, we do. You pay us, we tell you what the audience likes, and you do it." To that, I say, I'm not interested. I think that it's foul. I think it shouldn't make money. Entertainment relies on an interplay between familiar elements and surprise elements, and you can't give people what they want and be innovative and surprising. If you know that they want it, then you must have tried it on them once, and that means they've experienced it, and it's not new.

Have you had any problems with guys in suits? I'm picturing these guys coming to you and saying, this piece is just too creative for our purposes. Can you give us John Williams?

It usually doesn't express itself that way. When it's tricky, they'll say, "Just give us something really exciting and movielike." They want higher, louder, faster. The way it comes across is usually "simple aesthetics." They request the most obvious, brutal means of communication. When you do that … Well, *Jaws* is great. *Jaws* with a shark in every frame is not. We do a lot of the latter.

That's a great way to put it. I was thinking, "you've got too many strings on your guitar."

Yeah, once I got, "Well, George, piano just isn't an instrument that you would hear on aircraft carrier." Okay, so you want all bosun's whistle and an accordion?

Somebody actually asked me, "Can you have fewer notes, but more of them?" That didn't happen.

Let's talk about your musical training. How did you get the skills to become a professional game musician?

Bob Demmon gave me a cassette tape of the essential songs for a rock 'n' roll band. By God, we played just about every tune on that thing. He mentored us really well. He taught us not to give up—have pride, attitude, and go for it. It's really helpful to know someone who has had success, and know what the success attitude is, and decide whether you want to adopt it.

So, George, if a kid came to you, and asked for a tape of the must-hear game compositions, what would you put on the tape?

That's nice. Well, just because I know the material, I'd give him a lot of our stuff, just because of my relative ignorance of things outside of my skin. From Team Fat, I'd give them *Wing Commander, 7th Guest, Loom, Putt Putt Saves the Zoo*. That was our best stuff. We did it as a team and we pushed our producers to the limit.

Getting beyond ourselves—everybody agrees that the *Final Fantasy* music is great. It's a given. *Guitar Hero* is game music; I'm sorry.

I love the music to *SSX Tricky*. It's just one tune, over and over again, and a lot of dumb remixes. But the interactivity is great.

Monkey Island has got to be understood at least intellectually, if not at the heart level. Those guys put ten years and a million dollars into smooth transitions between the rooms. That was a noble task, and I don't know if anybody will ever be able to do that again.

I love the weird stuff, too. *Katamari Damacy*. It's evident that the producers were embracing the weirdness. They stepped off the conveyor belt.

What I don't like is when people just try to sound movielike. Nobody ever went to a movie because it was movielike. There is so much more to aesthetics than being just like a movie.

What can you do with game audio that you can't do with an orchestra, and why aren't more people doing it?

Let me get my head around that. Okay, there are things that you can do with game audio that you can't do with an orchestra—technically. There are barriers, a lot of barriers … For example, some composers don't want to do it. Or maybe a composer has an idea, but it doesn't fit the tools that are available. Or maybe the programmer has a tool for something interactive, but he has no regard for the musical intention or the value of what the value the musician brings to the table.

I think that every once in a while we run into something golden and that really speaks to us. Sure, there will always be people who just do what the client expects, and the client is just doing what he thinks the audience expects, and the audience just buys it wholesale. There's always going to be a lot of that. But we can be out of the ordinary as long as there's a great big ordinary out there.

There are exciting things happening at a low level always.

I can't sit in a meeting and listen to, "Well, we have a responsibility to the shareholders, and that's why we're firing this guy on Christmas even though his wife's pregnant." I can't bear it. I just can't bear it.

If we can step back in time a moment. I just listened to your theme for the 1980 Intellivision game *Thin Ice* (see Figure 12.2). What a great melody. How did you end up making compositions for Intellivision?

I had no self-confidence. I had just graduated from Occidental College, just a few years ahead of Barack Obama. The people who went to that school were real heavy-hitters, especially in the music department. I just wasn't that great of a musician. I got into the music department because I wanted our band to make it. I'm in there with all these people who

FIGURE 12.2 *Thin Ice*, released in 1980 for Mattel's Intellivision console, boasts one of The Fat Man's earliest melodies. He composed it with a reel-to-reel recorder.

can sight read, play all these different instruments, conduct, and hear entire scores in their head. I couldn't do any of that. But I did like playing videogames.

I went to talk to Dave Warhol, who was my brother's roommate in college. He was doing videogames. I told him that I wanted to get into that and would take his trash out for free or whatever he wanted. He said, "You're a musician, aren't you?" Well, yeah. "Then write me some music. I've got penguins ice skating."

I got out my reel-to-reel recorder and went doop-deep, doop-deep, doop on one track, and dum-de-dum on the other. I punched in every little phrase, and once I got it sounding good, I translated it into written manuscript, which was laborious even with just two voices.

I gave that to him, and he liked it. He translated it into code and put it into the game. And that's how I got into it.

I can't recommend this path to anyone anymore. I don't know if Dave Warhol is still accepting manuscripts [*laughs*].

Were you only interested in the music side of games, or were you also interested in the technology and engineering?

Not the engineering but the design. If the engineering was required to do the design, yeah. I thought that I might have what it took to be a game designer, but the second game I worked on was with Paul Edelstein, *Capture the Flag* for Atari (see Figure 12.3). It was one of the first first-person games, and John Romero was really big on it. I did the music; it's kind of an interactive soundtrack—this is 1984. After that, there's nothing else to do, so Edelstein teaches me Forth.

FIGURE 12.3 *Capture the Flag* was released for the Atari 400/800 computer. It's one of the earliest first-person games.

He set me up with a kit and a bunch of definitions, which is how you program in Forth. I was trying to design a game with it. I made some puzzles that were kind of neat, and Paul liked them. But it was nice to find out early that I'm not that guy. Doing that, though, loaded me up with respect for people who are that guy.

One person you really don't think is that guy, but he really is—Ralph Baer. That guy is that guy. He invented the idea of videogames. On top of that, he came up with *Simon*, an elegant freaking game. He's still out there, about 90, working on his soldering station. I set up my soldering station like his. I spent the night at his house one night—that was really nice. What he likes to do is go down into his room and solder LEDs to chips and makes himself little games. He made himself a reaction tester, so he has to shoot a gun before the light goes off. He's always designing these one-bit games. That's the core—that attention to elemental game design. I really respect that.

I'm sorry, but I could just never get it up to respect the plots of games. I see that as my own deficiency, because I know it affects people emotionally—especially games like *Portal* and *Deus Ex*. People really care about that stuff. That was never me. I went to UC Film School. I have an idea of what a plot is, and it's just different. I get picky, and the voices in my head get too loud, and I just can't enjoy that. But I can enjoy basketball or the LED racing games from Mattel.

You're probably better known as The Fat Man than by your own name. Do you ever have any regrets about that?

I have had. I think The Fat Man as a character is a successful part of my life. Even though I lost a lot of jobs on account of that character, looking back now—it's more complicated; it's not straightforward for the consumer. It's not what they want.

The only part I really regret is that I don't think it really served people as well as it could have. It was more for me than for them. If I could have refined that, and made it more exciting for other people to be part of The Fat Man, I would have changed that. As far as what jobs I did get on account of it, and what I got away with, and people who heard about The Fat Man and didn't know if I really existed—I really enjoyed that part of it.

I was thinking about The Fat Man, and the suits and everything, and realized it wouldn't be unusual at all in the rock and roll world. You see somebody like David Bowie and all his characters, for instance. It works great for them. Why is it considered so weird and bizarre for a game musician?

I don't know. That's a really mysterious thing to me. I thought that we would be more like hippies. I thought we would be a more artistic crowd. But somehow we went right from primitive nerds to Hollywood sellouts. There were some beautiful things in-between, but we didn't have our Woodstock. We went through corporate Woodstock with stuff like *Mario*, *Katamari Damacy*, and *Grim Fandango*. There are great abstract pieces like that out there.

But *Tempest* and *Missile Command* indicated to me that there was something great on the horizon that never showed up. The impressionism of those things isn't what caught on. The warlike part of it, the need for accuracy—that caught on.

What do you think? I didn't think there was anything weird about being The Fat Man until a few years ago. Then I realized it—nobody gets it, do they?

I think you've hit on it with the corporatization of it all, getting away from the artistic, creative aspect of games. I've talked to other game audio musicians, and they've told me about how you can listen to a Jimi Hendrix song now and nobody is going to think, wow, that's really obsolete. But that seems to be the norm in game audio. Those musicians might even be embarrassed to hear their early stuff. It's not about old and new to me; it's just artistic or it's not.

I was never ashamed of my eight-bit stuff. People don't get it sometimes; they say, "This stuff sounds better because it's on an orchestra." I ask them to listen to the composition. You'll find that the *Maniac Mansion* stuff—take "The Evil Dr. Fred" piece—that's really complicated stuff. I'm not saying Mozart would have been proud to write it, but maybe Bach or Danny Elfman would have. If you've only got one or two voices available to you—I think this really expresses a lot with just those two voices, and I'm really proud of it.

The musicians who think their music is obsolete—that's too bad. I think if you listen to old recordings of great musicians—I don't think Little Richard looks back and thinks, oh, if only had higher fidelity. I think he looks back and says, "Whoa, listen to me! I'm the King!" He's excited about getting music out there. I want to see people excited to get games out there … I don't want to see people playing sequels to games based on movies that didn't come out that well in the first place. But they think they have to buy it because all their friends are going to have it. *Smash Bros.* and *Brawl*, yeah, those are great games, get the sequel. They've earned your loyalty. But if you're hoping that *Daikatana II* is going to be better, don't do it.

Oh, poor [John] Romero.

Well, look, I have no idea about the quality of *Daikatana*. I've never played it; I've never looked at it. But if you say the word *Daikatana* among gamers, you'll get a laugh. It's just a cheap laugh at the expense of my friend. Sorry, John.

How have the different technologies available to make game music affected the creativity of the compositions? Do the tools make any difference?

That's a good question, but you've got to look at it with some perspective. I can make music in a number of ways—almost any way. Certain ways have certain sounds, and certain speeds, and certain amounts of care that you can and can't put into them. Some work well for some styles and don't work well for other styles. If you're doing Dixieland on all sequencers and keyboards, there's a problem.

When I was doing the Brat Pack stuff, I bought a saxophone and learned it, then used the modern tools to pitch shift around and fix my tuning. I put in trumpet, which I can play but not play high, and used the tools to octave it up. It sounds very cool.

But my friend Ron Jones, who does the orchestral score for *Family Guy,* sits down at a piano with a piece of paper and writes little circles and dots. Then he gives that to somebody else to make a MIDI score out of it. If that sounds good, they take it to the orchestra.

It's just like asking a painter how much technology has affected him. If he's painting, probably not that much. If he decides he wants to do something on the computer, maybe it has. But it's so minor compared to the vision. If he's excited about technology, then that technology is important. Otherwise, no.

Technology is there to remove obstacles. It's like when they first laid down roads across America and got all the cattle off of them. Then you ask someone, to what extent did cattle farms affect your drive across America? You say, I didn't run into any cattle farms. There! To what extent does technology influence you? I really didn't have any technical problems today. That's how it has influenced me. Though I have to say I have had weeks of technical problems in the past.

I'm thinking, for instance, of all the voices you have available now as opposed to the '80s.

Well, in the '80s, the MIDI was really nice. It depends on where you're aiming. I like composition more than tone generally. If you have a really good tone, you can play one note on your guitar and you're done. Dave Govett taught me that. When I was stuck on composing for *Sound Canvas* even when other technologies were available, he was hocking his car and buying Miroslav sound libraries. I said, "Man, that's just tones!" But he said, well, sometimes if you have good tones the songs just write themselves. I thought he was nuts. But with that attitude he wrote some of the most beautiful stuff I've ever heard.

For me, if I'm composing for *Survivor*, those big orchestra sounds are important. But so is the conch shell. [*Blows conch shell.*]

That'll wake you up!

Even if you have a patch library … [*Plucks a cello*]. If you're looking for something that has feel to it, you're never going to get a patch library [*plays some more*] … I'm making tens of decisions every second. I'm deciding how fast to move my finger, I'm reacting to what I'm hearing, I'm deciding how hard to pluck. I can hit the instrument. You can buy sound libraries that have one patch of nothing but hits. But all you're going to hear is this—the same thing over and over, like a bad game soundtrack. "Look, here they come! Look, hear they come!" If you get involved with the instrument, you can put more love, care, and attention into the sounds. There are long standing ways to make sounds that are expressive, they're tried and true, and still open to all kinds of experimentation. They exist regardless of sound libraries, and there is always old technology that allows you to record tones like that.

Where it becomes different nowadays is the extent that you have software that allows you to be interactive inside a game. And that is a dog's breakfast; just a mess.

You've got a lot of fans out there, George. You're probably well aware of this.

No, I'm really not. The way it appears to me is that every once in a while, somebody thinks I have fans, and they put me out there for an autograph session. It is the most embarrassing thing for everybody. I end up chasing people around and asking them to let me sign an autograph for them—"Hey, I'm famous, I'm famous."

What do you consider to be your masterpiece?

That's a neat question. I think that so far, not counting recent things I've written for my fiancé, I'd say "Viva La Resolution" is the coolest. It's not for a game, but there's a great story to it.

A rumor went around at GDC [Game Developers Conference] a few years ago that Microsoft was going to give the keynote address. It was going to be on the topic of HD. I immediately started e-mailing cynical messages to my friends: "Well, I'll tell you what the keynote ought to be: if you're still excited about technology and resolution, maybe you ought to remember that you're going to be dead soon." I'm not excited about technological improvements; I'm excited about gameplay improvements. I put that out there, and two hours later Mark Terrano, one of my good friends, called me. He was in charge of Xbox games at the time and was putting on the keynote. It was going to start with a video introduction, and he wanted me to do the music.

I said, okay, but I admitted that I wasn't excited about HD. He said they were just making a video that'd start off with 2D, bloopy bloopy, then move into 3D graphics from modern games—with more modern game audio stuff, then it'd go to HD. 2D, 3D, HD. I said, that's great. Is it all right if I put in words? Sure. Can I put in words that subtly try to affect the corporate vibe at Microsoft and make the culture less about technology and more about creativity? He said, yes! That's the best! He was the highest-up guy on the Xbox who doesn't wear a suit.

I set out to write "Viva La Resolution." It wasn't about technology, but what you were going to do with the technology. It's got lyrics like, "Did we do it for the dollar bills/or did we do it to be sharpening skills?" "Will you use it to make smarter troops/or will you use it to make great big jiggly boobs?"

The eternal question.

While I was writing it, I got a call from Verin Lewis. He said I had to write a new book because he wasn't in the first one. What did he have to contribute? "Legends and myths, man, legends and myths." So I said, okay. I put the earphones on the microphone, started the recorder, and he tells this story about how Microsoft unveiled DirectX and it crashed. But they'd gotten everyone drunk first, and handed out Gak and Frisbees. So all this Gak and Frisbees start flying and hitting the Microsoft guys, who say, "Hey, we gave you Gak, you can't do this to us!" It's a wonderful piece.

I gave it to Mark, and he said it was great. Then he calls back and says I have to take out the boobs. Okay, I've done harder things. That's fine. As I was doing that, he calls back and said that he played it for the Xbox team and they don't want Verin's story told.

I asked him then, well, if you own this tune, it's going to sit on a shelf somewhere and never get out. How about if I just give your money back and I get the tune? He says, fine. I get a call back from a legal guy—this is the best—he says, we'll sell it back to you if you take out that part at the beginning.

I said okay. I can understand how you can own the tune and have control over it. I can understand how you cannot own the tune and not have control over it. But this whole thing about not owning it and still having control over it—that doesn't work for me. [*Laughs.*]

Let's go back in time and talk about the *Wing Commander* soundtrack (see Figure 12.4). When I went back to listen to it, I thought it was just as good as anything John Williams ever wrote for *Star Wars*. It's beautiful stuff. Can you tell me about how it was composed?

That's a great question. I'd been working with Dave Govett, a young guy who was a bartender when I found him. He called me up one day and asked if he could look at my equipment. Then he wanted me to pick him up at a bus stop. I thought he was great, so I put him to work putting together some bloop-de-bloop stuff. He did some of the things in *Maniac Mansion*.

I got called in to do the *Wing Commander* music after trying hard to get that job. I was feeling really good. Chris Roberts asked me for something between *Star Wars* and *Star Trek: The Motion Picture*. I was feeling really big on myself, so I thought I'd start by farming off the first part of that to Dave Govett, because I was really so busy.

Dave said he had this tune that'd been sitting in his head since high school, so he'd go ahead and do that.

The next day I got this fanfare from him, exactly like you hear it in the game. He'd had that in his head and had never put it down before. The entire dogfight scene—zoop! All of it. He also did the briefings, but he didn't do the melodies that connected them. So I came in on top and did the "dum dum daaa dum," stretching the melodies out, putting them

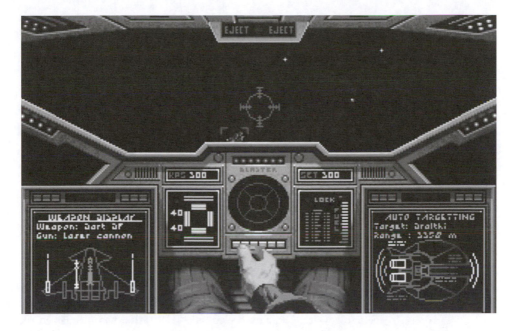

FIGURE 12.4 *Wing Commander* was a huge success and owes a lot to its fantastic soundtrack.

backward and upside down. We did about 50/50. I did the unifying and diversifying of it, and he nailed the John Williams.

I realized later that he didn't listen to pop music. His CD collection is John Williams.

Another game that people wanted to know about is *Ultima Underworld*. I think what's great about it is that it nails the atmosphere of the dank, lonely dungeon.

Again, Govett. Dave Govett. He took the first swipe at it, and he handed this thing in with the descending chromatic. I don't know what came first, but there's a huge similarity between that and *Phantom of the Opera*. I think that's where he got some of the chord structure. Of course, it's *Ultima Underworld*, so it's descending.

I did the intro tune, and he did the in-game music. I can't remember who did what first. Usually, Govett puts down this orchestra bit, but he wouldn't stick to a theme. I'd go in, pull out the melody, and stick it in the introductory fanfare and stuff.

Dave Govett is a cop now. He's a policeman, and he's a lot happier. He's a riot, having fun ruining lives. He's a brilliant practical joker, and he takes that to his police work. He's the one putting talcum powder on the ceiling fan. He used to tell me that he was a lot more worried about missing his deadlines than the thought of facing an armed criminal. It's more mellow to face physical danger than logging in to your e-mail and going, "Aw, crap."

Let's move into *The 7th Guest*. It must have been a great move when you had all the storage capacity of a CD-ROM to work with (see Figure 12.5).

I'd already been a little bit spoiled by using the MT-32 for *Loom* and *Wing Commander*, and I thought of myself as composing for that soundcard. You could get eight, sixteen

FIGURE 12.5 *The 7th Guest* was a runaway bestseller and helped CD-ROM drives emerge as a new standard for PC data storage. However, George used General MIDI rather than digitized recordings for most of the tracks.

voices out of it, and they were really nicely synthesized and sounded pretty good. The next step was the CD-ROM. For me, there were no technical advantages to the CD-ROM, because we were still writing for soundcards with MIDI. Some of them would require that I do a three-voice version, or a four-voice version, and another for FM. I'd have to rewrite the music five times. I was complaining about this to Tom White, a friend of mine at Roland. Tom said I should just write it for General MIDI. What's that? Aw, just get a Sound Canvas. What's that? Tom said, "Well, you can buy one …" So I did, and I wrote for it, making a big deal in the instructions about General MIDI. There was only one General MIDI card then, but there would soon be many others.

I wrote everything in General MIDI, then I wrote tones for the other devices. Between our tones and John Miles' drivers, everything would play on the different machines. We pushed it in that direction, and it really caught on.

As far as the music on the CD, well, I called Graeme Devine. Graeme, what is this thing coming out on? "CD-ROM." Is it like a CD? "Well, kinda, not exactly." If I wrote a bunch of regular recorded music for him for free, could he squash it into the game? "Sure, Fat Man, anything you say."

Only a couple of songs got into the game with a regularly recorded format. In fact, I have a fax document they sent just before releasing the game in which they give up on putting in any recorded music. They had technical problems and couldn't do it. Thankfully, they did end up figuring it out and putting it back in.

Graeme was kind enough to cut me some slack and let me do that. Later on, when they did the Mac and CD-i versions, they put in an extra CD. That felt really good.

Once we got recorded audio available to us, it was really fun, and it really quickly caught on. I suppose in the long run it really paid off.

Do you have any favorite tracks from it?

It depends on my mood. You can get the regular, biscuit CD from Amazon—it's called *7/11*. Make sure you play it in the right order, though. I always love listening to it in order, because there's a lot of richness and a lot of surprises in there.

I suppose that I feel best when "The Final Hour" comes on. It incorporates "The 7th Guest Theme" as a countermelody. It's a long piece, it sets a great mood, it has verbal puns—but not so many that it isn't musical. I think it's about my favorite.

"Mr. Death" is another great track from the game.

I won't give away the long-held secret about that. But I will say that the band that did it was European Sex Machine. It's two twins from Europe, Axel and Miles Dietrich, and they think they're playing blues, but they're really playing minimalist music. They think they owe all of their musical talent to the American black man. But they don't sound anything like them.

They wrote the song as part of a songwriter's challenge. It just happened to fit the game, and it really worked.

What's your advice for people who want to break into game audio?

I hate to hawk my goods so much, but all the good stuff is in my book. It's e-published on Kindle, so get it from Amazon.

The main thing is that there are a lot of butts and not many seats in the game audio business. It's a very, very competitive area. The secret is kindness. Be good to people, don't close any doors behind you, help people out, and get into the community.

If you want to be known as a good games music guy, be a good games music guy. Live for games music. Make it apparent that it's your life. Do the work and people will find you. Do what you love, and even if you never make a dime, at least you spent the hours of your life doing what you love.

Do you find that game audio people are happy doing it, or do they really want to be up on a stage performing with an orchestra or rock band?

There's an answer in my heart and an answer that comes from observation. The answer in my heart is a beautiful one, and the one in my heart is sad.

The observation is that there are a lot of people in the game audio world who are really beat down. They've accepted that they're third-class citizens who are providing a service. They have to deliver what people tell them to deliver, and they have to work really hard and not get paid very much. They provide a background to the game; they're not asked for opinions, they're not given the technology they need. They've succumbed to this idea that in the best of all cases, they'd be imitating something that's already been done. Nobody will notice them.

I don't think that's the best way to put music in a game. In my heart, I think there are people out there putting out small games, people who have confidence in their own artistic ability—there are plenty of opportunities to do something that's new and different. As game audio guys, we haven't had our Woodstock. A lot of us are just mining troglite under the cloud city.*

---

* A reference to "The Cloud Minders" episode of the original *Star Trek* TV series.

FIGURE 12.6 *Putt-Putt Saves the Zoo* features a full-on music video.

We can make the music we want, but we have to find the clients who will let us do it. When we do, people will hear it and catch on. Witness *Katamari Damacy*. That's really special music that's way out there. The producer let the music guy do whatever he wanted, and it came out great. There are other people falling in line.

If you want to be somewhere else and you're a game audio guy, go somewhere else, please. When I do my game music, I want to be doing what I'm doing.

If you're thinking about going into the business, don't let them clobber you. Figure out what you have to put on the table and keep pushing it up at notch. Keep making stuff better than what they ask for. Do stuff for free. Give them things they've never heard of. Do things you haven't been hired to. Make game music for a game that doesn't exist yet.

What was it like doing the music for Humongous Entertainment?[*]

That was fun. They gave us a lot of support. We were at our peak as a team doing the music for *Putt-Putt Saves the Zoo* (see Figure 12.6). They'd call us up, tell us what the musical requirements were—how much time each tune would be, what scene it would play during. The best thing was that they were quick about putting in the music and sending us back a playable version. We had a lot of feedback and a lot of freedom.

They'd sometimes send stuff that stimulated my competitive instinct. They sent me a couple of lyrics for a kid's tune, and I'd say, nah, that's no good—I'm going to write you a

---

[*] Question submitted by Hammond Cheese 309.

real tune, and you're going to do a video for it, and it's going to be the first music video in a game.

Ron Gilbert didn't like that attitude, but he knew it was a good idea. So he'd do it. I didn't charge them more for doing all that, but I did ask that they put my picture in the game somewhere. So he says to the guy sitting next to him, "Hey, Bill, you know that goofy looking billboard you're working on? Put a really goofy looking guy in a red cowboy suit on it and say it's "The Fat Man with Team Fat." That's in there.

A few years after the game came out, Ron sent me an e-mail and said that he hated me. Why? Because his niece was playing *Putt-Putt Saves the Zoo,* and all she wanted to do was click on the topiary creatures over and over.* I respect Ron, but he didn't like the idea of the music being more liked than anything else in the game. It was like being in a Lennon–McCartney situation.

Sometimes if people think your stuff is too good, they want you to take it down a notch. I think it's really healthy when they take their stuff up a notch.

Do you have any final thoughts or comments?

No, I don't think so, Matt. I'm really glad that people care about this stuff, and they care about it off the beaten track. They're not just worrying about the new first-person shooter. I really like this.

Hey, everybody, be nice to each other!

---

* Clicking on the creatures activates the aforementioned video.

CHAPTER 13

Mark Soderwall, Mentor to Graphic Artists

I first met Mark Soderwall at the Game Developers Conference of 2009. The first thing I noticed about him was his style; he wore his hair gelled up into a tidy pyramid and a leather jacket that wouldn't look out of place on Tom Cruise.

Of course, a keen sense of style makes sense for someone as heavily invested in the world of computer graphics as Mark, whose job is not just making things seem realistic (anybody can do that), but making them hyperreal; concerned with the sensuous rather than the sensory. It's not enough just to make something look realistic; it also has to be pleasing. That's where the "artist" part of "graphic artist" comes in.

I was happy to reconnect with Mark again in December 2011, this time focusing on his own career and history as a graphic artist. He's a veteran with over twenty years of experience and a résumé that includes *NBA Live 97* (1996), *Terminator 3: Rise of the Machines* (2003), *Forgotten Realms: Demon Stone* (2004), and *Stars Wars: The Force Unleashed* (2008). Like many of the veteran game developers I've talked to, Mark joined the industry fresh out of high school, learning all the skills he needed on the job, often without anyone to guide him. Convinced that there's a better way, Mark has dedicated himself to promoting best practices in the industry and fostering independent game development. To that end, he's prepared numerous online resources to help newcomers learn the trade and, perhaps more importantly, connect with professionals and like-minded people (see Figure 13.1).

I wanted to start off with your Game Creators Vault. It seems like a great source for anyone interested in doing games. What's the philosophy behind it?

I started it two years ago because I don't have a degree—no bachelor's, no master's, certainly no doctorate. I got into the games industry right out of high school, and I feel like I missed a great opportunity. I've learned on the job, from wonderfully talented people. Because of my lack of formal education, though, I wasn't able to teach at accredited universities. That really hurt my heart, as cheesy as that sounds, because I love giving back to students. I love seeing the light go on in people's eyes when they grasp a concept. Sometimes

FIGURE 13.1   Mark Soderwall is a graphics artist with over twenty years of experience in the games industry.

they just can't get it unless somebody gives them the spark, somebody who's been there—here's a best practice, why don't you try it this way? Suddenly, they're innovating, they're doing something magic. That's absolutely fantastic.

I figure that if the academic world is going to shut me out, I'm going to make my own destiny. We have this wonderful thing called the World Wide Web. I've got enough credentials, I've got enough game titles—I certainly know a lot of innovative people in the industry. I'm just going to do this thing called Game Creators Vault, I'm going to put it on Facebook, and I'm going to create a community to give back. I want people to share tools, ideas—students, professionals, indie, whatever. It's just a group of like-minded individuals sharing resources, breakthroughs, problems. It's a vehicle.

It's doing really well. I've got a group of guys who've jumped on board with me. Most of them are college students, some going for their film degrees, so they're running everywhere with their cameras. We're interviewing professionals, mining them for information, and then just post it all for free. It's been very well received.

Can anyone join?

It's completely free. The only thing I ask is that you not just go to the site and leech. Participate. It might be intimidating to throw a comment or question out there, but one of the main things I'm trying to foster is a safe environment.

People are here to learn. Check your ego at the door. We're all trying to get empowered and inspired. If you've got a rant, that's fair, but keep it objective. Don't put people down.

People are trying, and creativity is a process of a failure before you get to success. We need to be supportive.

What's that behind you, Mark? It looks like you've got some swords back there.

Oh, yes. [*Pulls out two awesome looking blades.*] These are Drizzt's swords from the game *Demon Stone* for Atari. I got them as a reward for finishing the game. I guess they're kind of a perk.

Whoa! That's a hell of a perk! I want some swords.

At Blizzard, they give you armor, gauntlets, and swords. Depending on how long you work there, it just keeps getting better and better. Eventually you have a full set of armor.

At some point they probably even give you a complimentary *WoW* [*World of Warcraft*] subscription.

[*Laughs.*] I don't know about that. I guess we'll see.

I saw in an earlier interview where you said that your mission is to make games better. What is it that you think is wrong with modern games?

I hate to slight anything, because there's always good in something—I'm a glass-half-full kind of guy. I wouldn't say there is anything wrong, but the gaming industry—at least the triple A developers and big publishers, they're just doing me-too games. Franchises are extended into their third cycle. That's not a bad thing, necessarily. *Modern Warfare 3* is making a killing, so obviously there's a fanbase out there for this stuff. But I've noticed that a lot of these developers—because they've invested so much money, and have such large marketing budgets, they want to keep it safe. They want to target a market that's a known quantity.

One of the things we're seeing that's terribly cool is the indie community. Students are creating these wild games that are very innovative, with brand new mechanics. They've got a little bit of a learning curve, but, boy, they're fun. They're very immersive. There are social and casual games that are generating communities. People who wouldn't touch a hardcore RTS [real-time strategy] or FPS [first-person shooter] are now able to find enjoyment in an interactive experience that's relational.

One thing I've noticed at a lot of conferences is that they're adding indie and student areas. They show off their games and projects, hopefully to get noticed. One of the things that's a big risk, though, is that you see corporate executives from big studios walking the perimeter and checking things out. They write down notes. God only knows what they're doing. They might be running back to their studios and saying, "Okay, we have a whole new mechanic we've got to work on."

I find it very ironic that a lot of the innovation we're seeing, and a lot of the new trends, are coming from nonprofessionals and students. And we see small bands of professionals who are saying, "Hey, we don't have to answer to anybody." They have small budgets and a lot of passion, and definitely have a lot of time. So they kick down the walls and see what kinds of mechanics they can come up with. It's awesome.

A lot of the game designers I've talked to recently see us in a golden age of game development. They point at all the iOS games, browser games. The costs are low; you don't have to go through a publisher. Do you think we're in a golden age?

Definitely. Look at all the accessibility, Matt. You've got UDK [Unreal Developer's Kit], this insane game engine, for free. You've got a vehicle like the Apps store, Android Market. You can put your game up there, they take a percentage, but it's okay. You've got Crytek releasing an engine. Of course, Unity is just blitzkrieging everywhere. It has the ability to transfer to different platforms with just a button click. Then you have all the development tools, art asset tools like Blender. There are all these tools out there that are free. So, yeah, you can create a game on a crazy budget. As long as you have an idea and a solid team of people who aren't flaky, who have ownership—show up and do their task, you can really make something happen. That's a golden age. I love this time in the industry. Everything is turned on its ear.

What are some of the games that have come out recently and really blown you away?

Obviously *Minecraft*. It's been talked about over and over, and I don't want to beat a dead horse, but it's insane innovation. The ability to create a sandbox, throw in some killer tools, and let people generate their own content—then post it back up. It's so cool, and so sophisticated. It seems like a simple mechanic.

I also admire *Super Meat Boy*. You have this little meat blob that is put in this insane platform environment with every kind of lethal bladed tool after you. The whole game is based on how many different ways you can die. It's so repetitive and so fast.

A game I'm having a ton of fun with right now is *Dungeon Defenders*. It's fantastic because it fits an ADD [attention deficit disorder] personality like mine. You've got tower defense meets action adventure meets RPG [role-playing game]. You've got this amalgamation of all these different genres all thrown into one. It's brilliant! Now I can actually have a gaming experience where I get all three for one.

There was one game made by a number of students at DePaul a few years ago. It was called *The Devil's Tuning Fork* (see Figure 13.2). The whole environment was black; you couldn't see a darn thing, until you generated out this sonar pulse that blanketed the environment with light for a short period of time. You could then see the scale of where everything was. It was just brilliant. Everything in the game was based on sound. That's the level of innovation I'm talking about.

A lot of gamers I talk to are very interested in doing their own games, and they get all excited at first. But eventually they fizzle out and their projects are never finished. What's your advice for motivating yourself all the way through to completion?

What it comes down to is to keep it simple. The thing that kills people is feature creeping. They solve a portion of the puzzle or the feature, and then they get excited that it's almost there—and they get distracted by something else. So it stays a half-baked idea.

If you're building a game, try to think of it this way. If you have a title, think about if there was a marketing pitch under it: "For the first time ever..." What is that? "For the first time ever, terrain transformation." With *Prince of Persia*: "For the first time ever, you

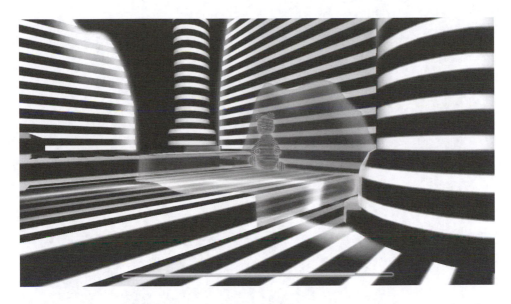

FIGURE 13.2   *The Devil's Tuning Fork* incorporates lighting and sound as key gameplay elements. It also looks fantastic.

control time." That is your hook. Spend all of your time prototyping and building up that core feature until you get it to a demo state that's very solid and unbreakable.

Once that building block is there, then you can pile on, using that as a platform. Innovate other features and ideas. But again, my advice: keep it simple.

That sounds great, but "for the first time ever …?" I don't know what I could do. What hasn't been done?

Where I heard that term came from a really good colleague from LucasArts named Harry Kinney. He got a lot of pitches across his desk. He had to have a very quick filtering system. So when he'd get on the phone with these guys, he'd lean forward on his desk and say, "If you've got on a box cover, 'For the first time ever,' how do you finish that sentence?" You'd be surprised how many times professional developers couldn't answer it. Because they've got a myriad of ideas for new features but no solid core foundation. That's what you need. So that's a best practice right there—come up with a solid mechanic first, then expand upon it.

I know you're a huge fan of the old coin-op classics. You told me once that you played them until your fingers bled. That's obviously a very different kind of game than what you ended up working on.

I literally did. I did daycare at an arcade—it was called the Electronic Corral. It was in Lakewood, California, at Lakewood Mall. My mom would drop me off at the Corral with five bucks. I'd use maybe a dollar of it. There were certain games that I'd play because I knew I was good at them—*Robotron 2084*. I loved that game. I'd sweat playing it. I'd end up having to leave it because my mom would show up, even though I still had tons of extra lives racked up. I'd leave it for some other kid, who'd get a free game with about twenty lives.

FIGURE 13.3 *Dragon's Lair*, released in 1983, featured traditional cel animation by celebrated animator Don Bluth. It used LaserDisc technology to store the images. The result was a game a decade or more ahead of its time.

Robotron was really great because it was really repetitive, not very deep. It was fire-and-forget. A lot of the other games were like *Tempest* and *Defender* …

Heart-attack-inducing games.

Yeah, they're just fantastic. But all these games I'm talking about dealt with speed. You had to be very quick and very reactionary. It was twitch gaming. When you're a kid, you like stuff that's very fast and intense.

When *Dragon's Lair* came out—it was fascinating (see Figure 13.3). It was actually story and art driven. I saw it at a fair, and I couldn't believe my eyes. I fell in love with that genre. *Space Ace*—oh, keep it coming! It was a great experience.

I never thought for a minute I'd actually be where I am now. Never even dawned on me.

So how did you end up doing the art and graphics for videogames? Are you just naturally talented at drawing and that kind of thing?

Yeah, I've got a talent. There are a lot of people out there who are better than me, no question about it. But I do love design. My real passion is character and foreground art. Environments take too long. I'm able to realize characters really quickly, and they hold a lot of personality for me. Two eyes, a nose, and a mouth—I can relate to that very quickly.

I was talking to a friend at Blizzard about environment art, and he asked me, "Mark, who's the biggest character on the screen?" [*Laughs.*] Okay, Azeroth. That put me in my place.

I could draw well, but drawing digitally didn't come natural. Photoshop didn't come out until the '90s. So it was all DPaint. When I graduated in '89, my art teacher submitted two pieces of mine to an art competition. She entered me as an amateur. I didn't think they had a snowball's chance of winning, but they did. One won first place. One of the judges on the panel did Nintendo games, and he called me up a few days later and asked if I'd like to come in for an interview at the studio. Was I interested in making art for videogames? I said I love to do that, but I don't know how. He said they'd teach me.

The interview went really well. Then I was doing artwork on graph paper [*laughs*]. It all snowballed from there. The tools just keep getting better. Autodesk, Maya, Max. All of these tools allowed me and lots of other guys and gals to realize the artwork at a level you see today—hyperreal.

Are people just born with artistic skill? If you're terrible at drawing, is that something you can learn how to do? Or do you either have the talent or you don't?

There's nothing that can take the place of just having the ability. There are a myriad of filters and tools, shaders, effects, that the software provides for you. A lot of people think artwork means being able to draw. But that's only part of it. There's composition, lighting, framing, telling a story visually. You look at storyboard artists—some realize very intense, very immersive illustrations. There are others that do chicken scratch. It's poo on a page, but they convey depth and action, motion, and pacing. Art is subjective (see Figure 13.4).

Really what it comes down to is whether you can communicate an idea. That's competitive; that's marketable. You might not be the best artist technically, but if you can com-

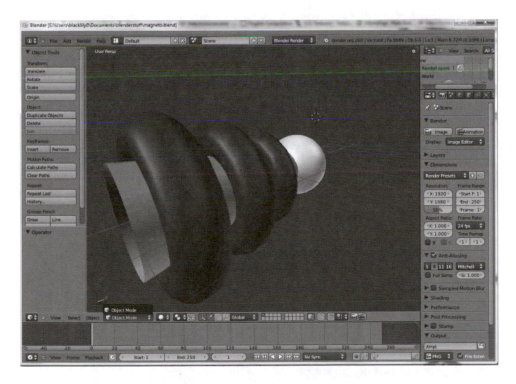

FIGURE 13.4 Nowadays, amazingly powerful graphics tools like Blender are available for free. You will, however, need to master the daunting complexities of the interface.

municate your ideas well and get other people excited about your vision, somebody will hire you.

What was your first job like, Mark? It was very crude, I'm sure.

Crude! We were dealing with 8-bit graphics and 256 colors, and a lot of the time it was only 255 colors because we had to leave one out for the alpha—a bright green or pink for the engineers to make nice edges. Working on graph paper … That was a real challenge. But this was the early '90s, and it's all relative—back then we thought it was cutting edge.

We'd be building a character and only have twelve-by-five pixels to realize Indiana Jones. Sometimes we'd only have two pixels for a head—a light flesh color and a dark flesh color. We didn't go into facial details. There were no hyperreal shaders, normal maps, no going into the pores of faces and seeing the water on the eyes—reflection, refraction. We didn't have any of that!

It was one thing to draw a little one-pixel character. But the real magic came when it got animated. Suddenly, life got breathed into this little pile of mush. When it started moving around, it was like, oh my gosh! It really does have personality. The emotion had to be made up from the animation. I couldn't tell just by looking at a flesh-colored pixel that the character was happy or sad. The only way I could tell is if he were upright when he was walking. If he was sad, he'd be hunched over and dragging his feet. It was a great collaboration between artist and animator.

What do you think about the relationship between graphics and gameplay? I've talked to some people who view graphics as window dressing. I don't think that's the right view.

There are lots of techniques you use when you're building out art and design for a game. You initially come out with the design … And also, I don't want to leave out audio. One of the things George Lucas told us at LucasArts was that 50% of a movie is visual, the other 50% is audio. That's why you have Skywalker Sound, and he'd work with really famous composers.

In games, it's the same thing. If you have a big open world game, you still need a way to drop breadcrumbs so players don't get overwhelmed. You need them to go to a point of interest to feel like they're progressing; you don't want them wandering like the Israelites in the wilderness. So we do a lot of things with color and lighting—it's typical. If you go into a dark room, and there's a light, you move toward the light. It's just instinctive. We utilize those fundamentals in games. A lot of color theory. We'll trade out warm colors from one environment and taper them off to more muted colors to set the mood. Then we complement that with the music; so now it's getting off-key and unsettling. There's only so much dark we can go with the art before players just can't see. But that's where sound comes in.

Even if you can't see the top of a large cave, you can give the illusion of that by providing lots of echo and ambient noises. You can give a sense of scale and ominous presence to make it foreboding. You really have to play nice to all areas of the development.

It sounds like you're talking about player psychology.

That's right. The minute something goes wrong, as subjective as it might be, the player will pick up on it. Like with animation. If you see a human character [moving wrongly], the

FIGURE 13.5 *NBA Live 97* offered an unprecedented level of detail for the time.

viewer might not be able to tell you what's wrong with it. But you can see it. The weighting just doesn't feel right. If the model is this big, ominous type of character, and he's moving really fast with no lumbering or weight-shifting … Those are the kinds of things I have to be very sensitive to as a director. There are lots of little nuances, but they do add up.

One of your early games was *NBA Live 97* (see Figure 13.5). I read that you put a lot of energy into making the characters look as much like the real athletes as possible. Did you ever hear back from any of them about what they thought of their characters?

No, not really. The main thing was the black players looked black and the white players looked white. That's the level we got to. There was no "make my eyes closer together." Now, with *Terminator 3*, that was a whole different story. Schwarzenegger had a whole bunch of things to say. Well, not so much him, but his agent.

With *NBA Live*, though, it was just so new to be able to show any kind of likeness. There wasn't really a benchmark. Ignorance was bliss. They were just excited to see their numbers on their jerseys. I don't think they realized the power they had to affect the process. Now, they are very aware. They've got a slew of legal and PR teams that manage everything. It's arduous.

What was the deal with Schwarzenegger?

It was really interesting. When we were constructing Arnold, we actually had cyberscan data where they'd basically laser scanned his body while he was in his underwear. We had good topological information on his structure. Even though that was a very high polygon, high frequency map of his body's contours, we had to dummy it down for the game.

Otherwise it would have run at two frames per second. As we started interpolating down the polygons, certain things would mess up or break. We had to reconstruct parts of his body.

Once we had those parts back to where the likeness was one to one, we'd get back into the game and I'd think—man, this is Terminator, right? It needs to have a larger than life appeal to it.

Long story short, after we massaged the topology we had to get approval. I looked at the game and thought it just doesn't look Terminator enough. Make his thighs bigger, widen his shoulders, make his chest broader. I really wanted to give him a hulk-smash kind of look. Even though Schwarzenegger is a big guy, trying to put his body into the game like that—there wasn't enough exaggeration there. So I made a visual call.

When we sat down with Schwarzenegger and his agent, his agent really had a hard time. "His eyes are too far apart, his nose is too wide." Arnold was sitting there. He said, "No, no, I look fine. It's okay." He liked the way it looked. His agent … man, he was such a tool. He had so many things to say. I understand it's his job; he's trying to protect his brand.

The funny thing is that the only thing Arnold really had to say was to make his chest a little bigger. I didn't have the heart to tell him that we'd already done that!

It was great. It's rare that when we're doing movie-to-game titles that we actually get to interact with the actors.

I was just reading about the whole "uncanny valley" phenomenon and how disturbed people can get when they're looking at robots that look too realistic. Do you encounter that in videogame work? Do you have situations where the characters are just too realistic?

I'm going to take flack for this, but I still have a hard time watching things in HD. It is so hyperreal. When I'm watching *Pirates of the Caribbean*, and I can see the makeup lines of Jack Sparrow's eyeliners—and all the little details. You see all those little imperfections. You see all of those things that film covered up before. Maybe I'm just a product of my generation.

Director Ridley Scott said that it's not important to give the viewer every detail. They need to make stuff up for themselves. That's one of the reasons *Alien* was so frightening. He didn't show all the alien. He wanted the viewer to make up the rest of that creature in their mind, because what made him afraid might not be what makes you afraid.

It's the same thing for games. Sure, we have the ability to put in those details. But should we? I believe we shouldn't. There are certain things, just like reading books—there are things you need to fill in. It creates immersion, because you have to invest some of yourself and your imagination into the game. That's very important.

Do you remember working on *Tegel's Mercenaries* in 1992? (See Figure 13.6). It was definitely one of the earliest real-time strategy games. Did you do any of the design work on it?

Back then, I really wasn't really a designer. I was just an artist. I got the tasks thrown on me—just impressions by the designers. Here's a sketch on the back of a napkin. "Make something that looks like this, and give it a mood like that, and make it blue." I had a lot of freedom. I'd take those very subjective impressions and do up some sketches, throw some digital art together, get feedback. It was back and forth.

FIGURE 13.6 *Tegel's Mercenaries* was one of Mark's earliest projects.

There weren't a lot of best practices back then. Artists weren't encouraged to look at the design doc. They weren't given a lot of the story or premise. They weren't even encouraged to play the game. Now, if you don't do that, you're an idiot. I can't put it any more bluntly than that. You're just stupid. You need to understand the story; you need to play the game; you need an intimate knowledge of what you're working on. Otherwise, how can you put heart into it? Soul? How can you make that character come alive? I always encourage artists and animators to understand the story, the level, the backstory. Get into these characters! Method art, if you will. I tell animators to get their butt out of their chair and walk around. Get in front of a mirror and videotape yourself doing the movements. Don't just do it in your head.

You also worked on *Siege* in 1992 (see Figure 13.7). What was that experience like?

That was very difficult for me. I was still very new and didn't know about tile graphics. "What do you mean by 'corner piece?'" I just didn't get that. It was brand new back then. There was a lot of trial and error, because there were no mentors. Everybody was learning it, and nobody had time for the new guy.

I had to learn a lot of it by looking over the shoulders of other artists and trying to mine them for information.

One of the things that was really prioritized was making sure the characters looked very different. You're working with a small amount of information, so color was huge. If a red colored faction was fighting another faction, don't have them be brown or tan. Go with purple or blue.

FIGURE 13.7   *Siege* is a 1992 real-time strategy for DOS. It is set in the *Magic Candle* universe.

You also worked on *Magic Candle III*. I get a lot of requests to cover it and have even seen requests to bring it back. I saw where you'd said in another interview that it had a hectic development with a lot of feature creep.

It started off well. It had a really great story. We had solid protagonists and antagonists. As we developed it, we had some breakthroughs, and saw some potential for new features if we wanted to wander a bit. Next thing you know, we were feature creeping. We explored new NPCs [nonplayer characters]. It got convoluted. We lost our way because we kept going off on all these vacuum-oriented side quests. You started to lose the foundation.

Coupled with that, our memory footprint got out of control. It was taking up more disks. The publishers were getting worried about how many 5¼-inch disks is this going to be on? It was costing us money.

It was up to sixteen disks at one point?

Yeah, it was ridiculous. The bigger it gets, the more QA [quality assurance] you need to vet it. When you have so many different NPCs, so many quests, and so many artifacts— grab this, go here, go there, get this key for that—it just gets nuts. That's why I have such a high respect for designers like Chris Avellone, who can do these amazing RPGs like *Fallout*. I don't know how they track all this stuff.

We ended up going back to our original design docs and asking, okay, what was the story? Who are the main characters? What are we trying to achieve? How can we get this down to fewer disks, so the user isn't waiting three hours to load it?

These are the kind of questions you need to ask early in the design. It's not enough just to have a lot of creativity. You need to ask what it's going to cost you on the backend.

You've done a lot of games based on movies. What's it like to work on a movie tie-in game, knowing that the media seems to be biased against them?

Obviously, we've seen bad games based on movies—and unfortunately I've worked on a few of those, sorry. But then you see some games lightly based on movies or comics, like *Batman: Arkham* that are amazing. I could talk for an hour about what that game did right, and if I talked about what it did wrong, I'd be reaching.

Movie games are really difficult because a lot of it is driven by marketing. I hate to throw marketing under the bus, but marketing is expensive. You can make a great game, but grassroots will only get you so far. If you have a movie coming out with some big names in it, like Arnold Schwarzenegger or Sylvester Stallone, a lot of the games publishers will want to capitalize on the hype surrounding the movie's release date. The movie studio will have billboards all over bus stops and freeways, and they'll have TV ads running. Usually at the very end of a TV commercial for a movie, you'll see a little ad for the game, too. So we're racing against the clock.

The big misnomer about movie production to games is that movies can be edited and reshot on the fly. Because movie studios are so secretive with their scripts, screenplays, and stories … Just because we're working on *Terminator 3* (the game) doesn't mean we have access to the script or screenplay. We had to travel to the studio, ask permission, and schedule time to sit down with the screenplay. We weren't even allowed to take notes. No pictures. It was all under lock and key at the studio.

We'd have to retain all we could and rush back to the studio, writing down everything we could remember. Then we'd find out three months later that a whole scene had been dropped from the movie. Dear Lord Jesus! We've had a crew of twenty people working on this environment for the past month. Now that's all shot to bunk?

That's why you don't see real hyper innovation in movies to games. You have to keep things very safe and very loose. You didn't want to go into it too deep because it might get thrown out. If you miss the date, you all get fired. Movie-to-game titles are all about survival, really.

Do game magazines tend to be prejudiced against movie-to-game titles?

I think so. We just have such a legacy of crappy movie-to-games out there. Everybody just chuckles under their breath; "Oh, we have *Green Lantern* coming out, who's the poor studio who's going to be doing that?" They're going to be thrown under the bus.

One of the nice things about working on *The Matrix* is that the Wachowski brothers actually wrote a brand new story for the game. It was a backstory that dealt with Niobe and Ghost. That was really cool because our game could have a story that intersected with the movie but go off and do its own thing. You always had a nice comfortable tie-in. We could expand the universe and the story and weren't just railed to a linear experience. A game is an interactive experience; a movie is a nonlinear, passive experience. They fly in the face of each other. You've got to be able to build to those different mechanics.

The Wachowski brothers really seem to have the right idea. I wonder why all movie to game titles aren't made like that.

Yes! The Wachowski brothers are just like us; they're big kids. They've got figurines all over their desks. They drink Red Bull and eat pizza. They love to have fun. They read comic books, play videogames. That's why their movies are so spectacular—they appeal to a generation.

***Demon Stone* is based on the writings of R. A. Salvatore. What was it like adapting that material?**

It was great. He's a great author. His Drizzt Do'Urden trilogy is fantastic; just awesome.

Personally, given the premise of *Demon Stone* … The premise was great, it was built on *The Two Towers* game engine. Great talent, great group of people. But it just seemed like overkill by way of story. It should have been a heavy RPG, not just a third-person action adventure. Look, you've got this guy Salvatore, who's written this fantastic trilogy—he's a great author who can realize worlds with words … and *this* is what we're doing with it? Really? It's like putting a Ferrari engine into a Pinto.

Sometimes a game gets put out when you know it could have been so much more; it's disheartening. It could have had more depth, more character realization—a better mechanic. But that's why you do a second version.

I feel your pain. I know you've got a deep background in the tabletop role-playing games, so all this simplification must be hard to take.

Yes, but it is what it is. As much as I'd like to consider myself an artist, and a fine artist at that, I'm a commercial artist. I hate to sound so insensitive, but it's a job. It's a business. It's a sad fact. For me to continue doing what I love, I have to produce product. I have to make sure the developer is making money, and I'm keeping my icebox full.

This focus on the bottom line—is that something that's always been there, or is it something that's been increasing over time?

No, it's increasing as time goes on, especially in this economy we're in now. The past two years have been very trying. We've found that we can bleed. The industry has traditionally been recession proof.

Gaming is a cheap form of entertainment. When you consider how much movies cost, and popcorn, and dinner—those are fine experiences. But you can spend forty dollars on a game and get twenty hours of experience—and if there's an online component, it exponentially increases. Throw in user-generated content, and the sky is the limit. Compare that to spending twenty dollars to go see a movie.

But the economy has still hit the gaming industry. I have a lot of friends getting laid off. But when these talented people get laid off, they start making indie games, and using the free tools. They have the passion and the talent, and actually get to make games they wouldn't get to make at a large studio because of the politics and all the money involved.

FIGURE 13.8 *Fracture* introduced a literal groundbreaking feature: Players can affect the terrain to secure a tactical advantage.

One of your most recent games is *Fracture*, which was released in 1998. From what I hear, its development seems worthy of its title (see Figure 13.8).

Yes. *Fracture* was a very unique game. Coming back to that "for the first time ever" hook on the box cover, this was "for the first time ever, you can use terrain deformation for a tactical advantage." Imagine playing *Call of Duty* or *Medal of Honor* and being able to suddenly drop the ground out from under an opponent or raise up a duck blind out of a mound of dirt. It was a very cool mechanic. All the weapons, grenades, vehicles—they all had ways of affecting the terrain. It was very physics based.

It started off as a first-person shooter. You never saw the character except in cut scenes. A few months into production, though, George Lucas had an idea. He thought the game had a rich story, but he didn't feel connected to the main character because you never see him. He told us to make the game third person. Okay! That turned development sideways for a few months as we broke things and put them back together. It was a challenge for sure. Then we went through the rigmarole of designing the main character; it got really detailed. What kind of uniform would he have, hairstyle ... We went through months just arguing about his hair. Green light groups, focus groups, all on the hair.

George Lucas gets obsessive about hair?

[*Laughs.*] I'm not going there.

Then it's like, should he have a mystery scar? Make him African American? It all got very convoluted. But I'm glad it did go third person, since we could have some scale reference. In a first-person shooter, your gun and your hand are so close to you—if you're doing

FIGURE 13.9 *Star Wars: The Clone Wars* features a graphics style patterned after the unusual artistic style of the animated series.

all this stuff with the environment, you don't have a good sense of the depth of a pit or height of a duck blind. But now you had a wider field of view and an open periphery.

It was a fun production, but there were a lot of technical challenges.

One of the things that came out of my interview with Jon Hare is his frustration about his best games becoming obsolete and forgotten. You don't really talk about a fine work of art or music as being "obsolete." What are your views on this?

It's relative. You can go back and look at the horse and buggy, or the old Ford cars with the spoked wheels and boxy shapes. They had candlelit lamps on the sides. Compare that to a Vector or Lamborghini Countach. It's very subjective.

I don't appreciate or like all art, but I do appreciate its creativity and evolution. I'm finding more and more, though, that the industry is coming full circle. It started off with 8-bit sprite art, and where are we now, Matt? We're right back to where we started. We're back to low polygon art on mobile titles and social games. Even though *Modern Warfare* and *Skyrim* is out there, right alongside them are these sprite games. The appreciation has come back; it hasn't been lost. It's found a new market and a new appreciation.

Which of your works are you most proud of as an artist?

One of the newer ones—I'd say *Star Wars: The Force Unleashed.* Or maybe *Clone Wars* (see Figure 13.9). The thing I liked about *Clone Wars* is that it was so highly stylized. In fact, when we started development on it, I set up a meeting at Skywalker Ranch with the directors and producers of the animated series and got into their head. What makes these characters and visual elements come alive? I wanted us to interpret that correctly in the game. If you look at the textures on the show, it's almost like a relief. You can see the brushstrokes. They're not refined or polished; it was meant to be distressed. Even the models of the characters have jagged edges.

It was a huge learning experience for me, even as the art director. It inspired me.

What do you say to the sixteen-year-old who comes up to you and asks what he or she can do to prepare for a career as a games artist?

My advice is that if you're an artist, you're always going to be an artist. They're going to continuously work on their skills and refine them.

If you really want to get in the games industry, start working with the games that have modding tools. Start downloading engines like UDK, Unity, and Crytek. Start working with Blender. As a student, you've got nothing but time, passion, and drive. Use it to your advantage. If you're not learning it at school, download them and learn them by yourself.

If you are in art classes, pay close attention to lighting. Lighting is very important in the games industry. We think what we're realizing now is amazing; imagine what we're going to have in five, six years. Lighting is next-gen. It's just as important as animation. It sets the mood for everything.

Get a feel for design. You should also start creating your own tabletop games. I still know designers who will toss an idea out the door if they can't realize it in a tabletop version.

How important is it for them to learn about the history of videogames?

It's very important. People play a game because it's fun. They want an experience. I can watch a movie to get artwork. I can listen to MP3s and get great audio. But games are about the experience.

Back in old-school days, you didn't have a lot of horsepower for audio and visuals. The only thing they had to rely on is the mechanics of gameplay. They had to do that really well. Even though you may not try to make the same kind of game today, there are still things you can extract from that. You can take those foundations and build on them.

One of the things I hear a lot from industry veterans is that they're not gamers. They don't play a lot of games. I wouldn't say it's a high percentage, but definitely a good percentage who aren't gamers.

That could explain a lot of games I've played …

Well, a lot of times you get into the mindset of, well, I'm developing a game, and I know it's fun because I'm the one developing it. It's the impression you get that, because you're a professional game designer, you know what's a good game and what's not.

I got busy. I have a family. Developing games takes a long time. I fell out of love playing games because I had other priorities. But you still have to touch games—you have to understand what makes them fun. I just had this realization a few years ago, I'm sad to say.

Now I'm playing everything. It's not that I have to play a game from start to finish. But I do pay attention and get referrals from friends—"Hey, Mark, you've got to download this from Steam." I get the trial versions, which are usually pretty good. I can get a good sense of where the game's going, of the core mechanics.

I'm always looking back. You need to look back to history and learn from it, so you can move forward, better educated and better aware.

CHAPTER 14

Megan Gaiser and Rob Riedl, Gamemakers for Girls

In 1998, Her Interactive produced *Nancy Drew: Secrets Can Kill* for Windows. Amazingly, from this humble beginning the company went on to produce a full twenty-six sequels—and the team shows no signs of slowing down.

Her Interactive's Nancy Drew games are point-and-click adventures based on the varied novels of the long-lived franchise for young readers. Nancy Drew, the "sassy detective," is a smart and capable young woman who enjoys solving mysteries with her friends Bess and George, her boyfriend Ned, and occasionally with help from the Hardy Boys. Self-reliant, resourceful, and confident, the character of Nancy has inspired generations of girls and young women (see Figure 14.1).

All of the games feature professional voice talent and high-quality graphics and music. Each game features two difficulty options: Junior, intended for children, and Senior, which is challenging enough for adults. While the primary demographic is girls aged 10 to 16 or so, plenty of grown-ups of all genders enjoy the games, too.

In August 2012, the twenty-five-member team launched a Kickstarter project to help fund the conversion of their game engine for use on smart phones and tablets. If successful, this move seems likely to greatly expand their audience beyond the PC and Mac gamers.

My wife and I have been playing the games for years, so it was a great pleasure for me to get to sit down in September 2010 with Megan Gaiser, CEO, and Rob Riedl, executive producer, and learn about the company's vision and approach to making games.

Megan, how did you get to be where you are?

Megan: How much time do you have? [*Laughs.*] I started off as a filmmaker. I was a producer and editor, and I really got interested in multimedia—the nonlinear format. I knew that Seattle was the hub for that, and I was in D.C. So I moved to Seattle, without a job. I worked at Microsoft for a while, then someone introduced me to the CEO of Her Interactive. They needed a creative director. They'd just gotten the Nancy Drew license.

FIGURE 14.1 Megan Gaiser, CEO, and Rob Riedl, executive producer, of Her Interactive.

I knew nothing about games, but I loved Nancy Drew and thought the idea of transforming that mystery experience into an interactive one was really exciting. So I took the job.

Do you know the story of Her Interactive and how we got into retail?

Yes, but I'd love to hear it from you. I read that it started off with Amazon self-publishing.

Megan: Oh, yeah. When I came on board, we were a small crew. I knew nothing about the games industry at the time; I didn't even know that there weren't any games for girls, which completely shocked me. But we were excited. We created this great game, and when we finished—it took us about a year and half—we went to the publishers to get it on the retail shelves. They said the game was quality, but girls are computer phobic and will never play videogames. They wouldn't take it. We were completely dumbfounded.

We knew that 51% of the population is females, and they're targeted by all other mediums: books, music, and films. So we decided to take it into our own hands and learned how to publish it ourselves. We learned how to do packaging, marketing, and PR. We sold it to Amazon.

Luckily, the sales really took off. The *New York Times* dubbed us the "Un-Barbie" of computer games, which we're so proud of. The publishers who rejected us earlier now came back, and that's when we got into retail.

But we thought, why are we letting the publishers make the lion's share of the profit? Why don't we just learn more about publishing ourselves? We found someone to teach us, and two years later we had our first profitable year—2002.

What about you, Robert? What brought you to Her Interactive?

Robert: I've been making videogames since I was a teenager. My first computer was a TI-99/4A. I played a lot of text-based adventure games and tried to create them as well. I've always been eager to try out new videogames and ideas, but I never thought you could get paid to do that.

I started with American Laser Games, which Her Interactive spun-off of, as an accountant. There was an opening in product development, and I said I'd be interested. I knew something about computer games and Nancy Drew, having two older sisters. That's what I had to read as hand-me-downs. That's how I got into this crazy world.

Growing up, I played a lot of Scott Adams text adventure games. I'm not sure why I didn't play the Infocom adventures; maybe they were just too expensive. In high school and college, I played lots of MUDs [Multi-User Dungeons].

I read that Her Interactive sent *Secrets Can Kill* to one of the Nancy Drew authors; apparently she was in her nineties. Can you tell that story?

Megan: There were many writers of Nancy Drew books; Carolyn Keene was a pseudonym they all shared. Mildred A. Wirt Benson wrote most of them. We found out that she was a reporter at the *Toledo Blade* in Ohio doing a column for sixty year olds and older. We sent her chocolates, flowers, and a letter signed by everybody on the team. We thanked her and told her she was our inspiration. She called me back and said something like, "That was my former life." She was very humble, but a total character.

She actually was Nancy Drew. She flew planes in the '30s. There's pictures of her on her Stairmaster at ninety-two in *People* magazine. She was going blind at the time, so she had her assistant play the game and gave us a plug in her column. It was really amazing.

I've heard stories about grandmothers connecting with their granddaughters over e-mail or the phone, helping each other get through your games.

Robert: It breaks down the generation gap. It's really cool.

Megan: When started out, we targeted girls ten to fifteen. That was our core audience. But since Nancy Drew is such an inspiration for women in America, the moms starting buying the games for their daughters to inspire them just like the books had inspired them as girls. But then the moms got hooked on the games, and they got their mothers into it. So now the age is eight to eighty-eight. We also have guys and boys who love the games.

And that's what got me interested. I'm a huge adventure game fan, and I kept seeing the Nancy Drew games on the shelf, and finally one day said, oh, what the heck. I took one home called *Danger on Deception Island* and really enjoyed it. Then I realized there are a lot of other games in this series. How many, exactly?

Megan: Twenty-three.

That's an amazing number of games for any series.

Megan: It is. Robert will remember that after the first couple of games, people would say to us, "People are going to get really tired of this. What are you going to do next?" None of us realized that this series would go as long as it has. There are over 350 books in the series, so there's really no limit.

What are your own favorite games in the series?

Robert: Curse of Blackmoor Manor is one of my favorites. I got to spend a lot of time on design, and it was neat creating this British family with a bizarre tradition. I enjoyed making the castle a puzzle unto itself.

I also like *Message in a Haunted Mansion*. That one was the first where we really put a spook factor into the game. It was great testing it and seeing the focus group members become afraid. I like the scary ones. *Ghost Dogs of Moon Lake* is another one. Some of the characters are so funny; it's one of my favorites. It's amazing what they did with *Shadow at the Water's Edge*. It feels so Japanese. Really, really nice treatment of the location.

Megan: The games are set in real-world locations, so there's a lot of cultural discovery. The team is incredibly talented and committed to high quality, which is one reason why I think we've lasted so long. They do a lot of research. They make sure that the folklore, historical elements, the look and feel—it's all absolutely perfect. We also have historical references and characters that we weave into the stories, both fact and fiction. For example, Houdini is in one of our games, and Marie Antoinette. That's something unique.

What is the relationship between the games and the books? I know there are some based directly on books, some on the "Case Files" series.

Robert: They're based on a wide range. Some are from the "Case Files" books, others from the old yellow backs. *Secret of Shadow Ranch* is one of those (see Figure 14.2). Then there are "Case Files" books Simon & Schuster produced. *Whispers in the Fog* was the basis for *Danger on Deception Island*.

Simon & Schuster give us great latitude. They're the owners and publishers of the books. Our games don't have to be literally based on them. A lot of times they're just used as springboards for inspirations. An example is *Curse of Blackmoor Manor*, which is based on *The Bluebeard Room*. The only things taken from that book are the name Penvellyn and the setting in England.

How do you decide which books to base new games on? Do you have a library of all the Nancy Drew books? Are some of the games based on your own, original stories?

Megan: Well, they're inspired by the books. There is something there. But oftentimes, we create the characters and transform the stories. We're all storytellers here, even though we all come from different disciplines; math, film, and history. What's been so exciting about working with this team is that we've mastered the art of creative collaboration. Just like in film—how do you explain how that happens? It's an organic process. Everyone feels comfortable with each other and sharing ideas. Whether an idea makes it in is another story, but the artists and programmers all give their special touch. It's a collective work of art.

One thing I've noticed about the series is that some of the games seem more educational than others. I'm thinking of one like *Secret of the Scarlet Hand*, set in a museum with exhibits and things. Do you have a policy there of doing an edutainment title on a regular basis?

FIGURE 14.2   *The Secret of Shadow Ranch* has a "dude ranch" setting and theme.

Robert: When we're concepting new ideas for the next two or three games, we look at it in terms of the overall mix of the series. We avoid situations where you just have scary castle, scary castle, scary castle. We want to have a mix of different genres—an action adventure, a detective/CSI adventure, a more social one. We're definitely considering the product line.

Megan: We always want to have that mystery element that's in every one of the stories. At the same time, though, we want every Nancy Drew adventure to be completely unique in terms of where it takes place and the characters. They're all different. (See Figure 14.3.)

Have they all sold about the same, or is there one or two that stand out?

Megan: Message in a Haunted Mansion has sold the best. It could be because it was the first game to launch in retail. But for the most part, the sales are pretty consistent. We get feedback from our fans and do usability. With each game, we have people come in to test the puzzles and artwork. We really take that to heart in our postmortems.

There's none that you regret?

Robert: No. Every time we beta test, we ask about attitudes towards the previous games, and there are some that consistently come up as an overall favorite. But we rarely get a situation where there's one that just didn't work.

Megan: We just want every game to be better.

FIGURE 14.3   This is a scene from the latest game, *Tomb of the Lost Queen*. It's set in Egypt.

One thing I've noticed about your website is a very active and very extensive forums community. How are you integrating this social activity into your game design?

Robert: With every new product cycle, we try to think of ways to improve it. One aspect we've looked at for quite a while is how to integrate that strong message board userbase with a game's content. We've come up with a variety of ideas and are working on a couple of initiatives.

Do girls prefer the PC as a gaming device over consoles?

Megan: It's not that black and white. Before the Wii came along, that was probably truer, since consoles have been marketed at males. But everything is upside down now. The industry, the business models, the platforms, it's all changed dramatically over the past few years, especially since Facebook. I think it's dangerous to make those kinds of presumptions. Many girls and women like a variety of consoles.

As long as the game is accessible and targeted toward their preferences, they're going to like it.

I notice there are some Nancy Drew games for the Wii and the DS. Are those platforms more accessible to females than the PS3 or 360?

Megan: Yeah. At this point, our audience [isn't as active on the 360 or PS3]. I don't think there's been a targeted effort to bring females in yet. The Wii is very natural and intuitive. The iPad is really going to take off, so we're very interested in that platform. And online as well.

So you're thinking about the iPad, then? Are there plans to release Nancy Drew games on that platform?

Megan: You're definitely going to see Nancy Drew games on the iPad. Yes.

Is there a feminist agenda at Her Interactive or at least a push towards a feminist mindset? Are there political overtones to any of it?

Robert: No. The reason we created Her Interactive was … well … At the time, we were looking for other markets we could tap into. With American Laser Games, we were getting competition from violent videogames, and the board and the company didn't want to go that route. So we asked if there were any untapped markets; any underserved populations we could serve and make money.

The purpose of Her Interactive was to make money. It was a gamble; the prevailing wisdom at the time was that girls just weren't interested in games after age ten. The stats did show that female computer game usage dropped precipitously at that time. So we set up focus groups with girls of that age group, ask them what they liked, why weren't they playing, what kind of content they'd like. And we created content based on what they told us. So our agenda was to make money and create content for this underserved market.

Megan: A completely ignored market. We were the pioneers in creating games for girls back in 1995. It was just so obvious. All other mediums served both genders, and it just seemed crazy that computer games didn't give access to females. It was interesting to us why other companies didn't start sooner.

I'm somewhat surprised to hear you answer like that, since when you look at other games for girls they do seem to pander. You're the "Un-Barbie." You don't pander to the stereotypes; the Nancy Drew games seem to be about empowering girls. You want your daughter to imitate Nancy.

Megan: Well, Nancy Drew does represent all those characteristics we aspire to. She's smart, she's resourceful, and in the end, she always wins. That's one piece of it. But of course, we're also a business and out to make money. We are incredibly committed, though, to empowering girls and women. That's been the heart and soul of what we're doing. We're creating something that's high quality and also inspiring. We're really proud of what we're doing.

We set out in the beginning to make great games—not necessarily girly games. I was asked in the early days why we were making games for girls. Now they're asking us how to make games for girls. But when we were starting out, they said that if you want to make games for girls, just make it pink, and they will come. We purposefully decided to make it un-pink, and they still came. So what we really care about is breaking down the stereotypes.

There needs to be as many games preferences as there are types of boys and girls. It's equally insulting to say, "All boys like violent games." I think there's a lot of creative opportunities that we have as game companies to take some risks and offer new choices and a variety of content.

Why do you think it is that so many girls seem to reject violent games?

Megan: Some do. We can only speak for our audience, but some of the feedback we've received is that our audience doesn't like to be depicted as victims. They don't like exaggerated body parts; they want real, eclectic characters.

Robert: Some of the research shows that they don't mind shooting someone if there's a reason for doing that. There needs to be a strong motivation to resort to violence. What I've noticed in the market is a resistance to using it as a mechanic. It's not seen as interesting or relevant; there's a desire to do something else with this world than just shoot things.

Megan: One of the things that I was so interested in back in our usability tests with girls back in 1997—because they'd never played games before, they had such fresh perspectives on what games could actually be. They helped us improve on existing gameplay rather than perpetuate existing stereotypes.

They told us that Nancy Drew was great but too perfect. She intimidated them. They asked if we could put acne on her. We took all these gems and used them to tweak the game, not only preserving the integrity of the brand, but also to make some great games.

We wanted to make a series from the beginning, so we took a lot of series formula from film. We wanted to make sure we could keep them coming back.

I've heard you mention film several times. Just on a side note, what did you think of the recent Nancy Drew movie?

Megan: Uh … It was … Well, the good part about it was that we rode the coattails of that movie and doubled our sales. It was great for brand awareness. In terms of the film, though, I thought it was too young. They missed their opportunity to really grab that timeless brand that spans generations. They chose to do a film for a six- to nine-year-old audience. There could've been another way of doing that. It could have caught on a lot more.

Robert: Yeah. It wasn't the Nancy Drew that I knew. It seemed like the writers and creators wanted to make her more accessible. I don't really know what their motivations were. But it was strange and out of sync with the content we've been creating, which resonates quite well with the image you get from the books.

Do you have plans to do other games beyond the Nancy Drew franchise?

Megan: Absolutely. Creating another IP [intellectual property] series is definitely on our list. We're in the process of creating that land right now. We've been very successful with Nancy Drew over the years, so we're just taking this opportunity to see how we can extend our expertise into another very exciting series that targets females and mystery lovers.

What are the long-term plans for the Nancy Drew series?

Megan: Our goal is to make Nancy Drew games accessible across platforms, social, console, iPad, iPhone. We want anyone to be able to play the game—including people who have never played games before. We're also appealing to mom and teen bloggers to spread the word about Nancy Drew. It's her eightieth anniversary this year, if you can believe it. So the word is really getting out.

I know one thing you did to celebrate was re-release *Secrets Can Kill* with an updated interface. Why did you choose to remake this game rather than make a new one? (See Figure 14.4.)

Megan: We wanted to honor the anniversary, and we thought it'd be fun to revisit our first game. We changed the ending, too. We did it for the fans, really; that was the impetus.

FIGURE 14.4 *Secrets Can Kill* was remastered in 2010. Shown on the left is the original with the remastered version on the right.

Robert: There's technical reasons, too. The old *Secrets Can Kill* was made with an older technology we no longer use. The remake allowed us to do more with it, including localization.

Are there plans to remake more of the early games?
Megan: We're talking about it. It's been very well received, and the fans really like it. People who have never played our games are trying it out, so it's been great.

My favorite in the series is *Stay Tuned for Danger*.
Megan: Why did you like that game?

I thought it was a really fascinating setting and loved the characters. I also thought *Danger By Design* was a lot fun. Annette saying everything was "so rude" was quite humorous.
Robert: Yes, it's fun making characters like Rick Arlen; this sleazy, self-involved, egotistical star. Annette was fun, too, this crazy, fashion character.

***The Secret of Shadow Ranch* was another of my favorites, too. The music was great. How do you get the music? Do you contract out for it?**
Robert: We've been working with Kevin Manthei from the start. He's a composer in the L.A. area who does film as well as game scores. He's got a huge list of credits. He's great to work with because he's always up for a new challenge. We're always going to a different locale and need different instrumentation, different ethnic sounds. For the one in Japan, he was hesitant to do J-Pop tunes, but once he started getting into it, he really enjoyed it. He's an amazing, gifted composer.
Megan: We've also been using the same woman to do the voice of Nancy Drew from the very beginning.

Ah, yes, Lani Minella (see Figure 14.5).
Megan: Yes! She's incredibly talented. She's done lots of other voices than Nancy Drew.
Robert: Yep, she can do parrots. Anything you can come up with.

FIGURE 14.5 Lani Minella, the voice of Nancy Drew as well as many other characters—and the occasional parrot.

She did the parrot? Wow.

Robert: Yep, she did Lulu the Parrot. It was amazing, because when I called her and asked if she could do a parrot, she asked if I meant African Gray, Budgerigar, or Scarlet Macaw. I'm a bird watcher. I know what these birds sounded like, so I tested her. She really did have the sense of each bird.

I think I'll forever associate her voice with Nancy. I hope there's not any plans to replace her.

Megan and *Robert:* No!

Robert: I'm glad she's not bored with us. She always enjoys her sessions.

What would you say to a student who was interested in a career in games design, particularly a female?

Megan: We're very big on that goal. We do lots of tours, bringing in troops of Girl Scouts and sit them down with female artists, designers, producers, marketing people. We give them a taste of what the person does and plant the seed early. There are tremendous creative possibilities.

Anyone interested in getting involved in gaming—I'd suggest contacting the companies who make the games you love playing. One of the things we really look for when we interview people is passion. You can learn the skills, but we look for that fire. That's really helped us over the years in overcoming obstacles: complete teamwork and passion, the commitment to doing something really high quality.

If someone is totally excited, that gets noticed in interviews. The fact that they haven't done something before is not that big of a deal. They can be trained.

Robert: I would recommend getting a well-rounded education and having an understanding of technology. It's a big debate in the industry whether you want someone well rounded and eclectic or someone who is very good at a specific task. In our shop, we want well rounded. In design, we really look for critical thinking, the ability to examine a game and deconstruct it, understanding how it works and why it works.

Is there anything in particular you look for on résumés? Let's say there's a girl in high school right now who is determined to work at Her Interactive. What she should be doing right now to prepare for her interview?

Robert: A lot of different things. Take advantage of what high school offers, but also extracurricular activities. Study abroad; learn another language. Participate in activities you enjoy such as sports, chess, or math club. I look for the well-rounded person who is looking at all life has to offer and brings some interesting perspectives.

Megan: And someone who is excited about learning and takes risks. In this industry, it's very creative, and there are many times when you need to turn on a dime. Creative problem solving is part of our daily lives. They can become risk takers by trying out lots of different things, expanding their knowledge. There are lots of opportunities to be beta testers for games, too. We have beta testers across the country. In Seattle we have an advisory board of girls and women. The girls participating in that are already getting a taste for getting involved, and it's great for their confidence. We're listening to them. In the early days, they didn't have much to say because they thought we wouldn't take them seriously. Now we can't get them to shut up, which is great.

It almost sounds like the perfect applicant is, big surprise, Nancy Drew.

Megan: [*Laughs.*] Yeah, she's smart, she's gutsy, she's resourceful.

Robert: She's traveled all over the world; she's suffered major head injuries.

Megan: But she always comes back. She always takes a second chance.

So how is Krolmeister fairing in this recession?

Robert: He's still doing very well. We still don't know he succeeds with all those odd contraptions he makes, user unfriendly creations. But there's got to be market for them.

How about Koko Kringle? How the heck did you come up with that?

Robert: That came out of *Treasure in the Royal Tower*. It was created by Ezra Wickford, the chocolate king from Wisconsin. We create crazy characters that we love and want to continue with, so we put Koko Kringle bars throughout our games. We decided in the *Twister* game to create a whole line of candy bars and solicited ideas from all over the office. The winners are good. Some of them we just couldn't put in for family reasons …

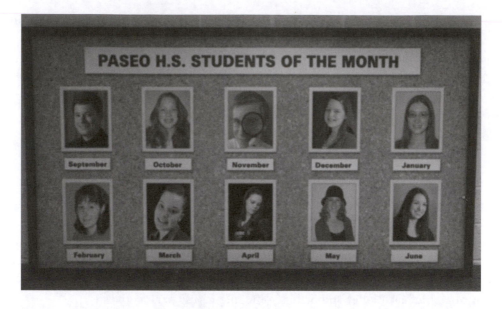

FIGURE 14.6 Her Interactive frequently uses real images of friends, fans, and family in their games. In this case, they chose to immortalize themselves as "students of the month."

I've noticed in some of the games there are pictures of actual people. Are those family members? Fans? (See Figure 14.6).

Robert: There are some friends and family members, contest winners.

Megan: In *Secrets Can Kill* there's a photo of everyone on the team at the time. It's the "Students of the Month." We named ourselves students of the month.

Robert: The student artwork is also submitted by actual users and players.

Megan: It's totally cool their artwork is actually in the game.

Well, that's all the questions I have. Thanks for your time.

Megan: Thank you, Matt.

Robert: Yes, and have a happy fall. I remember what it's like up north in Minnesota.

Sure, thanks! I hope I'll have a new Nancy Drew game to play once the snow falls!

CHAPTER 15

Paul Reiche and Fred Ford, the Toymakers of Gaming

Paul Reiche III and Fred Ford are the founders of Toys For Bob. At the time of my interview with Paul and Fred in March 2011, the duo were just finishing their *Skylanders: Spyro's Adventure* project, which combines traditional toy figurines with a videogame. It's been very successful, earning over $500 million in sales for Activision and making them very hot commodities indeed. Needless to say, I'm lucky to have caught them when I did!

Before *Skylanders*, Paul and Fred were probably best known for the *Star Control* series, sci-fi games that debuted in 1990 for DOS. Whereas the first *Star Control* is remembered for its fun multiplayer dogfight action, the second introduced a rich story with dozens of unforgettable alien races. *Star Control II: The Ur-Quan Masters* still enjoys a loyal and active fanbase, which has published an extensive wiki as well as an open source port of the game for modern operating systems.

Before cofounding Toys For Bob in 1989, Paul worked at TSR, Electronic Arts, and Free Fall Associates. During these years, he worked on such influential hits as *Archon* (1983), *Mail Order Monsters* (1985), and *Murder on the Zinderneuf* (1983) (see Figure 15.1).

I'm really happy to have had the chance to interview both men together. Their working relationship is one of those rare examples of perfect chemistry; two highly skilled and talented individuals who complement each other like peanut butter and jelly. Like all of the successful developers I've interviewed, they greatly enjoy their work and are deeply passionate about it. However, I could never see these guys doing anything but games. The thought of two men with this level of zany imagination doing anything else would just be an insult to humanity—and several extraterrestrial species, I'm sure.

I thought we could start off by talking about your top-secret new project.

Paul: It's *Skylanders: Spyro's Adventure*. It's an entirely original game we're creating, and we're focusing on the Wii version of it. What's really cool about it is that it uses actual physical toys that we've created. As you're playing the game, if you want to be a giant,

FIGURE 15.1   Fred Ford and Paul Reiche III back in the early '90s. (From the *Star Control* instruction manual.)

freaky robot, you just grab your giant, freaky robot toy and stick it on the platform—and magically you become that creature.

We've got a whole bunch of different toys, and it comes with three including Spyro. As you go through the game, like any traditional role-playing game, you get stronger and gain more powers. All of that is recorded in your toy automatically. You can take the same toy and play with different versions of this game, and hopefully upcoming games, and your character gets stronger, more detailed, and more customized as you move from game experience to game experience.

Fred: And let's face it … Who doesn't want to be a giant, freaky robot?

Paul: We are Toys For Bob, after all.

That brings up a good question. How do you guys view the relationship between toys and games? How closely related are the two?

Paul: I'll start. They both appeal to the same part of your brain, which is that fun, imaginative, play experience. Toys, because they've been isolated from the game experience, really live in the imaginative realm. They're very tactile; you hold them in your hand, you bite them, and you swallow them—then go to the hospital [laughs]. To me, they're very important, because they reflect an experience I had growing up as a kid. When my kids were growing up, I got to relive the biting the heads off toys and going to the hospital.

Now what we're trying to do is to combine the deep audio and visual experience of games with a "super toy," or something that not only comes to life but also remembers your experiences together. We're known for hybridizing, whether it's strategy and action or skateboarding and crazy downhill racing. This is continuing our focus on the hybrid edge.

Fred: So we're trying to ruin two industries at once.

Paul: Dominate, dominate.

Fred: Oh, dominate, I meant.

Paul: I think we will totally dominate the toy industry as soon as kids see that you can buy this toy for a price that's comparable to any other little toy of that size. When they see that there's a game in which it will appear, and they can give it a name—they're never going to want a dumb toy again. Hasbro and Mattel are going to be furious at us.

Does this have any similarities to the Webkinz toys?

Paul: In the sense that you can register them in an online experience, yeah. But we're going way past that. The key is that in those games there's a purely theoretical connection between the toy and the in-game experience in those other titles—you type in this electronic code, and then you have this totally separate electronic experience. Ours is constantly referencing back to the toy, putting memories in or getting them out. You're allowed to switch. You've had enough giant robot—now you want to be a screaming slime dragon. You can switch at any time you want, either for strategic reasons, or you just want to be the slimy dragon, or maybe you just bought it and want to see what it looks like. That's the big difference—a direct, immediate connection.

Toys are fun, games are fun. What is fun?

Paul: Well, if you ask me you'll get a different answer than you'll get from Fred. Fred has a darker sense of fun. It's an interesting question we've been asked before, and I try to give a different answer every time. One way to look at it is to think about your life and all the times you've been sitting somewhere thinking, "This is not fun!" Just check that off, and you get a Venn diagram of what's not considered fun.

On the one hand, though, it's got to be surprising on one level. There are enjoyable activities, but that's not really fun. There has to be some surprise or new information—freshness to the experience. It's hard for the same thing to be fun time and time again. That's why two-player interaction is great—because you always have the freshness of what your friend says when you blow up his spaceship or punch him.

Fred: I would say that it if it were easy to define, Paul and I would be rich and probably have a better video connection here. It's something that's elusive, and you just have to iterate over and over again until you get it right.

So is it like pornography, then? You know it when you see it, or I guess in this case when you play it?

Paul: No comment! [*Laughs.*]

Okay, then, let's talk about your tabletop days. Paul, you got interested in gaming from *Dungeons & Dragons*. Can you tell me how you moved from playing those games to actually creating your own?

Paul: Sure. There are actually many similarities between Fred and my background; we both had families that love to play games. I have a bunch of relatives who are gainfully employed as cattle ranchers, and playing cards and *Uno* are part of the life experience.

When I was at Berkeley, I took an art history class that gave me the choice of writing an essay or making a game on the subject. I thought, wow, I'll take game. I had no idea what to do, so I had made a hybrid bull fighting, art history, and abstract strategy game all in one. I don't think a single game was ever played from beginning to end, but it was called *What did Goya Die of?*

Back when I was in high school, I'd gone into chemistry one day and saw this dude with glasses and strange booklets spread out in front of him with fantasy illustrations on them. It was my *Napoleon Dynamite* moment—was I repulsed or attracted by this? I went with the attraction. I found out that he played *Dungeons & Dragons,* and this was the really early, early days. He and his friends were very thoughtful and creative, and one of them was Erol Otus, a guy I've worked on and off with to this day. He became one of the original artists at TSR, and I was fortunate to get to follow him to TSR as a writer and designer. We'd created some of our own books back in high school and published them. We made some money and got in trouble with the IRS because we didn't know what we were doing. We closed down the company and ran away. But those books were *Booty and the Beasts* and *The Necronomicon.* They're for sale on eBay at some ridiculous prices. They were a lot of fun, and they led to the career that I have today.

When we got to TSR, my first job was alphabetizing a bunch of glyphs, which I thought was impossible because they didn't have names. But I got through it. Then we worked on monster cards, a *Gamma World* module. I have a very soft spot in my heart for *Gamma World.* I love that game.

You're also the father of your very own TSR race, the Thri-kreen. I'm pretty sure everyone who's played enough *D&D* has encountered them at some point.

Paul: That goes back to the monster cards at TSR. As they often did, they'd motivate us with cash prizes. They wanted us to sit down with an artist and come up with some new monsters together. Erol and I had created some termite characters in *Booty and the Beasts*, and I thought mantises were the coolest insects in terms of fighting. So I wanted to create some mantis warriors. I also loved the weapon in one of the *Star Trek* episodes, the kligat, a spinning disc of death. I thought that'd be a cool thing to give mantises, since they don't really have hands. Then I had a vision of their history out in the desert, but on the monster card I didn't have much space for text.

Afterward, I found out that they'd taken off in the Dark Sun era, and some people had done some really wonderful, far more extensive designs on them. Those kind of mantis creatures also show up in *Star Control* in some of our insectoid races. They are still living in our brains—cool insect warriors. Are they going to chop my head off?

I notice that all of your games have extensive, original backstories. I'm wondering what you think about the relationship between story and game, especially since the backstories of your earliest games begin and end in the manual—and are not actually in the game at all.

Fred: Not all games give you an opportunity to tell a story. The first *Star Control* was mostly a tactical, strategic hybrid. There was some story there, but it was mostly in the manual. In *Star Control II* we made a conscious decision to tell more of a story. We specifically made an opportunity for ourselves to do that, and it became very important.

Paul: Up until that point, the games that had best-done stories were the text adventures, which I loved and still love. We saw that you need time to communicate text in chunks. We wanted to figure out where we had an opportunity to do that, because our player was going to be blasting someone—he's not going to want to stop and read a block of text.

A friend of ours, Greg Johnson, had designed a game called *Starflight*. I'd worked a few days on it with him, and thought it was very exciting. I love science fiction. What we explored was the communication system.

When we went into *Star Control II*, Fred and I were able to think about the ways you can use storytelling within a conversation between you and an alien. Little things popped up, like the statements made when you landed on a planet. Initially, those were really game driven, but we found them to be a funny little spot for reports from arbitrary, unseen heroes, like the poor Libermann triplets who get blown up on Pluto. Then we had a UI [user interface] built into the starbase for things you brought back to be scanned. The lab technicians took on a life of their own, talking about the things happening to them. We found niches that let us tell stories, and we filled them in.

It seems to me those "little" additions made the game a lot more innovative and immersive.

Fred: Yeah, they did. But the fact that we didn't answer all the questions has intrigued people for years.

Paul: We worked on the first two games, and some really nice guys worked on the third one. But they were coming in trying to answer a bunch of the questions that we'd set up. Looking back, we should have advised them, oh, God, don't do that! Come up with new questions. That's way more fun, easy, and stimulating.

When we do the next *Star Control* game, which we promise is coming soon, it's not going back and picking up with the Androsynth; what are the Shofixti up to? We'd like to touch on some of those threads, but it's also about bringing in new characters and seeing who's moved off stage. We want to add more life to it rather than just close it down.

Henry Jenkins has talked about this in his book *Convergence Culture*. Instead of trying to contain everything, you're trying to make more and more people curious about more and more things.

Paul: If you think about the best science fiction, there's always quite a bit at the end that you have to fill in with your own imagination. I think that's the big difference between reading and film. There are some people who just don't like to read, but those of us who do—Fred and I are big readers—we're projecting and fleshing out the experience. In fact, I'll recommend books to people who work here. They'll say, "I liked the book, but what about those parts you talked about? They weren't in the book!" I will have completely forgotten that I made all that up. My real-world state and my imaginative state are not entirely distinct. Same thing with dreams. I had a whole thing about polar bears being weasel related, not bear related, and isn't that a funny thing? I went on with this for years, until someone finally called me on it. Oh, that was just a dream.

Do you have a reading list of books and novels for aspiring game designers?

Fred: We're big Jack Vance fans. He's an old-time science fiction writer, but his work stands up remarkably well even today.

UNICORN (GROUND 4)

FIGURE 15.2 *Archon* was one of the first hits published by Electronic Arts. It's basically an arcade adaptation of traditional chess.

Paul: Absolutely. In the late '40s and '50s, he was writing fiction on a merchant marine ship somewhere. Those stories became the basis of the *Dungeons & Dragons* magic system, with memorizing spells, and spells having such fancy names. He was into setting up rules and systems in his fiction, and if you read them, you'll almost always find some component of structure that the characters manipulate to their own ends—and his characters aren't always good guys. Jack Vance is big for both of us.

In terms of dreaming large, games are usually larger than movies and often novels in scope. Space opera writers—and I'd classify Larry Niven in there, Orson Scott Card … I have a big list. Dan Simmons' *Hyperion* series is awesome. If you remember, we had a big list in the first *Star Control* manual where we did list people who inspired us.

I pity the people who have never read *Ender's Game*. Such a great book for videogamers.
Paul: Orson Scott Card is an interesting dude. He wrote one of the first reviews of *Archon*, actually (see Figure 15.2). He wrote a lot of the insult work for *Monkey Island,* too.

Our house is completely full of books. My wife keeps her Virginia Woolf books very far away from my science fiction.

Let's talk about Free Fall Associates. How did you get involved with them?
Paul: Free Fall starts with John Freeman and Anne Westfall. John has a long and interesting history. He's been in science fiction since it virtually began, attending fairs and writing novels. He wrote *The Playboy Guide to Games.* That led him to create Automated Simulations, which was one of the first game companies in existence. They did *Battle Fleet Orion* and *Starship Orion.* They later became Epyx and did *Temple of Apshai* and *Hellfire Warrior.*

I met them when they were showing off their PET version of *Temple of Apshai.* They had a booth at a *D&D* convention next to Erol's and my booth. We started talking, and I may have greatly exaggerated my programming abilities. But John didn't have any experience in

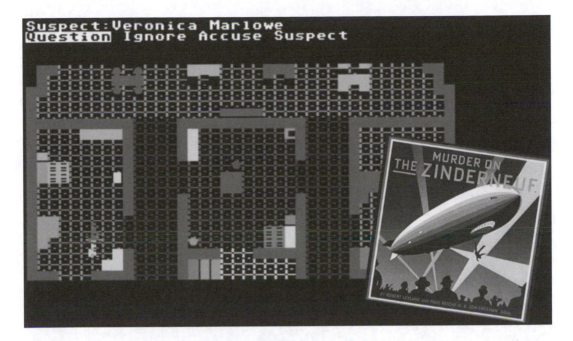

Suspect:Veronica Marlowe
Question Ignore Accuse Suspect

MURDER ON
THE ZINDERNEUF

BY ROBERT LEYLAND AND PAUL REICHE III & JON FREEMAN

FIGURE 15.3 *Murder on the Zinderneuf* is an intriguing murder mystery game set aboard a dirigible.

paper games, and he was really interested in what I was doing—and I was really interested in what he was doing with computers. So he hired me to do a follow-up to *Hellfire Warrior*. I sat in front of a TRS-80 for about three weeks, twenty hours a day, entering a game built within the *Hellfire Warrior* system.

Then there was a grand falling out at Epyx between John and his partner, and we split off with Anne Westfall—a great programmer—and Robert Leyland, also an Epyx dude, and formed Free Fall Associates. We came up with a famous list of twelve games and shopped them around. A strange little company called Electronic Arts was being founded. We went to a party of theirs where they had food, drink, and arcade games, and it was the first big, serious business party I'd ever been to. They had their manifesto printed by the door. Wow! This was weird, different, and kind of scary. It turned out to be Trip Hawkins' company.

We signed up to do *Murder on the Zinderneuf* and *Archon*, some of the first games they contracted (see Figure 15.3). We did those for a few months, and I made some money and was overwhelmingly seeing my future as how much money I was going to make. *Archon* only took three or four months and was probably day for day the most successful days I've ever had. After that, we did a sequel to *Archon,* and I started wanting to head off and make different kinds of games. One of my co-workers at TSR Hobbies, Evan Robinson, and his wife, Nicky Robinson, wanted to program games. They'd done a port of *Picnic Paranoia* for Synapse Software, and based on their knowledge of the Atari 800 and the Commodore 64, I'd wanted to make a game based on battling beasties. That became *Mail Order Monsters.*

After that, the industry crashed, so Evan, Nicky, and I were wondering what to do. We decided to make a really safe game—and that's how we ended up with the golf game. You

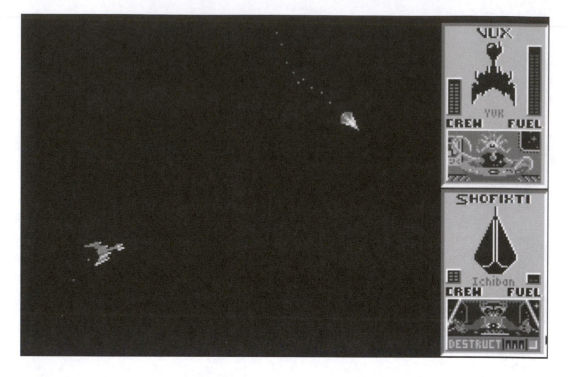

FIGURE 15.4   Shown here is one of the famous space dogfighting sequences in the original *Star Control* game.

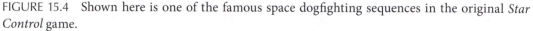

can see how we struggled with that, because there's a dinosaur in there that they didn't want. He'll eat your ball. Later, I met up with Fred. Fred, what were you up to during this time?

Fred: Well, while he was at TSR, I was making games for a Japanese personal computer. That was while I was still in college. That company went out of business, and I ended up programming in the corporate world. When I got sick of that, that's when Paul and I got together.

Paul: Fortunately, Erol and Robert Leyland were involved in the company Fred was working with, and it was really awesome timing. We were both ready to tackle something new, and we both had the time.

One of the things that made *Star Control* different was that we just stopped talking to the publisher about what we were doing (see Figure 15.4). They stopped paying us, which was fair enough, so Fred floated the company for a few months. But we just made the game we wanted to make. Eventually, when we were done, they published it. It's really hard to overestimate how important that is.

I know you've had creative conflicts with publishers before. You originally wanted *Mail Order Monsters* to be a serious and gritty game.

Paul: We had this vision in our head of giant monsters, and you were in the future genetically engineering these creatures. When you actually looked at the game, grr! They had semicute monsters. You don't always control the conception you create, just the materials that create the conception. What we had to do was realize that we had a successful experience, just not the one we had in our heads. So we embraced this more robust, *Gamma World* type fiction. We had fun with it.

Erol is famous for making the worm look shiny.

Toys For Bob, then. How did you get the name?

Paul: I'm glad you asked that. I'm looking at you, Laurie, my wife. We were looking for names, and Laurie recommended "Toys For Bob" because it's playful and people could project something of themselves into it. She's a poet, so she thinks about words very carefully. It works marvelously well. I can't tell you how many people desperately want to know the real truth behind "Toys For Bob."

The company rule is that each of us has to come up with our own Bob, and then act like that is the only Bob—thus further confusing people. It's a discordant approach. Somehow, though, Toys For Bob has survived being a partnership, a division of Crystal Dynamics, a corporation, and now a studio within Activision. We've just pulled it along with us.

My personal Bob is the subgenius.

What about you, Fred?

Fred: I'd have to go with myself, since my first name is actually Robert.

Paul: Since we're being funded entirely by Activision, "Toys for Bobby Kotick" is also not unreasonable.

Star Control is probably one of your biggest hits to date. What's the story of its development? Do you see it is as an evolution of ideas that began with Archon and Mail Order Monsters?

Paul: The answer is yes. The original name was *Starcon*. I had done a fake ad to pitch it, and the idea was 3D space combat with the sort of asymmetrical match-ups we'd done with *Archon*. Some reviewer called it "rock, scissors, vapor," which I always thought was appropriate. Learning about the match-ups and the individual characters really matters. You'll see that in all of our games.

The first game that Fred put together was just flying spaceships around and blowing up asteroids. It was a two-player game with the Yehat and the Vux ship. We started playing it, learning how to maneuver and fire weapons. The whole universe is built around that play experience.

We'd create a ship through paper illustrations, then implement powers that made sense for it. Then we'd step back and think about who was flying the ship. If a ship has an odd, robotic kind of top to it, maybe DEVO is flying it. So the Androsynth evolved out of this idea that it'd be really cool if DEVO was flying around in spaceships.

Later on, in *Star Control II*, we created very simple visual stories with the captain's images, the spaceships, and the loose pairings of the two different sides. We dug ourselves out of this creative, narrative hole.

Fred: Sometimes the ship designs would drive the story and sometimes the other way around.

Paul: [Take the] Mycon ship design, which was organic. How do you rationalize this concept of an organic structure with high-energy plasma? Well, what about these creatures that live in that molten discontinuity between the interior of a planet and the crust? How did they get there? Someone must have made them, since no creature would evolve there.

FIGURE 15.5 *Star Control II* added a great story campaign with lots of fun, highly imaginative alien races. Paul and Fred's unique humor is felt throughout the game.

What would they be doing there? Obviously they were making volcanoes. My imagination often tells the story, and I just have to write it down.

I've heard you have a special love for the Spathi race. (See Figure 15.5.)

Paul: They're me to a large extent; the distilled philosophy of self-preservation at all costs. Fred and I were once talking over lunch about what we'd do if we were rich. I started talking about how I'd like to have a beautiful house in the woods. But woods have scary things—bears and monsters. While I would want to take walks, I'd always want walls tall enough to keep out monsters. Monsters, being tricky, would get over those walls from time to time, so I'd need backup plans. I like to climb trees, so I thought, maybe we could tailor the trees to my climbing ability. If a monster was sitting at the bottom of a tree, it might be sitting there for a long time. So it makes sense to have rocks stored in each of the treetops, of sufficient size for my flimsy arms to throw them—and yet big enough to annoy a monster to make it go away. So, all I had to do was take this fantasy I was having over Chinese food, and give it to the alien. Running away and throwing rocks has been one of my strategies.

Fred, do you have a special place in your heart for any of the aliens?

Fred: None of them represent me perfectly, but I like how extreme the Ilwrath and the Druuge are.

Paul: They're very passionate. I drew the starbase captain based on Fred. That's one of his bits in there.

Fred: The Pkunk ship regenerates energy through insults. I gave that power to the ship because, for some reason, I was really mad at Paul one day.

Paul: We just recorded a string of insults from Fred focused at me. It soothed the situation and explained why these guys, whose are so philosophical, are going around insulting people. But it's the idea of being so nice that it wraps around and becomes very evil. Your morality is a signed value. We like the idea of never being too good—minor insults, pinching people. That'll keep you safe.

What about the music of *Star Control II*? I know there's an interesting story there.

Fred: As Paul mentioned, we weren't getting paid toward the end. We had a very limited budget to buy all the music for our game, and since we had so many races and wanted each one to have an individual piece … It got to be upward of forty themes. We just didn't have enough money to pay full price for all of them. I think it was Paul's idea to hold a contest with a decent first prize and a pretty wimpy second prize.

Paul: But lots of second prizes!

What were the prizes?

Fred: Fifty dollars, I think [laughs.]

Paul: We ended up finding a gentleman, Dan Nicholson, who'd done one of the really cool themes. The contest hadn't gotten us all the music we needed. So we got together with him. He had a great talent for doing really awesome techno music in MOD format. What we didn't know is that he wasn't even eighteen yet. But the cool thing about computers is that it doesn't matter how old you are.

You've released *Star Control* as open source. Are you a big supporter of the movement?

Fred: We feel bad that we haven't made a sequel yet, so we thought the least we could do is release the source code and let the fans revive it on modern computers.

Paul: Some people have made their own extensions. Our policy has been to let people do whatever they want, as long as they don't turn our characters into mass murderers or make money with it. If you're making money with our stuff, we'd like a pizza. Pizza is a good unit of exchange.

The game has been ported to a bunch of different platforms, including the Mac and iOS. I don't think I've actually played one yet. One of them is using our art, but I haven't been able to track him down. I'm going to get him one of these days.

How do you feel about abandonware? A lot of older games such as *Mail Order Monsters* are difficult to play legally nowadays.

Paul: As long as people are doing it out of love and for all the right reasons, we really like it. I may be violating contracts with previous publishers for saying that, because they're probably still in effect. We don't have a way to sell *Mail Order Monsters* now. If we want it to still make people happy, somebody else is going to have to do that.

If someone wanted to make *Mail Orders Monsters II* and were going to make millions of dollars off of it—we'd get snarky. But in general, we want people to enjoy our creative work. We do it to make people happy.

Fred: Send pizza.

FIGURE 15.6 *The Horde* featured full-motion video sequences. Kirk Cameron, shown here, plays the role of Chauncey.

We should setup a pizza contribution fund for everyone who downloads your old games.

Paul: I wanted to play *X-Com* recently, and I was having a heck of a time getting any of the DOS emulators to run the version I had. I was really happy that Steam was offering it again. I know there was an open source version of it in high resolution, but I thought the original was a much stronger experience. It's just a great piece of art. You can say the same thing about *Master of Orion. Monkey Island* has been revised and brought back, but the original EGA version was great and worth playing by itself.

Let's talk about the '90s era. You released *The Horde* in 1993, a full-motion videogame starring Kirk Cameron. How do you feel about that game now? (See Figure 15.6).

Paul: Good!

Fred: It was a cleansing of the palate after *Star Control II*. Accolades came to us after we finished and, having not paid us for six months, asked if we could do *Star Control III* for the same amount of money we gave you for *II*. We decided to do something different.

Paul: We created *The Horde* entirely on the PC, with the game experience of building up your town and taking care of your cows. Then we decided to move it to the 3DO, and thought—whoa, cool, now we could add full-motion video. We'd never made a movie before. We took a stab at writing the script, then it got rewritten, then it got really long and had to be cut back.

It was the first time casting came up as an issue for us. The head of the company had formerly been part of the film industry, and he walked by and asked who had the role for Chauncey. We'd picked Martin Short. He's like, "Box office poison. Please rethink." We kept finding people we really wanted, but they were too famous and wouldn't talk to us. Finally, we decided we didn't need a huge star so much as we needed an authentic, nice guy that you could root for. Kirk Cameron was perfect for that.

We actually had a couple of people who wanted to join Crystal Dynamics after that because *The Horde* was such a weird and different kind of game.

I bet there are plenty of gamers out there now who have never heard of 3DO or even full-motion video (FMV), for that matter. Why do you think FMV games didn't last?

Fred: It's hard to tell an interactive story that way. You pretty much get what you film. Sure, you can do the *Dragon's Lair* thing, with punctuated moments where you switch to a different track…

Paul: Part of it had to do with the hardware chase. We started off with four colors on the IBM, then sixteen, then two hundred fifty-six. Then we started being able to animate faster and faster. People wanted to jump ahead. Hey—you want to make a movie; that's where you're headed. Of course, that wasn't us. There were a whole lot of people who said, "Hey, they're doing movie games. We know movies!" So it became a Hollywood production. We got off track. Thankfully, there are games that synthesize their graphics. *Call of Duty* does an excellent job of having an interactive game that transitions to a filmlike experience.

But really, the core fun is always about the gameplay. We know that if you get bored, you're just going to click through it. "Oh, no, that was $250,000 and they just clicked through it!" We're very reticent to spend big money on that stuff. We really try to avoid those click-through moments.

In 1999, you made a game called *Little Witching Mischiefs* for the Japanese audience. I haven't had the chance to talk to many developers who have worked with that audience. Can you tell me what it was like? How does the Japanese market compare to the American? (See Figure 15.7).

Paul: Wow. I think you're way overestimating our competence to answer that question.

Fred: Just how that project came to be is an interesting story.

Paul: We'd done *The Unholy War*, and we really liked the way the combat in that worked out, but we had a strategy and story component that got cut out at the last minute. So we felt there was an unresolved potential there.

We'd been playing these games called the *SD Gundam*. We thought, we have a game where instead of just watching canned combat, you could actually go into battle with these robots. So let's go get that license. The president of our company said he knew people at Bandai and could make it happen.

The message that we got back was that Bandai loved *The Unholy War* and thought it was a great idea. But they said they have an even bigger license we could use; a huge one. What could it be? So we signed the contract. We didn't know anything about it until the fax started churning out images. When we got the fax, it was this girl from the '60s with a magical makeup kit. We were like, huh?

And they just kept coming and coming. It's hard to understand, but it was a retrospective, nostalgia piece that combined these witch girl characters from the '70s and '80s … I guess it was like our *Scooby Doo* or *Johnny Quest*. But theirs were these girls born in another dimension, where they're princesses. They have magic powers. For some reason,

FIGURE 15.7 *Little Witching Mischiefs* was sadly never released in an English version.

they're sent to our world, and the only way they can invoke their powers is through their makeup—or some other object for which a toy gets made and sold in the real world.

We got these great design docs for level design, but couldn't read them because they weren't in English. And the only person who spoke English on the Bandai side quit. For a long time, we couldn't understand each other. At the very end of development, the bugs tend to get very technical. It's stuff like unplugging the joystick while plugging the memory card in and out while opening the disk box. Even in English, it's confusing. And the fax would just keep rolling with all these bug reports in Japanese. Eventually, we just shut off the fax machine. That was the end of the development—we thought it was good enough, and we're not talking anymore. It was definitely the weirdest game development we've ever had, and we've never met a single person who's played it.

We were talking earlier about designing games for kids. When I was a kid, I was playing games like *Archon* and *Mail Order Monsters*, which weren't explicitly designed for kids. What is it like designing games specifically for kids?

Paul: There's always a risk of being condescending, and that's the worst thing you can do. Kids are extremely smart, and they learn faster than us older people do. Their vocabulary, in language and symbols, isn't complete, so you have to be careful about using references and shortcuts that a teenager would understand. Since they don't have the vocabulary, they might not know the concepts if you just throw out something like, "The horror of war." But they might get the concept if you communicate it in a different way.

The core experience needs to be fun and compelling, at least as much as in a game for adults. Kids are notoriously impatient with boring stuff, as they should be. It focuses you on getting to the good stuff fast, and it makes you not rely on bizarre vocabulary—in text and symbols, and you need a fast feedback loop.

Then there's the ratings issue. For example, in the first *Madagascar*, they wanted an E-rated game, but it became E-10 because Gloria had a butt bounce. We didn't want to change its name, because clearly she was bouncing on people with her butt. Because we used the word "butt," it became an E-10 game. It's amazing, but we spent hours arguing about Gloria's butt. What a job! We had to argue about a hypothetical hippo's butt.

You've mentioned making a new *Star Control* game. How similar will it be to the previous games in the series?*

Paul: There needs to be enough there that when you enter the experience it feels like a fairly continuous moment from the last game. Twenty or twenty-five years might have passed between them, but I don't think we're saying "generations later, in an entirely different area of space, with all new ships." That's not why people will want to play this game. This isn't a game we'd sell for the same reasons we'd sell a first-person shooter. It's for people who like *Star Control II* and want to continue that experience. We'd pick up pretty close to where that story ends, and keep enough of the races and ships that it feels familiar. As the game goes on, we'd introduce new races.

I really want to know what the Druuge have been up to. Our technology has changed so much since that time, that the game has to reflect the fact that people are walking around with way more advanced computers in their hands than we imagined people owning two hundred years from now. The whole issue about how movies from fifteen years ago would be different if they'd known we would have cell phones—entire movie plots would fall apart. We have to reflect the change in our understanding of technology and also try to bring in what really pisses us off about this modern world we're living in. Stuff like intolerance, people being unnecessarily warlike, the price of gas, political parties—the earth revolting upon us.

That's all the questions I have. Is there anything else you wanted to add that I didn't ask about?

Paul: You mean, besides stay in school and don't do drugs? I don't know. Have a good time. Cut each other some slack.

Fred: Hopefully we'll be here in a few more years.

Paul: Hopefully we'll be talking about how much people are loving the new *Star Control* game.

---

* Question submitted by Cameron Goble.

Index

A

Abandonware, 4, 127, 147, 213
Abrams, Michael, 13
Accessibility, 176
Activision, 31, 63, 71, 203, 211
Adams, Douglas, 144, 145
Adams, Scott, 140, 193
ADD personality, *see* Attention deficit disorder
        personality
AdLib, 17
Adventure, 8
Adventure International, 14
Age of Empires Online, 83, 94
Alignment, 79, 80
Alpha Protocol, 75, 82
American Laser Games, 192, 197
Amiga, 43, 64, 66, 105, 117, 120, 150
Angry Birds, 110
Apple II, 5, 6, 11, 27, 62, 140, 143
Apple Spice, 140
Arcanum, 45, 55
Archon, 203, 208, 209, 211, 216
Assembly language, 8, 9, 141
Atari, 29, 56, 98, 143, 150
Atari 400/800, 141, 162
Atari 2600, 11, 27, 29, 102
Atari 5200, 141
Atari ST, 117
Attention deficit disorder (ADD) personality, 176
Avalon Hill, 27, 30
Avellone, Chris, 75–82, 184
    alignment, 79, 80
    Alpha Protocol, 75, 81, 82
    BioWare, 79
    blank slate, 80
    CAD programs, 77
    Chrono Trigger, 78
    clichés, 79
    computer role-playing game, 80
    death, 79
    defying conventions, 76
    Descent to Undermountain, 75
    Diablo, 79
    Dragon Play, 77
    Dungeons & Dragons, 75
    espionage RPG, 82
    Eternal Dagger, 77, 78
    Fallout 3, 82
    Fallout: New Vegas, 75, 82
    Icewind Dale, 81
    Interplay, 78, 81
    Kickstarter, 75
    Lionheart: Legacy of the Crusader, 75
    MCA, 75, 76
    nonplayer character, 76
    Obsidian, 75, 77
    Planescape: Torment, 75, 80
    Ravel, 81
    rule set, 75
    System Shock 2, 77, 78
    vision points, 79
    Wasteland, 78
    "wow" moment, 76

B

Baer, Ralph, 129–136
    background, 129
    "Brown Box" prototype, 133
    Coleco, 129, 130
    copyright, 131–132
    documentation, 131
    family games, 135
    German trait, 136
    Google, 132, 134
    licensing agreements, 130
    Magnavox, 129, 132, 133
    National Medal of Technology, 130
    Nintendo, 134
    patents, 129, 131
    pioneering work, 129

Pong, 129
recordable talking books, 132
Simon, 129
spreading of misinformation, 134
violence, 135
Wii, 134
YouTube, 132, 133
Baldur's Gate, 58, 61, 72, 91
Ball Blazer, 140, 147
Bard's Tale, 27, 32, 35, 37, 39, 41, 47, 61, 63, 64, 65,
    66, 70, 77, 78
Bard's Tale I, 35, 36
Bard's Tale II, 36, 37, 65, 78
Bard's Tale III, 27, 35, 36, 37, 38
Bard's Tale IV, 37, 38, 39, 41
Bard's Tale Construction Set, 47, 49, 54
BASIC, 8, 9, 85, 140
Battle Chess, 66, 67
Battlechess, 39
Berry, Danielle Bunten, 1, 4
Bethesda, 57, 70
Bible-Belt driven company, 125
Big Blue Disk, 14
Bioshock, 40, 108
BioWare, 72, 79
Bitch advertisement, 22, 23
Bitch-X, 23
Blender, 176, 179, 189
Board games, 89
Boone Corporation, 30, 34
Boyarsky, Leonard, 53, 55
Burger, *see* Heineman, Rebecca

C

C (programming language), 47, 85
Cadillacs & Dinosaurs, 151
Cain, Tim, 45–60
    Arcanum, 45, 55
    Atari, 56
    Baldur's Gate, 58
    Bard's Tale, 47
    Bard's Tale Construction Set, 47, 49, 54
    Bethesda, 57
    "bloody mess" trait, 48
    bridge game, 45, 46
    C (programming language), 47
    CD-ROM, 54
    Civilization, 47
    consoles, 57
    dark social themes, 45
    digital distribution, 54
    disillusionment with status quo, 45

Dragon Age, 54
drugs, 48
Duck and Cover film, 52
Dungeons & Dragons, 58
Electronic Arts, 45
EPROMs, 47
Fallout, 45, 48, 49
Forced Evolutionary Virus, 57
gay, 48
GECK, 53
governments, 53
GURPS, 50
Hellcat Ace, 47
Interplay, 53
Lord of the Rings, 50
Massively Multiplayer Online, 58
nonplayer characters, 58, 60
octogenarian vegan, 58
"open-world" dynamics of games, 45
resumes, 59
science fiction, 59
seminal role-playing game, 45
social commentary, 52
steampunk, 51, 55
stupid features, 59
Temple of Elemental Evil, 47, 49, 56, 57, 60
touchstones, 59
triple-A product, 56
Troika, 50, 55, 58
turn-based games, 47, 57
Ultima series, 47
unique role-playing game, 48
Vampire: The Masquerade, 58
Vault-Tec, 52
violence, 48
Wasteland, 48
Cakes, 28
Call of Duty, 72, 108, 109, 110, 187, 215
Canada, 86
Cannon Fodder, 105, 106, 113, 116, 121, 122, 127, 128
Capital Computers, 7
Card, Orson Scott, 139, 208
Carmack, John, 5, 12, 18, 20, 32
Castle Wolfenstein, 15
Catacombs, 13, 16
Cavedog Entertainment, 88
CD-ROM, 2, 54
Celebrity Squares, 116
CGA, 13, 144
Championship Manager, 119
Choplifter, 15
Chrono Trigger, 78
Civilization, 47

Clone Wars, 188
Codemasters, 126
Coleco, 129, 130
Command & Conquer, 83
Command & Conquer III, 40
Commander Keen, 11, 12, 14
Commodore 64, 6, 12, 15, 27, 64, 87, 89, 105, 112,
    114, 117, 120, 143, 147, 150, 209
Computer role-playing games (CRPGs), 61
Consoles, 57, 71, 196
Copyright, 35, 121, 131
Copyright Infringement, 13, 14
Corona SDK, 153
CP/M, 6, 8, 140
Cranford, Michael, 35, 36, 63, 65
Cromenco, 11
Crowdsourcing application, 3
CRPGs, *see* Computer role-playing games
Crytek, 176, 189
Curse of Blackmoor Manor, 194
Cut the Rope, 110

D

Daikatana, 21, 22, 164
Danger on Deception Island, 193
Dangerous Dave, 13
Dark Castle, 15
Darwinia, 40
Day, Shelley, 88
Day of the Tentacle, 157
Dead Space, 40
Demmon, Bob, 158, 159
Demon's Forge, 31, 61
Demon Stone, 173, 175, 186
Deus Ex, 162
Devil's Tuning Fork, The, 176, 177
Diablo, 79, 83, 91
DirectX, 14, 15, 166
Disneyland, 139, 157
Distinctive Software, 86
Doom, 5, 68, *see also* Romero, John
Dragon Age, 54
Dragon Play, 77
Dragon's Lair, 178, 215
Dragon Wars, 27, 37, 39
Drugged Out Hippie, 126
Drugs, 48, 126
Dune II, 122
Dungeon Defenders, 176
Dungeons & Dragons, 35, 45, 58, 75, 89, 205
Dungeon Siege, 83, 95
Dungeon Siege 2, 91

E

Easter eggs, 138
EA widow, 85
EGA, 13, 16, 144, 214
Electric Eggplant, 153
Electronic Arts, 39, 40, 45, 66, 208, 209
Electronic Corral, 177
Ender's Game, 139
EPROMs, 47
E-rated game, 217
Espionage RPG, 82
E.T., 97, 102, 103
Eternal Dagger, 77, 78
EULA, 95
Europe, 70, 106, 113, 118, 122, 151, 169
Evil Avatar, 23

F

Facebook, 3, 95, 174, 196
Fallout, 45, 48, 49, 68, 79
Fallout 2, 53, 72
Fallout 3, 51, 70, 82
Fallout: New Vegas, 75, 82
Fan remake, 148
Fargo, Brian, 27, 31, 34, 61–73
    Activision, 63, 71
    Amiga, 64, 66
    Apple II, 62
    arcade machines, 63
    Bard's Tale, 65
    Battle Chess, 66, 67
    Call of Duty phenomenon, 72
    computer role-playing games, 61, 72
    consoles, 71
    dead license, 69
    Demon's Forge, 61–62
    Electronic Arts, 66
    Europe, 70
    Flash, 71
    genius coder, 65
    GURPS, 68
    Hunted: The Demon's Forge, 73
    Icewind Dale, 72
    Interplay, 62, 71
    inXile, 66
    iTunes, 71
    Kickstarter, 61
    licensed games, 69
    LucasArts, 66
    Mindshadow, 63
    moral ambiguity, 67

nonplayer characters, 68
old-school games, 70
passion, 73
Pong, 70
royalty, 72
Saber Software, 61–62
sensibilities, 62
Star Trek, 69
Stonekeep, 68, 69
top-seller, 64
Ultima, 67
violence, 68
Wasteland, 68, 70
Wizardry, 64
Fat Babies, 23
Father of videogames, *see* Baer, Ralph
Fat Man, The, *see* Sanger, George
FEV, *see* Forced Evolutionary Virus
FIFA, 119
First-person shooter (FPS)
clones, 15
consoles, 92
Daikatana, 21
Doom, 19
expert level, 21
id Software, 5
key controls, 17
levels, 109
Mass Effect 2, 108
Portal, 40
relational interactive experience, 175
RPG, 57
scale reference, 187
Star Control II, 217
System Shock 2, 78
Wolfenstein, 17
women, 23
Flash, 71, 94, 110, 127
FM Towns, 149
FMV, *see* Full-motion video
Football Manager, 119
Forced Evolutionary Virus (FEV), 57
Forgotten Realms: Demon Stone, 173
FORTRAN, 98
4D Boxing, 88
Fox, David, 137–153
abandonware, 147
Amiga, 150
animation, 138
Apple II, 140, 143
Apple Spice, 140
assembly language, 141

Atari, 143, 150
Atari 400/800, 141
Atari 5200, 141
Ball Blazer, 140, 147
brainstorming, 144
Cadillacs & Dinosaurs, 151
CD-ROM, 152
CGA, 144
Commodore, 143, 147, 150
conversion process, 143
Corona SDK, 153
CP/M, 140
Disneyland, 139
Easter eggs, 138
EGA, 144
Electric Eggplant, 153
Ender's Game, 139
Europe, 151
fan remake, 148
FM Towns, 149
fractal geometry, 141
Germany, 150
hamsters, 150
Incredible Machines, 138
Industrial Light & Magic, 140, 152
internal references, 150
iOS, 138, 144, 153
iPad, 144
iPhone, 144
Kickstarter, 148
Koronis Rift, 143
Labyrinth, 144
LISP, 143
Loom, 137, 149, 150
LucasArts, 137, 147, 148, 150
Lucasfilm, 137, 140, 142
Maniac Mansion, 137, 145, 148, 150
Marin Computer Center, 139
Myst, 152
pinup, 150
piracy, 146, 147
Rescue on Fractalus!, 141, 142
risk, 142
Rube Goldberg, 137, 138
SCUMM, 143, 145, 147
Sierra On-Line, 150, 151
6502 assembly, 141
Sol, 139, 140
Spectrum Sinclair, 143
Sun microcomputers, 143
tabloid stories, 146
UNIX, 142, 143

VAX computers, 143
Zak McKracken and the Alien Mindbenders, 137, 138, 145, 147
FPS, *see* First-person shooter
Fractal geometry, 141
Fracture, 187
Free Fall Associates, 203, 208, 209
Freeway, 31
Full-motion video (FMV), 215

G

Gaiser (Megan) and Riedl (Rob), 191–202
    advice, 200, 201
    Amazon self-publishing, 192
    American Laser Games, 192, 197
    books, 194
    consoles, 196
    Curse of Blackmoor Manor, 194
    Danger on Deception Island, 193
    dude ranch, 195
    Facebook, 196
    favorite games, 194
    feminism, 197
    grandmothers, 193
    Her Interactive, 191
    iPad, 196, 198
    iPhone, 198
    Message in a Haunted Mansion, 194, 195
    Multi-User Dungeons, 193
    Nancy Drew, 191, 193, 198, 199
    primary demographic, 191
    risk takers, 201
    Secrets Can Kill, 198, 199
    "students of the month," 202
    Tomb of the Lost Queen, 196
    "Un-Barbie," 197
    violence, 197
    Wii, 196
Game Center, 111
Game Creators Vault, 173, 174
Game Developers Conference (GDC), 25, 165
Gamma World, 206, 211
Garriott, Richard, 157
Gay, 22, 48
GDC, *see* Game Developers Conference
Gebelli, Nasir, 6, 8, 11
Genesis, 108
Germany, 126, 136, 150
Gilbert, Ron, 89, 145, 151, 171
Girls, gamemakers for, *see* Gaiser (Megan) and Riedl (Rob)

God of War, 110
Goldberg, Rube, 137, 138
"Golden Age" of gaming, 3
Google, 3, 132, 134
Govett, Dave, 157, 164, 166, 167
Graphic artist, *see* Soderwall, Mark
Grim Fandango, 163
Guitar Hero, 160
GURPS, 50, 68
Gygax, Gary, 4, 47, 56

H

Half Life, 42
Half-Life 2, 58
Half-Life III, 41
Halo, 93, 108
Halo Wars, 93
Hardball 2, 85, 87
Hare, Jon, 105–128
    abandonware, 127
    accelerometer, 116
    Amiga, 105, 117, 120
    Angry Birds, 110
    Atari ST, 117
    Bible-Belt driven company, 125
    Bioshock, 108
    Call of Duty, 108, 109, 110
    Cannon Fodder, 105, 106, 113, 116, 121, 122, 127, 128
    Celebrity Squares, 116
    Championship Manager, 119
    Codemasters, 126
    Commodore 64, 105, 112, 114, 117, 120
    copyright, 121
    Cut the Rope, 110
    Drugged Out Hippie, 126
    drugs as game mechanic, 126
    Dune II, 122
    Europe, 106, 113, 118, 122
    FIFA, 119
    Flash, 110, 127
    frustration, 108
    Game Center, 111
    Genesis, 108
    Germany, 126
    God of War, 110
    GTA, 125
    Halo, 108
    iOS, 110, 126
    iPad, 110, 126
    iPhone, 106, 109, 110, 116, 126

Kick-Off, 123
Leisure Suit Larry, 125
Mass Effect 2, 108
Mega-Lo-Mania, 122
Nemesis, 115
NTSC, 117
Ocean, 112, 115
open source project, 126
paradox, 110
Parallax, 106, 112, 114
piracy, 127
politics, 112
Renegade, 118
Rock Band, 125
royalty, 118
Score Loop, 111
Sega Megadrive, 108
Sensible Golf, 123, 124
Sensible Soccer, 105, 106, 119, 125, 126
Sensible Software, 105, 106, 107, 112, 113, 114,
    123, 124, 126
Sensible World of Soccer, 119, 124
Sex 'n' Drugs 'n' Rock 'n' Roll, 105, 107, 116, 124,
    125, 128
Shoot'em Up Construction Kit, 116
Smurf Hunt, 116
Speedball, 109, 110, 116, 126, 127
Speedball 2: Evolution, 126
star developers, 120
3D programming, 105, 118
Tiny Wings, 107, 109
Wizball, 106, 112, 115, 117, 125
Wizkid, 115, 117, 125
Word Explorer, 106, 108, 110
World of Warcraft, 110, 111, 175
ZX Spectrum, 107
Heineman, Rebecca, 27–44
    Activision, 31
    Apple II, 27
    Atari, 29
    Avalon Hill, 27, 30
    Boone Corporation, 30, 34
    Burger, 34
    cakes, 28
    Commodore 64, 27
    copyright, 35
    cult classic, 33
    Dragon Wars, 27, 37
    Dungeons & Dragons, 35
    Electronic Arts, 39, 40
    female characters, 36
    gay, 22
    Half Life, 42

humor, 41
id software model, 39
indie games, 40
Interplay, 27, 31, 35, 40
iPhone, 37
Kinect, 27, 43
London Blitz, 27
Macintosh, 27, 42
markswoman, 28
Merlin, 35
Monty Python, 36, 39
Need for Speed, 40
Neuromancer, 39, 40
Orca/M, 35
personal life, 28
Portal, 29, 40
Quick Draw, 35
reverse engineering, 31, 43
role-playing game, 32
Softdisk, 32
Space Invaders, 29
Tass Times in Tonetown, 27, 33, 40
Time Warner, 30
TRS-80, 31
Ubisoft Toronto, 27
Uplink, 40
Wasteland, 28, 36, 38
Wizardry, 32, 35
World of Goo, The, 40
World of Warcraft, 32
Xonox, 31
YouTube, 40, 43
Hellcat Ace, 47
Hellfire Warrior, 209
Her Interactive, 191
Hewlett-Packard, 98
Honoring the code, 1–4
    abandonware, 4
    crowdsourcing application, 3
    culture, 1
    duty, 4
    gaming legacy, 4
    "Golden Age" of gaming, 3
    jon interview, 2
    Kickstarter, 3
    online activity, 3
    paradigm shifter, 2
    pioneers, 4
    poorly punctuated e-mail, 4
    technical skills, 1
Horde, The, 214, 215
Horizontal scrolling, 13
Hovertank, 17

Humor, 14, 41, 151, 212
Hunted: The Demon's Forge, 62, 70, 73

I

Icewind Dale, 72, 81
id Software, 5
Impossible Mission, 15, 89
Incredible Machines, 138
Indie games, 40
Industrial Light & Magic, 140, 152
Infocom, 14
Intellivision, 86, 160, 161
Internet Relay Chat (IRC), 20
Interplay, 27, 31, 35, 40, 53, 62, 71, 78, 81
inXile, 66
iOS, 110, 126, 138, 144, 153, 176, 213
iPad, 110, 126, 144, 198
iPhone, 6, 37, 89, 106, 109, 110, 116, 126, 144, 198
IRC, *see* Internet Relay Chat
IRS, 206
iTunes, 71

J

Java, 94
Javascript, 94

K

Kassar, Ray, 98, 102
Katamari Damacy, 160, 163, 170
Kellner, Charlie, 141, 143, 144
Kick-Off, 123
Kickstarter, 3, 61, 75, 148, 191
Kinect, 27, 43

L

Lawrence, Daniel, 4
Leisure Suit Larry, 125
Level editors, 20
Licensed games, 69
Licensed titles, 39
Licensing agreements, 130
Lionheart: Legacy of the Crusader, 75
LISP, 143
Little Witching Mischiefs, 215, 216
Lode Runner, 7, 15
London Blitz, 27
Loom, 137, 149, 150, 167
Lord of the Rings, 50

Lucas, George, 66, 137, 141, 180, 187
LucasArts, 12, 66, 89, 137, 147, 148, 150, 177, 180
Lucasfilm, 137, 140, 142

M

MacDonald, Jay, 88
Macintosh, 15, 27, 42
Magnavox, 129, 132, 133
Mail Order Monsters, 203, 209, 210, 216
Maniac Mansion, 137, 145, 148, 150, 155, 157, 158, 163, 166
Mass Effect 2, 108
Massively Multiplayer Online (MMO), 58
Math, 86
Mega-Lo-Mania, 106, 112, 113, 122, 123
Meier, Sid, 47
Merlin, 35
Message in a Haunted Mansion, 194
Microsoft, 94, 191
    advanced technology group, 29
    DirectX, 166
    Kinect, 43
    rumor, 165
    Softcard, 8
    Task compiler, 9
MIDI, 164, 168
Military, 134
Miller, Scott, 14
Mindshadow, 63
Minecraft, 40, 176
Minella, Lani, 199, 200
Mirage, 151
MMO, *see* Massively Multiplayer Online
Mobile revolution, 2, 95
Modding, 95, 189
Monkey Island, 160
Monty Python, 36, 39
Moriarty, Brian, 149, 152
MRB (marijuana review board), 99
Ms. Pac-Man, 99
Murder on the Zinderneuf, 203, 209
Myst, 152

N

Nancy Drew, 191, 193, 199
NBA Live 97, 173, 181
Nemesis, 115
Neuromancer, 39, 40
Nintendo, 13, 134
Nonplayer characters (NPCs), 58, 60, 68, 76, 184
NPCs, *see* Nonplayer characters

O

Obsidian, 75, 77
Ocean, 112, 115
OpenGL, 14, 15
Orca/M, 35

P

Pac-Man, 1, 7, 93, 104
Paint select, 93
Parallax, 106, 112, 114
Patel, Jay, 31, 63
Patents, 129, 131, 156
Pavlish, Alan, 28, 30
Pegasus, 7
Pinball, 86
Piracy, 89, 127, 146, 147
Planescape: Torment, 61, 75, 80
Player psychology, 180
Politics, 22, 112
Pong, 2, 70, 86, 99, 129
Portal, 29, 40, 162
Portal 2, 91
Prince of Persia, 176
Prototype
    Brown Box, 129, 133
    flying over a fractal landscape, 141
    Sierra, 55
Putt-Putt Saves the Zoo, 160, 170, 171
Pyramids of Egypt, 14

Q

Quake, 4, 5, 20, 22, 24
Queen of the Hill tournaments, 24
Quick Draw, 35

R

RadioShack, 89, 140
Real-time strategy (RTS) games, 83, 90, 92, 175
Reiche (Paul III) and Ford (Fred), 203–217
    abandonware, 213
    Activision, 203, 211
    Archon, 203, 208, 209, 211, 216
    backstories, 206
    books, 207
    Call of Duty, 215
    Commodore, 209
    conflicts with publishers, 210
    Dragon's Lair, 215
    Dungeons & Dragons, 205

EGA, 214
Electronic Arts, 208, 209
E-rated game, 217
feedback loop, 217
Free Fall Associates, 203, 208, 209
full-motion video, 215
Gamma World, 206, 211
Hellfire Warrior, 209
Horde, The, 214, 215
Humor, 212
iOS, 213
IRS, 206
Little Witching Mischiefs, 215, 216
Mail Order Monsters, 203, 209, 210, 216
Murder on the Zinderneuf, 203, 209
Napoleon Dynamite moment, 206
SD Gundam, 215
self-preservation, 212
Skylanders: Spyro's Adventure, 203
Star Control, 203, 204, 206, 207, 211, 213, 214, 217
Starflight, 207
Star Trek, 206
Synapse Software, 209
tabletop days, 205
Temple of Apshai, 208
Thri-kreen, 206
top-secret project, 203
toys, 204
Toys For Bob, 203, 211
TSR, 203, 206, 209, 210
Unholy War, The, 215
Webkinz toys, 205
Renegade, 118
Rescue on Fractalus!, 137, 138, 140, 141, 142, 151
Resumes, 59, 73, 201
Reverse engineering, 31, 43
Reviews, 91, 93, 208
Riedel, Rob, see Gaiser (Megan) and Riedl (Rob)
Risk, 92, 142, 201
Robotron 2084, 177
Rock Band, 125
Rocket Science Games, 152
Role-playing game (RPG), 32, 112
    action, 83
    ADD personality and, 176
    baby analogy, 93
    computer, 61, 77, 80
    critically acclaimed, 75
    death, 79
    espionage, 82
    Fallout, 184
    FPS, 57
    Icewind Dale, 72

pitch, 50
RTS sensibility, 90
seminal, 45
story, 32
turn-based, 58
unique, 48
Romero, John, 5–25, 32, 105, 161, 164
   advice, 24
   Apple II party, 11
   arcade machines as design templates, 8
   assembly language, 9
   attitude, 24
   biggest questions asked, 25
   bitch ad, 22, 23
   breakthrough technology, 14
   Burroughs computers, 6
   Capital Computers, 7
   Catacombs, 13, 16
   CGA people, 13
   challenges, 17
   clones, 15
   Commodore 64, 15
   computer lock-up, 10
   conflict, 22
   Copyright Infringement, 14
   Daikatana, 21
   DirectX, 14
   Doom, 17, 19
   enthusiasm, 5
   expert level FPS, 21
   favorite multiplayer game, 19
   first-person shooter, 5, 19
   goal, 8
   home computer, 8
   horizontal scrolling, 13
   Hovertank, 17
   independent study class, 11
   internal politics, 22
   Internet Relay Chat, 20
   Keen, 11
   level designer, 7
   level editor, 18, 20
   Lode Runner, 7
   magazines, 9
   mainframe terminal, 8
   networking, 25
   Nintendo game, 19
   OpenGL, 14
   Pac-Man, 7
   pioneering Apple II programmers, 6
   programming, 6
   QA team, 7
   Quake, 20, 21
   sabotage, 23
   scripting change, 20
   shareware, 15
   shooter-formula-type game, 21
   Sirius Software, 11
   social aspect, 12
   source code, 11
   team, 14
   teenage hackers, 5
   U.S. Air Force base, 10
   vault, 10
   Windows 95, 25
   Wolfenstein 3D, 15, 16
   women, 23, 24
   Xevious-scrolling background, 13
Royalty, 72, 118
RPG, *see* Role-playing game
RTS games, *see* Real-time strategy games

S

Saber Software, 61, 62
Sanger, George, 155–171
   Atari 400/800, 162
   Capture the Flag, 161, 162
   CD-ROM, 168
   corporatization, 163
   Daikatana, 164
   Day of the Tentacle, 157
   Deus Ex, 162
   DirectX, 166
   Disneyland, 157
   Europe, 169
   Fat Man, The, 156, 163
   game audio, 160, 169
   Game Developers Conference, 165
   Grim Fandango, 163
   Guitar Hero, 160
   Humongous Entertainment, 170
   Intellivision, 160, 161
   Katamari Damacy, 160, 163, 170
   Loom, 167
   Maniac Mansion, 155, 157, 158, 163, 166
   masterpiece, 165
   MIDI, 164, 168
   minimalist music, 169
   Monkey Island, 160
   Moog synthesizer, 158
   musical training, 159
   patents, 156
   Portal, 162
   problems, 159
   Putt-Putt Saves the Zoo, 160, 170, 171

7th Guest, The, 155, 157, 160, 167, 168
slot machines, 155, 156
soundtracks, 157
SSX Tricky, 160
technologies, 164
Thin Ice, 160, 161
Ultima Underworld, 167
Wing Commander, 155, 157, 160, 166, 167
Xbox games, 165
Z80, 157
Schwarzenegger, Arnold, 181, 182, 185
Science fiction, 58–59
Score Loop, 111
Scout Search, 9
SCUMM, 143, 145, 147
SD Gundam, 215
Secret of Mana, 11
Sega Megadrive, 108
Sensibilities, 62
Sensible Golf, 123, 124
Sensible Soccer, 105, 106, 125, 126
Sensible Software, 105, 106, 107, 112, 113, 114, 123, 124, 126
Sensible World of Soccer, 119, 124
Serf, Christopher, 144
7th Guest, The, 155, 157, 160, 167, 168
Sex 'n' Drugs 'n' Rock 'n' Roll, 105, 107, 116, 124, 125, 128
Shoot'em Up Construction Kit, 116
Sierra On-Line, 150, 151
Simon, 129
Sirius Software, 11
68K assembly, 12
6502 assembly, 31, 141
Skylanders: Spyro's Adventure, 203
Slot machines, 155
Smith, Douglas, 7
Smurf Hunt, 116
Social commentary, 52
Social life, 12
Soderwall, Mark, 173–189
  accessibility, 176
  ADD personality, 176
  advice, 176, 189
  artistic skill, 179
  attention deficit disorder personality, 176
  Blender, 176, 179, 189
  bottom line, 186
  Call of Duty, 187
  Clone Wars, 188
  coin-op classics, 177
  Crytek, 176, 189
  Demon Stone, 173, 175, 186

Devil's Tuning Fork, The, 176, 177
Dragon's Lair, 178
Dungeon Defenders, 176
Electronic Corral, 177
Facebook, 174
first job, 180
first-person shooter, 175
Forgotten Realms: Demon Stone, 173
Fracture, 187
Game Creators Vault, 173
graphic artist, 173, 174
history of videogames, 189
iOS, 176
LucasArts, 177, 180
magazine prejudice, 185
Magic Candle III, 184
Minecraft, 176
modding, 189
movie tie-in game, 185
NBA Live 97, 173, 181
nonplayer characters, 184
player psychology, 180
Prince of Persia, 176
real-time strategy games, 175
Robotron 2084, 177
Siege, 183
Star Wars: The Clone Wars, 188
Star Wars: The Force Unleashed, 173, 188
Super Meat Boy, 176
Tegel's Mercenaries, 182, 183
Terminator 3, 173, 181, 185
UDK, 176, 189
"uncanny valley" phenomenon, 182
Unity, 176, 189
Unreal Developer's Kit, 176, 189
World of Warcraft, 175
Softdisk, 11, 12, 32
Sol, 139, 140
Soundblaster, 17
Space Invaders, 29, 86
Space Siege, 93
Spectrum Sinclair, 143
Speedball, 109, 110, 116, 126, 127
Speedball 2: Evolution, 126
SSX Tricky, 160
Stackpole, Michael A., 28, 35, 67
Star Castle, 100, 101
Star Control, 203, 204, 206, 207, 210, 213, 214, 217
Starflight, 207
Star Trek, 69, 206
Star Wars, 18, 75, 66, 188
Star Wars: The Clone Wars, 188
Star Wars: The Force Unleashed, 173, 188

Steampunk, 51, 55
Steed, Paul, 4
Stonekeep, 68, 69
Substalker, 12
Sun microcomputers, 143
Super Meat Boy, 176
Supreme Commander, 83, 93
Supreme Commander 2, 93
Suzuki, Tony, 12
Synapse Software, 209

T

Tank, 99, 100
Tass Times in Tonetown, 27, 33, 40
Taylor, Chris, 83–95
  Age of Empires Online, 83, 94
  Baldur's Gate, 91
  BASIC, 85
  board games, 89
  C (programming language), 85
  Canada, 86
  Cavedog Entertainment, 88
  Command & Conquer, 83
  creative freedom, 89
  Distinctive Software, 86, 87
  Dungeon Siege, 83, 90, 95
  Dungeon Siege 2, 91
  EA widow, 85
  8088, 85
  end user license agreement, 95
  EULA, 95
  farm, 84
  first-person shooters, 92
  4D Boxing, 88
  Gas Powered Games, 83, 85, 94
  Halo Wars, 93
  history, 85
  Impossible Mission, 89
  industry, 84
  Java, 94
  Javascript, 94
  math, 86
  miniatures-based games, 89
  mobile evolution, 95
  modding, 95
  older generation, 91
  Pac-Man, 93
  paint select, 93
  pinball, 86
  Portal 2, 91
  raising money, 95
  real-time strategy, 83, 84, 90
  reviews, 93
  Space Siege, 93
  Supreme Commander, 83, 91, 93
  Supreme Commander 2, 93
  toolkits, 95
  Total Annihilation, 83, 89
  turn-based games, 95
  Utopia, 86
  Wizardry, 86
  Xbox 360, 83, 92
Teams, 54, 112
Temple of Apshai, 208
Temple of Elemental Evil, 47, 49, 56, 57, 60
Tennis, 12
Terminator 3, 173, 181, 185
3D programming, 105, 118
Thri-kreen, 206
Time Warner, 30
Tiny Wings, 107, 109, 110, 127
Total Annihilation, 83, 89
Toymakers of gaming, *see* Reiche (Paul III) and
    Ford (Fred)
Toys For Bob, 203, 211
Troika, 50, 55, 58
TRS-80, 31, 85, 89, 209
TSR, 72, 203, 206, 209, 210
Turn-based games, 47, 57, 95
Twister: Mother of Charlotte, 113

U

UDK, *see* Unreal Developer's Kit
Ultima, 47, 67
Ultima Underworld, 16, 68, 167
"Uncanny valley" phenomenon, 182
Unholy War, The, 215
Unity, 94, 176, 189
UNIX, 142, 143
Unreal Developer's Kit (UDK), 176, 189
Uplink, 40
Utopia, 86

V

Vampire: The Masquerade, 58
Vance, Jack, 207, 208
VAX computers, 143
Violence, 48, 135, 197
Vivid Games, 110

W

Wal-Mart, 107, 125

Warhol, Dave, 157, 161
Warner, 97, 98, 108, 113, 124
Warner, Silas, 15
Warshaw, Howard Scott, 97–104
    Arpanet, 98
    Atari, 98, 99
    Atari 2600, 102
    "Big" Warner, 97, 98
    blue-collar workers, 99
    coin-op games, 100
    "Crash Christmas," 97
    E.T., 97, 102, 103
    FORTRAN, 98
    Hewlett-Packard, 98
    ion zone, 101
    marijuana review board, 99
    Ms. Pac-Man, 99
    Pac-Man, 104
    pits, 103
    Pong, 99
    RAM, 99
    Tank, 99, 100
    Yar's Revenge, 97, 100, 102, 103
Wasteland, 28, 36, 38, 68, 70, 78
Wii, 134, 196
Windows 95, 25
Wing Commander, 4, 155, 157, 160, 166, 167
Winnick, Gary, 145

Wizardry, 32, 35, 64, 86
Wizball, 15, 106, 112, 115, 117, 125
Wizkid, 115, 117, 125
Wolfenstein 3D, 5, 15
Women, 23
Word Explorer, 106, 108, 110
World of Goo, The, 40
World of Warcraft, 32, 58, 110, 111, 175

X

Xbox 360, 83, 92, 165
Xevious, 13
X-Factor gaming, 110
Xonox, 31

Y

Yar's Revenge, 97, 100, 102, 103
YouTube, 40, 132, 133

Z

Z80, 8, 85, 157
Zak McKracken and the Alien Mindbenders, 137, 138, 145, 147
Zenith, 11
ZX Spectrum, 107